# SACRED SURVIVAL

**Jewish Political and Social Studies**
Daniel J. Elazar and Steven M. Cohen, editors

# SACRED SURVIVAL

The Civil Religion of American Jews

JONATHAN S. WOOCHER

INDIANA UNIVERSITY PRESS
BLOOMINGTON & INDIANAPOLIS

Manufactured in the United States of America

Library of Congress Cataloging-in-Publication Data
Woocher, Jonathan S.
Sacred Survival.
(Jewish political and social studies)
Bibliography: p. 227
Includes index
1. Jews—United States—Politics and government.
2. Judaism—United States. 3. Civil Religion—United
States. 4. United States—Ethnic relations. I. Title.
II. Series.
E184.J5W88    1986        305.8'924'073        85-45790
ISBN 0-253-35041-7
1 2 3 4 5 90 89 88 87 86

# CONTENTS

# PREFACE

This book lies at the intersection of two domains of inquiry: the sociology of religion and Jewish political studies. It deals with the American Jewish community and with the faith which animates it, but from a perspective which has thus far been missing from most portraits of American Jewry and Judaism. Its central thesis is that the religion of American Jews may be found not only in the realm of synagogue and denominational life, but in the activity and ideology of the vast array of Jewish organizations which are typically thought of as "secular."

For several decades, students of American religious life have paid close attention to what the sociologist Robert Bellah has called America's "civil religion." Civil religion is anchored and focused not in America's churches and synagogues (though it may be found there as well), but in the national community and polity itself. It is the system of beliefs, values, and rituals through which America the nation relates itself to its ultimate horizons and destiny.

The organized American Jewish community is not a nation, but it is, as Daniel Elazar has conclusively demonstrated, an imposing voluntary polity in its own right. Through their ostensibly "secular" organizations, American Jews have undertaken to govern themselves as a component of *k'lal Yisrael*, the peoplehood of Israel. In so doing they have achieved unity, purpose, and identity as a moral community which transcends (without excluding) the overtly religious ideology and practice of the denominational movements of American Judaism. They have given expression to this sense of purposive unity in a characteristic set of beliefs, myths, and rituals which legitimate the work of the American Jewish polity and which mobilize support for its endeavors. In short, American Jews have created their own civil religion, what we call in this book "civil Judaism."

This book represents the first scholarly attempt to document, describe, and interpret American Jewry's civil religion. It is the outgrowth of several years of intimate contact with and detailed study of the leadership and activities of the North American Jewish federation movement. The federations do not constitute by any means the entirety of the American Jewish polity. They have emerged, however, as its central force, the single most comprehensive and representative expression of American Jewry's political and moral unity. The federation movement in its largest sense embraces not only the roughly 225 local Jewish community federations which today claim as their constituency approximately 95 percent of American Jewry, but the network of social service and educational agencies which federation-raised funds help to sustain in the United States and around the world. The federations constitute as well the "action arm" of the United Jewish Appeal, probably the single most widely visible and supported institution in American Jewish life. Thus, it is appropriate that this initial effort to define and to analyze the religion of the American Jewish polity takes the federation movement as its focus.

*Sacred Survival* traces the evolution of the guiding ideology of the movement from its origins as a value system emphasizing philanthropy and Jewish adjustment to American life to its current status as an encompassing set of beliefs which legitimate Jewish survival and activism in the modern world. Largely through the words of the leaders of the Jewish polity, this volume lays out th fundamental tenets, the worldview and ethos, of today's American Jewish civil religion. Citing evidence gathered in surveys of several hundred young federation activists, it shows how this religious ideology lies at the heart of the Jewish commitment of a significant segment of American Jewry. It identifies the central myths and rituals of civil Judaism which enable it to function as a powerful prism through which American Jews envision their place in contemporary history, in the surrounding society, and in the unfolding destiny of the Jewish people.

The scope of this book is at once narrow and broad. It is narrow in the sense noted above: It does not pretend to be a comprehensive account of the belief systems characteristic of every component of the American Jewish polity, nor even of all of the diverse ideological strands which may be found amoung federation leaders and activists. Much less does it claim to be a history or sociology of American Judaism as a whole. Civil Judaism represents but one piece of the elaborate mosaic of American Jewish religious life. Our aim in this book is to rectify the relative inattention paid to this piece in other treatments of American Judaism, not to contend that it is the whole picture.

In another sense, however, the ambition of this book is far-reaching. It is not sufficient simply to present civil Judaism as a feature of American Jewish life without attempting to assess its significance in relation to the larger context in which it resides. American Jewish civil religion plays a unique and important role in defining the character and self-understanding of American Jewry today. It helps American Jews to achieve their most notable aspiration: to survive and to thrive precisely as *American Jews,* as loyal members of an ancient people with a proud tradition, and as full participants in a great new society- and nation-building endeavor. Civil Judaism merits, therefore, serious evaluation as a religious meaning system. It occupies an important place in the two-centuries-old Jewish struggle to validate and to direct Jewish existence in the modern world. An examination of civil Judaism in this context, tentative and speculative though it must inevitably be, forms the conclusion to this book.

As is always the case, many individuals deserve credit for helping to stimulate the ideas, support the research, and shape the words which have gone into this book. They share in whatever merits it may possess, though they have no responsibility for its defects. First and foremost, the contribution of Daniel Elazar must be acknowledged. This book rests on the solid foundation of his work on the American Jewish polity in every respect. It was he who published my first article on civil Judaism and who has encouraged me to pursue the theme in depth. He has been a continual source of insight and counsel in numerous private conversations. I owe a great debt of gratitude as well to Charles Liebman. He is responsible for critical insights into American Jewry which underlie this book and for many valuable comments on its contents. In addition, his work together with Eliezer Don-Yehiya in describing and analyzing the civil religion of the state of Isreal provided a valuable model for much of what appears in this volume.

A number of colleagues have served as sounding-boards and thoughtful critics of both the ideas and language of this book over the years. Deborah Lipstadt has been both a good friend and an unfailingly enlightening, scholarly co-venturer into the Jewish federation world. I have benefitted both intellectually and psychologically from our countless conversations. Steven M. Cohen and Peter Medding have provoked me to rethink and to rewrite much that needed rethinking and rewriting during the gestation process of this book. My colleagues at Brandeis University, especially Bernard Reisman and Marvin Fox, offered both encouragement and support in working out a schedule which permitted me to bring this project to fruition. Others who deserve my thanks include Irving (Yitz) Greenberg, my former colleagues at Carleton College—especially Richard Crouter and Daniel Sullivan—the staff of the Computer Centers at Brandeis and at Carleton, and Prime Computer Company of Natick, which developed software, lent equipment, and donated computer time for the content analysis of documents. Robert Mandel at Indiana University Press offered encouragement from the outset and sage counsel on how to translate a concept into a publishable manuscript.

My special thanks go to numerous volunteer leaders and professional staff of Jewish federations, the Council of Jewish Federations, the United Jewish Appeal, and other Jewish organizations who assisted me in my empirical research, filled out my survey questionnaires, and serve as the living examples of the values and commitment I describe. They are more than the "subjects" of this study, they are my co-workers and friends. Among the many who deserve to be listed I must single out for specific mention Jack Mayer, Ted Comet, Larry Rubenstein, the members of the Leadership Development Committee of the Council of Jewish Federations, and my fellow members of the Young Leadership Cabinet of the United Jewish Appeal.

My final words of gratitude must inevitably and appropriately be reserved for my family. My parents, Howard and Ruth Woocher, and my parents-in-law, Harold and Terry Fleisher, have done more than nurture me, and continue to provide sustenance (physical and spiritual) and support while I have worked on this book. They have been, as well, models of Jewish concern and devotion who have reinforced my desire to explicate what makes American Jews and the institutions of the American Jewish community so special. My wife, Sherry, has shared with me her considerable professional talents as a writer and editor in helping to mitigate the ponderousness of my prose. This, however, is the least of her contributions, far outweighed by her calm acceptance of my travels all over the continent (and abroad) and by her love which continually reminds me of what is truly valuable and precious in life. Finally, my children, Meredith and Benjamin, exercised remarkable patience and forebearance throughout. They dealt with my incessant pleas to give me five more undisturbed minutes at the computer keyboard with tolerance and good humor—even when the five minutes stretched into fifty. But more important, they make my life constantly joyful and fulfilled. They will be the inheritors, just as their grandparents have been the builders, of what American Jews have helped to create in this land. I dedicate this book to my family—past, present, and future of a people whose sacred survival I passionately believe in.

# *I*

# CIVIL RELIGION AND THE MODERN JEWISH CHALLENGE

## The Modern Challenge to Judaism

For two centuries Jews have struggled with a dual challenge: how and why to remain Jewish in the modern world? The questions "how" and "why" be Jewish are not in themselves new. But for the modern Jew they have carried an urgency and an uncertainty greater than that which most of his ancestors experienced. The post-Emancipation, post-Enlightenment history of Jewry and Judaism is one of continuous reformulation of the meaning of being Jewish. The process of reformulation has been complex and often contentious. Its products—the diverse forms of Jewishness manifest today—constitute tenuously successful responses to the dual challenge of Jewish self-definition in the modern world. But the challenge itself persists and repeatedly thrusts itself forward. It is the fundamental Jewish reality of our time, the text, as it were, to which modern Jews are writing and rewriting ever new commentary.

The story of this challenge and the Jewish responses to it has been recounted by numerous historians and social scientists.[1] Until the latter part of the eighteenth century, the vast majority of the world's Jews lived a life circumscribed by the authority of a corporate communal structure and a traditional religious culture. Jews were, in both a social and a psychological sense, in the world but not of it. The traditional community, the *kehillah*, mediated between the individual Jew and the surrounding society. This Jewish community was both a political and a religious entity. It served as the framework for Jewish self-governance (within boundaries permitted by gentile authority) and for the collective self-understanding which sustained and made meaningful the persistent Jewish struggle for continued existence as a distinctive national and religious group.

The *kehillah* was, in effect, a "state within a state." In pre-modern Europe, still largely comprised of social systems based on corporate subgroups, each with a distinct status, a semiautonomous Jewish collectivity was politically functional for both Jew and non-Jew. But the *kehillah* was not simply an externally dictated accommodation to the social structure of the period. For the Jew, it was a traditionally sanctioned instrumentality for maintaining a thoroughly Jewish way of life. Its source of authority was the *halakhah*, the Jewish legal system whose origins were traced back to the divine revelation of the Torah at Mt. Sinai. Thus, though Jews maintained economic and limited social relationships with non-Jews, they regarded themselves as a people apart. The religious and social institutions of the *kehillah* expressed, sustained, and symbolized that separateness.

The distinction between Jew and Gentile was accepted by both, and theologically legitimated by both. From the Jewish perspective, Jews were God's chosen people, living in exile from their homeland due to their own sins, but faithfully awaiting the expected messianic redemption which would vindicate their loyalty to Torah. For Christianity, the presence of Jews as a visible but subservient minority was living evidence of their rejection by God for having spurned his Son. Both theological perspectives demanded that Jews be marked off as a separate group. Thus, though Jews surely did not choose their living conditions, they could willingly accept them, as long as the traditional religious ideology which legitimated their distinctiveness held sway, and the surrounding society offered no alternative except repudiation of their Jewishness.

The revolution which transformed the Jewish world altered both of these conditions. The infiltration of new ideas, known generically as the Enlightenment, and the offer of a new civic status through political emancipation, beginning in the last years of the eighteenth century, set loose a wave of change which within a century would completely undermine the old order in Europe. Slowly, often in fits and spurts, but inexorably, Jews were drawn out of their traditional insulation. The autonomy and legal authority of the *kehillah* were increasingly circumscribed and eventually abolished. Intellectual modernization and secularization tore away at the fabric of the religious tradition itself. Most important of all, Jews became, at times reluctantly but often eagerly, participants in the dynamic cultural and social changes of the age. Their horizons were no longer those of a small group living, as it were, beyond time, but of actors on a vast stage filled with historical possibility.[2]

We cannot attempt here to describe this process of dramatic change in detail.[3] We can, however, identify four critical and closely linked areas in which the Emancipation/Enlightenment experience posed far-reaching challenges to European Jewry. The first was the question of identity: What does it mean to be a Jew in the new era? How does a Jew behave? What does he believe? How does he perceive the nature and significance of his Jewishness? The traditional religious answers to these questions were no longer persuasive for many Jews, but new answers were by no means obvious. As Jews entered the larger society they began to assume other identities as well—as Germans or Frenchmen, or later as liberals or socialists. Jewishness no longer was an all-encompassing identity, yet neither could its reality be entirely ignored. The post-Emancipation, post-Enlightenment Jew was forced to shape his Jewish identity in deliberate fashion, to "define its sphere and harmonize it with the other components of self," as historian Michael Meyer put it.[4]

At the same time as the individual Jew struggled with his or her identity, the collectivity of Jews struggled with its integrity and unity. In the pre-modern period, "Halakha provided the dispersed nation of Israel with a common religious framework that assured an enduring commonality and continuity to Jewish life despite the disparity of geography and of culture among the respective communities of the nation."[5] What the legal tradition did for Jewry as a whole, the political and social institutions of the *kehillah* did for the Jews in a given locality. But with the decline in the authority of the *halakhah* and the removal of authority from the *kehillah*, what could remain as a basis of Jewish unity? In the post-Emancipation environment, that unity rapidly gave way to diversity and even conflict, as partisans of various ideological programs sought to establish their authenticity as continuators of the Jewish tradition and to find new institutional bases for communal integrity.

The Emancipation confronted Jews with a further task of redefinition: redefining their relationship to non-Jews. Prior to Emancipation, that relationship was reasonably clear: the non-Jew was the "other," to be kept at arm's length. But such a relatinship was impossible once Jews sought and received their rights as citizens. Napoleon asked the Assembly of French Jewish Notables which he convened in 1806 whether they regarded other Frenchmen "as brethren or as strangers." The notables answered unequivocally, "as brethren."[6] Yet, in the same set of responses, they expressed (delicately, to be sure) their continuing reluctance to countenance intermarriage with these "brethren." The dilemma of these notables was to be felt by nearly all Jews in many ways during the ensuing decades. The dominant thrust of Enlightenment ideas and Emancipation legislation was to minimize, if not to eliminate entirely, the distinction between Jews and non-Jews. Many Jews leaped eagerly at the chance to take their place alongside their new fellow citizens, to become part of the national body politic. They were not, however, prepared to give up completely a sense of Jewish distinctiveness, if only in religious terms. This posed a practical as well as theoretical question: How were they to maintain this distinctiveness and at the same time behave truly as "brethren" in their relationships to non-Jews? How could they be both a part of society and apart from it?[7]

The final question which the Emancipation and Enlightenment posed

for the Jews was—and is—in many ways the most far-reaching in its implications. Why should Jews continue to seek to survive as Jews at all? In
the face of a benighted and unwelcoming Christian world, and possessed of the certainty of his own special divinely-ordained place in the
universe, the traditional European Jew need hardly have asked such a
question. But for the modern Jew the question proved very real. What
did the Jew gain by holding on to his or her Jewishness? As Joseph Blau
points out, the secularization of society and the development of a "hy-
phenated," compartmentalized Jewish identity almost inevitably raise
this question:

> If modern life is divided in this fashion, and if the compartment that con-
> tains a man's religion is just one box among many, and if this box is the
> only one in which a man differs significantly from other members of his
> society, it will not be long before he will question the need and the desir-
> ability of maintaining this distinctiveness.[8]

Any satisfactory Jewish ideological response to the Emancipation and
Enlightenment had, therefore, to tell the Jew not only *how* to be Jewish
under the radically new conditions of modernity, but *why* to be Jewish
as well. The dual challenge was acute. For a Jewry increasingly cut off
from traditional values and mores, without the support of authoritative
and unifying communal institutions, the modern world was treacher-
ously open. That openness was exhilarating for many who had felt stifled
in the often narrow and decaying structures of the old order. But it demanded that Jews seek new landmarks and bulwarks if they were to survive at all in the new world of perpetual change.

### Responses to the Challenge

The Jews of Europe responded to this challenge in diverse, even
contradictory ways. Two responses need not concern us here: those of
the Jews who believed that no essential change was called for, and of the
Jews who were prepared to abandon Judaism altogether to ease their
entry into the modern world. Between these two extremes, however,
there remained a variety of programs which sought to blend accommodation to the modern world with fidelity to some interpretation of
traditional Judaism. These programs were the progenitors of the contemporary Jewish religious denominations: Reform, Neo-Orthodoxy,
and Conservatism. Each reprsents a particular strategy for meeting the
interrelated challenges we have outlined above.

For the self-proclaimed Reformers who began to appear in Germany
during the first half of the nineteenth century, the preservation of Jewish life demanded a radical reshaping of its substance and terms of refer-

ence. The program of religious reform which took hold in parts of Central Europe and spread to America as well had both practical and ideological components. The traditional liturgy and forms of worship were modified, with the introduction of regular sermons, prayer in the vernacular, mixed seating, choirs, and instrumental music, and the elimination of textual references to the return to Zion. Dietary laws and other practices which restricted participation in social intercourse were abandoned. Some radical Reformers even attempted to shift the Jewish Sabbath to Sunday.

Underlying these changes was a more far-reaching ideological innovation, one which redefined the nature and bases of Jewishness. Jews, the Reformers came to argue, must no longer regard themselves as a national group, but as a religious communion. They were now to see themselves as fully German, or Austrian, or American, differing from their fellow citizens only in their religious beliefs. These beliefs themselves, and the practices which accompanied them, were to be critically examined and modified where necessary in light of modern philosophical standards and spiritual sensibilities. The binding authority of the *halakhah* was denied. Instead, Reform leaders placed their emphasis on Judaism's "prophetic" ideals, the ethical values which were the essence of religion in their view and, therefore, perhaps not incidentally, the common possession of all enlightened religious individuals.

Perhaps the most significant change which Reform introduced came in response to the challenge of providing a rationale for the continued existence of Jews and Judaism itself. This challenge was especially acute for the Reformers precisely because they had rejected so much of the traditional differentiating structure of belief and practice. To validate the survival of Judaism without giving up their belief in the full integration of Jews into modern society, the leaders of Reform redefined a Jewish "mission" in the world which required precisely that involvement. They repudiated the traditional view of Diaspora existence as exilic punishment, and proclaimed it rather the divinely-ordained condition for the fulfillment of a Jewish mission to spread the ethical and spiritual ideals of Judaism among the nations. Freed from the necessity of maintaining an independent political existence, Jews could function as a pure religious group bringing the message of ethical monotheism to their fellows in every land. This concept of a universal mission represented a profound revaluation of the meaning of the traditional Jewish idea of "chosenness." Like the other innovations of the Reformers, it was offered not as a rejection of the Jewish past, but as a higher form of continuity with Judaism's religious ideals.

In looking back on the vigor with which such fundamental changes were pursued, it is easy to draw the mistaken conclusion that the Reformers were merely assimilationists in disguise. This, however, would be a significant misunderstanding of Reform's intent. The Reformers, by and large, acted out of a sincere belief that only substantial changes could preserve Judaism in the new era, and out of a genuine sense that, in the words of an early Reform group in Berlin, "our religion failed gradually to give us that satisfaction which was the comfort and the happiness of our ancestors."[9] The choice, many Reform leaders believed, was between change and complete disintegration.

In their own way, these leaders were often sensitive to the threat their efforts represented to Jewish unity. They sought, through frequent Rabbinic synods, to preserve a measure of unity at least among those with some sympathy for their platform. But ultimately, the entire thrust and tenor of their position, placing the authority to redefine Jewish practice and belief in the hands of those who could claim to be most in tune with the times, rendered this hope unrealizable.

That this would be so became clear from the vigorous opposition which the Reformers received, not only from those who rejected change in any aspect of Jewish life, but also from forces which accepted the idea of accommodation with modernity, but not the Reform program for achieving this accommodation. The reality of the challenges which Jews confronted required that this latter group restate the premises of the traditionalism which they wished to maintain, as well as the terms under which they would participate in post-Emancipation, post-Enlightenment society. The most notable such restatement came from Samson Raphael Hirsch, the nineteenth century German rabbi generally regarded as the founder of modern Neo-Orthodoxy. Hirsch took as his motto the Talmudic phrase *"Torah im derekh eretz,"* which he translated as meaning "traditional Judaism together with the civilization of the times." Traditional Judaism meant unswerving fidelity to the *halakhah.* The civilization of the times meant acceptance of citizenship, social intercourse with non-Jews, and philosophical exploration of the meaning of Jewishness in and for the modern world.

Like the Reformers, Hirsch believed that Jews had a mission among the nations which required their dispersal and an effort to bring together the values of modern society and of Judaism. Unlike the Reformers, he believed that Jews must maintain a spiritual segregation from the world in order to fulfill their mission, and that Torah must remain the standard by which modernity is judged rather than vice versa. Thus, the Neo-Orthodox insisted that *halakhah* continue to serve as the basis for Jewish unity and the vehicle through which Jews pursued their mission of demonstrating how man must and can devote his life to divine service.

Despite this assertion of continuity with the past, Hirsch himself confronted the necessity of defining Neo-Orthodoxy as a party within a divided Jewry, no longer the unself-conscious religious expression of a unified community. When the official Jewish communal institutions in several German cities were "captured" by Reformers, Hirsch did not hesitate to advocate secession from these communities. The Neo-Orthodox fought for government recognition as a separate religious grouping, and in so doing they helped to reemphasize the distance which Jews had traveled in the post-Emancipation period. If religious ideology and practice were the fundamental defining characteristics of a Jew, then, indeed, one could question whether Reform and Neo-Orthodox still constituted a single religious group. To be sure, the sense of commonality among Jews even of different denominational loyalties never dissipated entirely, but such an absolute split was conceivable within the terms of reference which both the Reformers and their Neo-Orthodox opponents employed.

Not all those, however, who were uncomfortable with Reform's open dismissal of the authority of *halakhah* were prepared to assert the Law's unchanging character. Nor were all rabbinic leaders sympathetic to the need for change ready to discard the notion that Jews constituted a people with a national homeland. Standing between the Reformers and the Neo-Orthodox there developed a third program of response to the challenges of modernity. In Germany it was called the Historical School; in America it became the Conservative movement. The core of its position rested on a new understanding of the character of traditional Judaism. Utilizing the tools of the new "scientific" approach to history, the Historical School found in Judaism a continuous process of evolution guided by the internal dynamics of a developing *halakhah*. Change was, in effect, built into the tradition, and therefore could be effected without denying the tradition's authority.

But what was to be the mechanism for determining which changes were in fact acceptable and which violated the tradition's spirit? Since, according to the proponents of this viewpoint, Judaism represented the record of the Jewish people's divinely inspired responses to their changing life experiences, it would be the people—what American Conservative leader Solomon Schechter called "catholic Israel"—which would serve as the ultimate arbiter. This position was not quite as democratic as it seemed, because the ideologists of the movement generally added an important qualifier: the people in a position to decide were only those who accepted and identified with the tradition and could therefore presume to accurately represent its spirit.

Despite this qualification, the Conservative movement, as it developed, came to place far more emphasis than either the Reform or Neo-Orthodox on the maintenance of Jewish community as a vital response in its own right to the challenges of modernity. In effect, it placed its faith not in ideology—whether liberal or traditionalist—but in the primoridal affinity of Jews for one another and in their common history as the vehicles for sustaining Jewish identity and unity in the modern era.[10] The ambiguity of its own ideology enabled Jews with diverse beliefs and practices to gather under its banner, but that banner could not embrace those on either side who sought a clear break with the past or its unequivocal reaffirmation.

## From Religion to Nationhood

Reform, Neo-Orthodoxy, and Conservatism were philosophical and denominational antagonists, but in several respects they were in fact ideological allies. All affirmed the possibility and necessity of maintaining Jewish identity and communality in the modern world. At the same time, all affirmed that the social and intellectual canons of modernity could be embraced by the Jew without undermining his Jewishness. They differed on how to maintain Jewish identity and communality and on the terms under which modernity could be appropriated, but they shared a fundamental strategy for Jewish survival in the post-Emancipation world: the reconstitution of Jewry as a religious group.

In the context of nineteenth century Germany, most of the rest of Western and Central Europe, and the United States, this strategy appeared to make sense. As a religious community Jews could justly assert an undivided nationality, that of their homeland. They could locate their distinctiveness in an arena—that of faith—which accorded it social legitimacy without demanding social isolation. And by linking that distinctiveness to spiritual and ethical values, they gave it a prima facie rationale as purposive, not merely accidental and therefore dispensable. Bitter though the dispute among the denominational proponents may have been, it was, to borrow the traditional Jewish phrase, "for the sake of heaven," for a conception of Jewish life in the modern world which placed religion at its center.

Such a strategy could not, however, appeal to all Jews. Even in the West, the inroads of secularizaton rendered a Jewish religious identity irrelevant to those who had rejected religion itself. Further, the fundamental proposition underlying religious reconstitution—the assertion that as a religious group Jews would find full acceptance in the emerging post-Emancipation national societies—proved problematic. Not only did religiously based disabilities disappear more slowly than anticipated, but the entire intellectual atmosphere of Europe was transformed by the emergence of a more romantic form of nationalism which emphasized "folkist" and even racial conceptions of national identity from which Jews were excluded.

In Eastern Europe, where millions of Jews lived, the entire drama of challenge and response which we have sketched out above was played out in very different terms. Jews living under the Czar (as most did after the Polish partitions of the late eighteenth century) did not experience even the promise of freedom which the Emancipation offered their

Western counterparts. Instead, they were subject to a policy which sought to undermine their traditional communal institutions, transform their economic role, and often forcibly assimilate them to Russian culture, while keeping them restricted geographically and socially. Religious reform, as such, held little attraction or utility. Neither, for most, did assimilation to a Russian culture which was not notably superior to their own and was characterized by a deep strain of anti-Semitism. In the multiethnic, multicultural milieu of the Czarist empire Jews retained a stronger consciousness of their distinctiveness in these domains, even as their communities began to disintegrate and their religious traditionalism to weaken in the face of spreading secularism.[11]

Thus, the responses of Eastern European Jews to their crisis of modernization were by and large different from those in the West. There were efforts to reinvigorate religious life, primarily within the framework of traditionalism (for example, the Musar movement which sought to revitalize Jewish ethical piety through educational reform). There were also Jews who sought a radical transformation of the Jewish condition through social and political revolution. For some of these radicals the continuity of Jewish identity was irrelevant. They embraced instead the ideals of proletarian internationalism and, in practice, Russian culture. For others, the vocabulary of Jewish culture was a language through which to reach the Jewish masses, of instrumental if not ultimate value. Other socialists, however, regarded revolution as a precondition for the free development and expression of a secular Jewish culture, which retained significance in its own right.

Undoubtedly the most important response to modernity within Eastern European Jewry, however, was the emergence of Jewish nationalism. Jewish nationalists took what was in their eyes a self-evident fact, that Jews possessed a distinct ethnicity and culture in addition to their religious faith (or lack thereof), and made it the cornerstone of a program for revitalizing the people and securing a place for it in the modern world. Jews, they believed, should seek acceptance and self-respect as a ethno-cultural-national group alongside other such groups. The national culture would replace traditional religion as the glue holding Jewry together. Its values would provide the spiritual substance necessary to sustain Jewish morale. This program was as far-reaching in its context as religious reform had been in the West in terms of redefining the basis and nature of Jewish identity and communality. The redefinitions proposed were in apparent diametrical opposition, but the goal of each strategy was the same: to enable Jews to live in the modern world on its terms, but as Jews.

Several forms of Jewish nationalism existed, often—as among Jewish socialists—in bitter rivalry with one another. One group envisioned Jews as a culturally autonomous minority enjoying full individual civic and political rights within the countries in which they lived. Others went further and championed some form of minority political, in addition to cultural, autonomy. The most radical form of Jewish nationalism to emerge in Eastern Europe was Zionism. Russian Jews were not the only ones to embrace the conclusion that Jews required a national homeland of their own. Theodor Herzl, Zionism's first great political leader, was, after all, an assimilated Western Jew. But Eastern Europe provided the soil within which the Zionist seed could take root and flourish. More than a decade before Herzl fashioned his proposal for a Jewish state, the *Hovevei Zion* (Lovers of Zion) movement had already taken shape in Russia, and Pinsker had already published his pamphlet "Auto-Emancipation," which anticipated many of Herzl's ideas.

Historians have often debated how to characterize Zionism as an ideological movement. Does it represent, as many have suggested, a revival in a secular vein of traditional Judaism's messianic aspiration for a return to the national homeland in Eretz Yisrael? Or is it primarily an echo of nineteenth century European nationalism, a Jewish *risorgimento?* Does Zionism provide a basis for continuity with the Jewish past, or is it a revolutionary repudiation of what has gone before? [12] Regardless of exactly how one assesses the relationship of Zionism to traditional Judaism and modern nationalism, it is clear that, as Joseph Blau has asserted, it must "be understood as another of the constructive attempts of Judaism in confrontation with the modern world."[13] Zionism, like the other such attempts we have outlined, sought to permit Jews to live in the modern world with the same rights and civil status as others enjoyed, while preserving a measure of Jewish distinctiveness and communality. The Zionists argued that these conditions could never be met as long as Jews were a dispersed minority, that neither political emancipation, religious reform, social revolution, nor cultural autonomy could overcome the dual specter of assimilation and anti-Semitism. Only in a Jewish national home could Jews be secure, be "like all the (modern) nations," and at the same time express their unique national spirit.

These claims made Zionism highly controversial in its early years. More than most modern Jewish ideologies, it was itself internally differentiated, with multiple visions and versions of the core ideology competing for hegemony within the movement. Zionism was wedded to socialism, to liberalism, to religious Orthodoxy, to vitalism, producing a bewildering array of variants. Even more, it was the target of attacks from virtually every other camp in the increasingly divided Jewish world. Like nearly all of the responses to modernity's challenges which preceded and accompanied it, Zionism held forth a vision of a united Jewry, but took its place as one among many competing programs which insured that Jews would, with respect to fundamental issues of self-definition and direction, remain disunited.

Yet, in another sense, the development of Zionism reinforced an underlying thrust in the several major Jewish responses to modernity which casts their admittedly substantial differences in a somewhat different light. The original Reform program for reconstituting Jews as a denationalized religious community and the Zionist program for building a modern, secularized Jewish nation-state stood in diametrical opposition to one another. Yet, as Jacob Neusner has noted, in one respect at least, they shared a common focus. Both concentrate

> upon the meaning of great events. Reform Judaism and Zionism take with utmost seriousness the history of the modern world, each interpreting that history, those events, in its own way, but in common agreeing that the world was changing and moving towards a climax.[14]

Reform Judaism and Zionism were in this sense messianic ideologies. They took the fundamental fact of modern Jewish existence—the Jewish return into history—and made it the focal point for their programs of internal revitalization and external adjustment. They averred that Jews could, through a self-conscious effort to restructure their relationship to the world, meet the challenges of modernity, and indeed play a central role in the world's progress.

Not all of the programs of response which we have outlined above were quite so bold in this assertion as classical Reform Judaism and Zionism. But nearly all shared the conviction that the return to history offered Jews an opportunity to enjoy the fruits of a new-found freedom, while rediscovering a purposive focus for their continued Jewishness. When it came to the point of defining the terms under which this vision might be consummated, the various ideological programs took their disparate paths. But in their belief that the modern world could accommodate an ongoing Jewish presence, and in their conviction that Jews could make that presence a satisfying and meaningful one, they were more united than their respective partisans might ever have acknowledged.

### Ideological Diversity and Jewish Civil Religion

In this Jewish world of active, but not necessarily eternal, disharmony, American Jewry began to come of age. The Jews who came to America throughout the nineteenth and early twentieth centuries brought with them every program and ideology which European Jews had devised. In America the partisans of these programs encountered one another in an atmosphere of unprecedented openness to Jews and to Jewish self-expression. With no old order to assault, no official community structures to seize or contest, no government arbitration of Jewish disputes, America provided a virtual blank slate on which Jews could write whatever story they wished about who they were and why they were.

And so they did write. As the waves of immigration—from the West and then the East—ebbed and flowed, ideological or ethnic groupings made their grasp for hegemony and unity, and fell back in face of the stubborn diversity of America's Jews. Reform leaders proclaimed the inevitable triumph of their theological standpoint, while proponents of Jewish national identity invoked, with equal confidence, their vision of American Jewry's destiny. In 1908, David Philipson could assure his Reform rabbinic colleagues that the Russian Jewish immigrants would soon be Americanized; that ghettoism, neo-nationalsim, and Neo-Orthodoxy would soon fade, "and that which shall remain will be the great fundamental ideal of the mission of Jews . . . as a people of religion and of Judaism as a religious force through all the world."[15] Seven years later, the writer and activist Chaim Zhitlovsky could predict with firm conviction that "the basis of our life in America will not be the Jewish religion, but rather our Jewish nationality."[16]

Again, however, it is not only the utter divergence of these predictions that should be noted, but a hidden commonality as well: in this case, the belief that American Jews must find a basis for unity which would at once locate them securely in their American environment, and legitimate their continued existence as a group. Both the fact of Jewish diversity and the American emphasis on freedom of belief made unity behind any of the ideologocal programs of the day impossible. In the American context neither religion nor ethnicity alone could serve as the foundation for encompassing Jewish community. Yet neither were American Jews prepared to abandon the sense that they were, ultimately, members of a single group. They were, therefore, unwilling to give up the quest for at least a partial expression of that unity.

Joseph Blau describes how the leaders of the Historical School in America sought to grapple with this problem. They came to recognize that for American Jews "unity would have to be one that transcended differences in the interpretation of Judaism, and that recognized the right to differ in belief, and even in practice, as a fundamental right of the Jew."[17] What had to be emphasized were those things which American Jews did have in common:

> All Jews, regardless of their "party" affiliations, shared in the millennial Jewish tradition, had a common concern for the fate of Jewry in the present age, and bore a responsibility for the transmission and preservation of Judaism in the future. Historical continuity itself is the factor transcending contemporary divergences and, therefore, the constitutive principle of the Jewish community.[18]

The leaders who recognized in this approach a path to unity were, in fact, accurate in their assessment. But even the Conservative movement was too particularistic in its own ideological program to serve as the vehicle for its realization. A basis for American Jewish unity indeed existed, but none of the specific religious or national ideologies arrayed alongside or against one another could effect or adequately express that unity.

The dilemma which American Jews faced, and continue to face, is not unique. One of the fundamental realities of the modern era is religious pluralism—members of the same society espouse different, even conflicting, ultimate meaning systems. Yet, they recognize themselves as participants in a common social order as well. Out of this sense of unity may arise a new religious quest: an effort to endow the commonality which is felt and the actions which are undertaken as a society with transcendent significance in their own right. Where this quest takes hold, "civil religion"—a religious meaning system which symbolically expresses and sustains the unity of the society (or nation, or group), even in the face of religious diversity—emerges.[19]

For the Jews of America, the quest for a shared religious self-understanding could not be met by any of the Jewish ideological movements which competed in offering systems of meaning. Yet the possibility existed for the emergence of something else—an American Jewish civil religion, a civil religion which would draw out the meaning implicit in those domains of experience and activity where Jewish commonality *was* manifest, and define an overarching identity for American Jews which would transcend the divisions of belief and practice that characterized American Jewry.

## The Nature of Civil Religion

The concept of civil religion has emerged as a major theme in the contemporary sociology of religion and in the study of American Religious history. The publication of Robert Bellah's seminal essay, "Civil Religion in America," in 1967 initiated a wave of discussion about the nature of civil religion, the historical and intellectual roots of the concept, and its applicability to a variety of phenomena ranging from contemporary American political rhetoric to medieval Japanese society. While there is even today no consensus on many of the historical and interpretive issues which have arisen, there is sufficient agreement on the reality of civil religion that we can feel comfortable in attempting to utilize the concept to illuminate the American Jewish experience in this century.[20]

The fundamental nature of civil religion can perhaps best be understood in terms of Durkheim's conception of religion in general as the symbolic expression of a group's sense of unity: "Men who feel themselves united, partially by bonds of blood, but still more by a community of interest and tradition, assemble and become conscious of their moral unity."[21] Religion—belief and ceremony—serves both to represent this unity and to reinforce it by linking the group to a transcendent order of reality. The group comes to envision itself not merely as a conglomeration of individuals, but as a moral community, a purposive entity with shared values and conceptions, with a life and destiny of its own beyond that of the individuals who comprise it.[22] That sense of transcendentally rooted and purposefully directed group unity becomes available to the group as it seeks to legitimate its collective endeavors and mobilize individuals' support for them. Religion is thus, in effect, the cement which bonds a group together. Where unity exists, religion arises; and where religion takes hold, unity is reaffirmed.

Modern society, however, is characterized, as we noted above, by a disjuncture between the unified political order of the nation-state and the plurality of religious meaning systems generally espoused by its citizens. Religious pluralism involves more than simply the existence of multiple religious groups in society. It means the presence within the social order of different, sometimes (though certainly not always) conflicting, frames of reference concerning the "moral architecture" of social life. Because religion defines the fundamental understandings that individuals and groups hold of their place in the world and supports their moral commitments, religious pluralism constitutes a potential threat to social discourse and to the unity of the political-social order itself. As long as that order is not entirely undermined, however, the desire of even a religiously diverse people to invest their common undertakings with meaning keeps open another unifying option. The political-social order itself may become the focus of religious sentiments. Alongside and apart from whatever religious convictions individual citizens and sub-communities (e.g., churches) may profess, the nation-state and/or its political institutions can themselves serve as the bases for the elaboration of a religious meaning system.[23] Such a system of shared beliefs and public rituals, defining and symbolizing the nation or polity as a moral community, is a civil religion.[24] United by such a civil religious faith, a society is assured of securing the degree of shared moral commitment required to tolerate a plurality of private meaning systems.

The great force of Bellah's original article on American civil religion lay in its demonstration through the citation of key historic texts that American political leaders spoke of the nation—of its origins, its trials, its purposes, and its destiny—in unquestionably religious, but not denominational, terms. The American civil religion is, as Michael Novak has defined it,

> a public perception of our national experience, in the light of universal and transcendent claims upon human beings, but especially upon Americans; a set of values, symbols, and rituals institutionalized as the cohesive force and center of meaning uniting our many peoples.[25]

The civil religion speaks to Americans not as members of particular faith communities or ethnic groups, but as participants in a common national historical venture. It sacralizes and interprets the elements of that common experience so as to link them to transcendent purposes and moral values. In so doing, the civil religion neither challenges the legitimacy of the churches as they continue to address questions beyond the purview of the civil religion's concerns, not does it merely adopt the common denominator of the churches' beliefs. Rather, the civil religion operates in a sphere of its own, that of the nation's identity and destiny, and seeks to invest that sphere with religious meaning. Often, it borrows its language —its symbols and metaphors—from the vocabulary of the religious traditions of the churches (especially the Bible). Often, the churches themselves share in the attribution of religious meaning to the national experience. But the American civil religion, Bellah and others suggest, is a meaning system in its own right, with a unique vision and a unique role to play in shaping American life.

Although America has provided the setting for most discussion of the phenomenon of civil religion, the concept has, as we noted above, been applied in a variety of other contexts as well. Charles Liebman and Eliezer Don-Yehiya, for example, have utilized the notion to illuminate the changing ideological underpinnings of the Israeli polity. They define civil religion in functional terms, "as a symbol system that provides sacred legitimation of the social order."[26] More specifically, civil religion helps to perform three major functions in and for the social-political order:

> (1) integration (uniting the society by involving its members in a set of common ceremonies and myths, which are themselves integrative and in turn express a sense of a common past, a common condition, and a common destiny on the part of the participants); (2) legitimation (transmitting the sense of an inherent justness or rightness in the nature of the social order and in the goals pursued by the society); and (3) mobilization (galvanizing the efforts and energies of society's members on behalf of socially approved tasks and responsibilities).[27]

Civil religion, like traditional religion, serves to link the ethos of a group to a worldview which renders that ethos supportable, and which is at the same time itself made plausible by the behaviors and sentiments it inspires.[28] The beliefs which a civil religion propounds and the mode of conduct it prescribes sustain one another and together offer a coherent way of understanding and responding to the conditions of group life. These beliefs are often embodied in myths, sacred stories which recount paradigmatic events in the life of the group. They are reinforced in rituals which call attention to the special character of particular values and moments in the group's experience and invest these with symbolic meaning. Civil religion integrates, legitimates, and mobilizes by producing in its adherents the sentiment that the society or group is tied to a sacred order, that its history and activity point beyond themselves to a higher realm of purpose and significance. Thus, the members of the society are induced to support its endeavors, to protect its unity, and to find meaning for their own lives through identification with the collective's ventures.

Not every group or social-political order either requires or is capable of generating a civil religion. Societies which are religiously homogeneous may draw sufficient legitimation from traditional religious institutions and ideologies. For centuries, traditional Judaism served also, in effect, as the "civil religion" of the Jewish people. Conversely, groups or societies which lack (or lose) the sense of themselves as moral communities will be unlikely to generate a civil religion (or to sustain one inherited from the past).[29] Other means of integration may be available for such societies, e.g., integration through the domination of a ruling class or caste, or through the functional relationships of the economic system. The vision of society as a moral community is itself not the only possible ideological standpoint. In the political realm, the position which regards the polity as a moral entity contests with at least two others: the liberal constitutional view, which sees the primary function of the state as the preservation of public order and maintenance of the conditions in which a free marketplace in goods and ideas can flourish; and the welfare state philosophy, which defines the role of the state in terms of the satisfaction of citizen demands and mediation among interest groups. It is unclear whether either the liberal or the welfare state approach is, by itself, conducive to the development of civil religion within a society.[30]

Where civil religion does develop, it assumes a functional and structural configuration much like that of traditional religion, but with two critical distinctions. First, civil religion's focus and locus is in the civic and political institutions of the community, not in the conventionally religious realm. Though it may invoke the concept of divinity, civil religion is not primarily concerned with God (or the Transcendent). It is concerned with the ultimate meaning of social and historical experience, especially as that experience is focused in the political domain. The prime bearers of civil religion are thus not, as we have noted, clergy or religious institutions, but the institutions of the polity itself and political leaders. Civil religion exists because the social-political order has a particular self-understanding as a moral entity which it seeks to sanctify and to legitimate. Civil religion provides a "meta-ideology" for the political community in a sacred key.

By introducing this transcendent component, however, civil religion also differentiates itself, at least partially, from the political regime at any given moment, and even from the political order and nation itself. Civil religion is a statement about the meaning of society's political in-

stitutions in an ultimate frame. Thus, it transcends any specific institution's or leader's political program or vision.[31] To be sure, this differentiation in theory is not always achieved in practice. Nor is the character
of the transcendent component which civil religion introduces into the
polity's self-understanding fixed. Writing of the American situation,
Martin Marty has suggested that there are "two kinds of two kinds of
civil religion." One axis of differentiation, Marty proposes, divides the
civil religion which "sees the nation 'under God,'" from that which
stresses "national self-transcendence." In the former there is an objective transcendent reference point which stands beyond the nation; in
the latter, the vocabulary of transcendence and faith is retained, but it is
the nation itself and/or its political values which are seen as embodying
transcendent significance. The second line of distinction separates
"priestly" civil religion—"celebrative, affirmative, culture-building"—
from a "prophetic" mode which is dialectical and often judgmental.[32]

These categories are, of course, analytical constructs. Specific articulations of civil religion do not always fit easily into one box or another.
Nevertheless, Marty's typology is a valuable reminder that a civil religion may embrace several variants with different theological shadings
and social implications. Civil religion, like traditional religion, is less a
single unchanging set of ideas than a family of beliefs and sentiments capable of multiple interpretations.[33] In nearly every instance, however,
civil religion establishes a context of meaning for group life which transcends the political situation of the moment, even as it helps to illuminate that situation. Civil religion constitutes the nation's or polity's
window on the larger reality beyond it. If it lacks traditional religion's
capacity to depict the human situation from a trans-human perpsective,
it can at least enable a society to see itself in a light projected from beyond its own present boundaries.

The second major way in which civil religion differs from traditional
religion is linked to the first, but is even more far-reaching. Because civil
religion is concerned primarily with the integrity and meaningfulness of
the social-political order, its scope is narrowed and its impact truncated
in comparison with traditional religion. The social-political domain is,
after all, only one of life's spheres. Often it is of relatively little immediate consequence to many individuals. Traditional religion reaches to
embrace the totality of human existence and of life's concerns. Civil religion generally does not. That is its strength as a social "meta-ideology."
Because it seeks to embrace only that part of life which is public, it can
integrate individuals and groups with diverse personal beliefs and tolerate the existence of alternative meaning-systems. But this is also civil religion's weakness. It cannot hope to displace these alternative systems,
nor can it anchor its own claims convincingly in an all-embracing worldview which promises personal as well as social integration and fulfill-

ment. Lacking such a worldview, civil religion rarely develops an elaborate or systematic theology. At most, one can expect to find a few theological tropes; often, civil religion is theoretically mute.

For these reasons, it is common for civil religion to establish a modus vivendi with traditional religious institutions. What the civil religion requires from these institutions is essentially reinforcement of its themes in the areas of its concern. This is usually not difficult to obtain. Civil religion, where it succeeds in taking hold, cannot be simply an artificial construct. It expresses the genuine integration and self-understanding which a group or society has achieved. As such, it generally enjoys a base of popular support. Indeed, civil religion often draws upon popular religious sentiments—the "folk religion"—for some of its central content. In this respect, its theological inarticulateness may indeed be an asset, since it can reflect and utilize folk myths and ceremonies without having to subject these to rigorous intellectual critique. Traditional churches and denominations have, at least in the American case, found it acceptable and at times advantageous to identify with the civil religion and offer it support.

At the same time, however, traditional religious institutions and leaders can play other roles with respect to the civil religion. Martin Marty has drawn the distinction between civil religion and "public theology."[34] The latter represents an attempt to elaborate on the theological import and meaning of civil religious themes and symbols. It is a public, but "unofficial" effort to add depth and substance to the vocabulary and content of civil religion, which its own articulators from within the political system often leave vague. This public theologizing may emanate from particularly thoughtful leaders in the political domain, but often it comes from church leaders who accept the fundamental direction of the civil religion, but wish to see its insights sharpened and critiqued. When the civil religion itself becomes too "priestly," or the sense of being "under God" threatens to become lost, it may be from the domain of "public theology" that a prophetic voice is heard. Such need not be the case; in American history some of the most celebratory, uncritical, and expansive visions of national self-transcendence have emanated from church leaders. But the relationship between civil religion and traditional religion can be dialectical without becoming oppositionary.

That dialetical relationship—and the inherent limitations of civil religion—are evidenced in other ways as well. We noted above that civil religion often relies upon and borrows from traditional religion for its primary symbols and metaphors. The prominence of biblical images in American civil religion—indeed America's core religious self-understanding as a "new Israel"—are evidence of this. So too is the use of traditional Jewish symbolism by contemporary Israeli civil religion.[35] The way in which such symbols are employed varies. Sometimes they are explicitly revalued, i.e., given radically new meanings and stripped of their old ones, as, for example, the socialist pioneers in Israel did with the festivals of the Jewish year. More often, they are assimilated to the new situation they are intended to significate without their original meanings being denied. This process is important in achoring civil religion to a familiar religious vocabulary and in intensifying the emotional resonances it produces. Civil religion "borrows" legitimacy from traditional religion in this fashion, but also gives these symbols new potency and immediacy. Traditional religious institutions must then decide if they too will accept the new symbolic referents, or risk having their symbols captured altogether by the civil religion.

As civil religion moves to incorporate elements of traditional religious symbolism, however, it also highlights its own weakness as a generator and interpreter of religious meaning. Because the force of transcendent reality is often attenuated in its own beliefs, myths, and rituals, these rarely have the same impact on the lives of adherents as do traditional forms on those who accept them. Coupled with civil religion's failure to address the full range of personal human concerns, the limited impact of its self-generated symbols places civil religion in a tenuous position. Its fortunes as a meaning system are very much linked to the events and social environment of the day. At a time when the political atmosphere is highly charged and the history of the hour dramatic and compelling, civil religion can dominate the consciousness and commitment of an entire society or nation. When events become routinized and concerns more private, then civil religion may fade into the background.

## Civil Judaism: The Civil Religion of American Jews

American Jews did not set out to develop a basis for unity in the midst of their ideological diversity by deliberately fashioning a civil religion. Yet, with the benefit of hindsight, we can see that over the course of the last century just such a Jewish civil religion has emerged. American Jews shared in all of the problematics of Jewish existence in the modern world. They confronted the problem of identity—of how to define their Jewishness. They faced the challenge of establishing their relationship to non-Jewish Americans and to American society as a whole. They asked the question "why?"—why seek to maintain a distinctive Jewish identity, why not accept the implicit invitation to immerse themselves in the most inviting melting pot the world could offer. The programmatic answers which nineteenth century Europe bequeathed to American Jewry were helpful, but insufficient. Above all, those answers could not enlist the common assent necessary to sustain their plausibility in the American environment. Each had something to offer, to at least one important segment of American Jewry if not to all. None had the power to express both the commonality which American Jews, despite their differences, felt, and the mix of certainties and uncertainties which characterized their attempts at a unique *American* Jewish self-definition.

Without fully recognizing that they were doing so, American Jews embarked on a strikingly successful venture in the early decades of the twentieth century. They began to create an American Jewish polity, a matrix of voluntary organizations and associations which carry out functions of communitywide concern.[36] The initial steps in this direction were relatively small and seemingly without significant ideological consequence. But the development of a Jewish civil sphere, institutionally distinct from (though not in opposition to) the domain of religious activities conducted by the synagogues and rabbinic leadership, constituted a critical point of departure for the development of something else: an American Jewish civil religion.

As the American Jewish polity evolved and took shape, it began to express, as well, a characteristic understanding of who its "citizens" were, of what purposes it pursued and what kind of world it pursued them in. It discovered a raison d'être and a mission, and these in turn became central to large numbers of American Jews who otherwise remained divided in their denominational loyalties and affiliations. The evolving ideology of the American Jewish polity became a type of American Jewish common faith, a "civil Judaism." This faith expressed and sustained the unity American Jews felt among themselves, legitimated the endeavors of the community to maintain Jewish group life while promoting maximal involvement in American society, and inspired Jews to contribute to the support of other Jews and the pursuit of social justice. In this civil Judaism many American Jews have found persuasive answers to the fundamental questions which have vexed modern Jews since the Emancipation. The American Jewish civil religion prescribes a model of Jewishness which synthesizes ethnicity and religiosity and places both firmly within the embrace of American pluralism. It links American Jews to the totality of the Jewish people at a level beyond ideological diversity. Perhaps most important, it gives Amercan Jews transcendent purposiveness by holding out to them a vision of Jewish destiny and mission in which they have a central role to fulfill.

American Jews do not constitute a nation or a society in their own, right. To speak, therefore, of an American Jewish civil religion may seem to be stretching the use of the concept beyond reasonable boundaries. Yet, we would suggest that no other concept makes as much sense of the constellation of beliefs and practices, myths and rituals, which animates the organized American Jewish community today. That community is indeed a sophisticated political system, with hundreds of local and national organizations operating through a complex network of linkages to raise and expend hundreds of millions of dollars to carry out the "public" business of American Jewry: support for the state of Israel, assistance to Jews abroad, maintenance of social welfare, recreational, educational and cultural programs for American Jews, insurance of Jewish security and involvement in American society. This voluntary political system is the expression of American Jewry's identity as a moral community. The American Jewish polity embodies American Jewry's sense of purpose and priorities, its conviction about the type of world Jews live in and the response to it they are called upon to make. It is, therefore, not really surprising that polity institutions and leaders have come to give voice to these convictions in civil religious terms. In the statements of these leaders and institutions, in the symbols they evoke, we can locate American Jewry's shared understanding of its place in the world and its part in Jewish destiny. This understanding in turn gives transcendent meaning to the work of that polity and to the lives of the individuals who share in it. It is American Jewry's civil religion.

The remainder of this book will examine this civil religion and its significance in contemporary American Jewish life. It will do so primarily in the words of the leaders of the American Jewish polity themselves. These men and women were and are not "religious" thinkers, and certainly not theologians. They are Jewish activists, who found in their work in the Jewish polity a cause worthy of their devotion. Their efforts to articulate the meaning of that cause are our best guide to the substance of the civil Jewish faith. That faith did not emerge fully formed in early decades of this century. Rather, it evolved as the polity did—slowly, fitfully, with ample divergence in viewpoint. Eventually, however, a consensual civil religion did emerge and became consolidated as the transcendent meaning system of the polity. It is to this process of emergence and consolidation that we turn in the next chapter.

# II

---

# FROM PHILANTHROPY TO POLITY, FROM ADJUSTMENT TO SURVIVAL

### Federated Charity and The Quest for Communal Unity

The development of an American Jewish civil religion did not really begin until the growing diversity which accompanied successive waves of immigration made it impossible for the synagogue to function as the sole religious center of a unified community. During the first two centuries of American Jewish life the synagogue had generally played this role. Perhaps the first clue that American Jewry would not remain a community of congregations—and hence that traditional religious institutions would not serve as sole definers of its self-understanding—was the founding in 1843 of the Order of B'nai B'rith. The establishment of the fraternal lodge as an alternative locus for pursuing Jewish solidarity and practicing Jewish values constituted a radical break with traditional Jewish forms. "At its heart," according to historian Deborah Dash Moore,

> lay a bold new vision of the nature of Jewish identity in America. B'nai B'rith's establishment gave Jews an alternative mode of affiliating with the Jewish community and a potential Jewish polity. It synthesized the components of Jewishness and Americanism into a unique amalgam that assumed the benefits of emancipation and affirmed the value of being Jewish.[1]

Despite its aspirations toward primacy, B'nai B'rith itself never became the institutional core of either the American Jewish polity or its civil religion. Its reach was simply not broad enough to encompass the "community" as a whole, especially after the arrival of millions of Eastern European Jews.

For several decades after B'nai B'rith's establishment and the nearly concurrent founding of the first Jewish charitable associations independent of single religious congregations, it was by no means clear that syna-

22

gogues would not, in fact, remain the focal point for Jewish communal organization. It seemed possible that a version of traditional religion (perhaps Isaac Mayer Wise's moderate Reform) would serve as American Jewry's common faith. Both the Board of Delegates of American Israelites (comprised of congregational representatives and focusing its activities on what today would be called "community relations") and the more ambitious (and successful) Union of American Hebrew Congregations sought to solidify the role of the synagogue as the building block of an American Jewish polity. These efforts ultimately failed (at least in their most ambitious aims) because the synagogue simply could not serve as a basis for comprehensive unity. Congregations and their leaders were themselves increasingly divided over issues of fundamental religious ideology and practice. More important, however, was the radical transformation in the character of the American Jewish community which was brought about by the mass immigration which began in the last decades of the nineteenth century.

The influx of Jews from Eastern Europe challenged the institutions of American Jewry both practically and ideologically. The practical challenge was to take care of the overwhelming numbers of new arrivals. This demanded—and produced—an explosive growth of philanthropic agencies and services: relief societies, children's homes, schools for teaching trades and good character. The ideological challenge was to transmit to the immigrants and their children a model of Jewish identity and behavior which would promote their rapid adjustment to American society, and thereby not undermine the hard-fought status gains achieved by their earlier arriving coreligionists. In this way—by promoting a common adjustment to the American environment—a measure of internal unity among Jews could be attained as well.

Documents from the period attest to the seriousness with which these challenges were taken by the established, largely German in origin, American Jewish leadership of the time. Many bemoaned the loss of homogeneity which accompanied the arrival of new immigrants. Louis Wirth cites the plaint of a Chicago rabbi as early as 1874:

> Scarce two decades have elapsed since all Israelites of this city were living as in the bonds of one family and circle. Each knew the other. All worshipped harmoniously in one temple and shared others' woes and joys. How great is the change! Thousands scattered over a space of nearly thirty miles, in hundreds of streets, divided by pecuniary, intellectual, and social distinctions, provincial jealousies, and even religious distinctions and differences. . . . Dissolved in the mass of our population, we are losing the consciousness of our homogeneity and the strength gained for each individual by concerted action.[2]

The desire for unity in the face of overwhelming disintegrative forces was both pragmatic and ideological. America's German Jews remained justifiably insecure about their position in American society as social discrimination waxed in the post-Civil War period. They feared that large numbers of Jews—some destitute, all "foreign" in their ways— would constitute an uncontrollable force, draining their own resources, undermining the image of the Jew, retarding the process of Americanization to which they were committed. More than once, leaders of charitable societies expressed dismay at the flood of immigrants. August Levy, secretary of the Hebrew Emigrant Aid Society, bemoaned that "only disgrace and a lowering opinion in which Israelites are held . . . can result from the continued residence among us . . . of these wretches."[3]

At the same time, many among the German Jewish leadership retained a genuine sense of solidarity with the immigrant Jews and a sincere desire to see them uplifted to their own state of "enlightened" American Jewishness. "Shall we shirk our duty to our unfortunate coreligionists?" asked a leader of Jewish charitable work in Boston. "God forbid that the holy flame of Charity which illuminated and warmed the Jewish heart should have lost its heat and lustre among the Jewish residents of this city."[4] Since the immigrants were not attracted to the religious institutions which the settled Jews had created (nor would they likely have been accepted into them), another approach to meeting their pressing socio-economic needs and to solidifying the community—thereby achieving a measure of social control, as well— was required. The answer was the vast expansion of philanthropic services which took place during the last two decades of the nineteenth century and the nascent attempts to make these the basis for communitywide Jewish organization.

By 1900 the American Jewish community was far different than it had been at midcentury. As a retrospective written twenty-five years later put it, "The synagogue had lost its place as the center of communal life, and had been supplanted by a network of institutions, philanthropic and educational, which now commanded first place."[5] Philanthropy has always been a source, as well as an expression, of Jewish unity. It links donor and recipient into a common bond, even as it differentiates their status. Philanthropy provided German Jews with a way of affirming their own Jewishness, while seeking to influence the way in which their fellow Jews adjusted to America. Both of these motivations for philanthropic activity must be taken seriously. As the expression of a noblesse oblige, even condescending, attitude toward the immigrant Jews, German Jewish philanthropy has at times been deprecated. Yet the organizers of the many charitable and educational endeavors which sprang up during this period believed that they were fulfilling a Jewish obligation to fellow Jews, and rarely questioned whether they were so obligated. American Jewish mythology points to the pledge made by the first Jewish settlers in New Amsterdam, never to permit their brethren to become a public charge, as one source of this obligation. But even if one believes such a special burden to be inconsistent with enjoyment of the full rights of citizenship, as Julian Mack, a prominent communal leader of the day, suggested, "nevertheless, [the Jew] conceives it to be his duty—no longer to his fellow Americans, but to himself, to his religion, his fellow Jews—faithfully to carry out this pledge given by his ancestors."[6]

The proliferation of philanthropic agencies designed to redeem this pledge constituted, however, a problem in its own right. Diverse, uncoordinated initiatives were often perceived as inadequate to the needs, wasteful of resources, and unseemly in the image they presented. American Jews were by no means ready for unity on any substantial scale which would embrace religious practice or broad-scale political activity, but they were beginning to show a readiness to move toward greater coordination within the philanthropic sphere. Several decades earlier, mergers of charitable agencies within localities had begun to take place with the goal of incorporating wider segments of the community in their work. When the United Hebrew Benevolent Association of Boston was founded in 1864, for example, it aimed "to secure if possible the cooperation of the Jews of every nationality residing in or near Boston."[7] An even more explicit plea for unity in philanthropy was made by leaders of Milwaukee's Hebrew Relief Society in the next decade:

> It has been characteristic of our race to . . . always car[e] for our indigent and poor. It is desirable that we should keep on in this good labor, and show by our deeds that while we may differ in our opinions as to dogmas, be they orthodox or reform, we do stand united on the rock of charity and benevolence.[8]

Still, the situation by the end of the nineteenth century was one of considerable confusion, marked by a proliferation of what one observer described as "loose, benevolent but spasmodic organizations"[9] One response was the organization of a National Conference of Jewish Charities in 1900, to try to introduce principles of "scientific charity" into the work of Jewish agencies and to provide a forum for discussing common issues and problems. What would ultimately prove to be even more significant was the introduction in 1895 of a new concept in local organization of philanthropy: the Federation of Jewish Charities, first instituted in Boston and Cincinnati.[10]

Federations were originally designed primarily as financing mechanisms, reducing the costs and easing the burdens on potential contributors of multiple charitable campaigns. But federations, as we have implied, were also part of a larger movement seeking to unify American Jews in their philanthropic endeavors. The federation form (as opposed to outright merger of agencies) acknowledged the reality of diverse interests and loyalties, but it also recognized philanthropy as a potentially powerful—at the time perhaps the only—basis for communal unity. Speaking on the eve of the founding of the Boston federation, Mrs. Jacob Hecht, a leader in Boston's German Jewish community, implored her colleagues: "We must be as one family, coming each from his separate society, as from the privacy of his own apartment to the general table where the family come together to talk over in a friendly fashion that which is of equal interest to all."[11] What immigration and its pressures had pulled apart, the Federation of Jewish Charities was designed in some fashion to restore.

Philanthropy could serve as a basis for (relative) unity because it was a precept of Jewish religion on which all could agree. Furthermore, it was functional for those who engaged in it. It accorded status, both within and beyond the Jewish community, and it helped advance a program of immigrant adjustment which donor Jews viewed as highly beneficial to their long-range interests as well as to those of the recipients. Philanthropy as practiced by the German Jews did not, to be sure, completely bridge the gap between the donors and the Eastern European Jews who were predominant among the recipients. The early federations were, by and large, leagues of the German Jewish charities only. But the immigrants, too, founded agencies for mutual aid and financial assistance, especially as some among them prospered financially. Thus, two sets of parallel institutions often emerged, and, despite the pleas of some leaders, it would in many instances be decades before these became part of a single communal philanthropic system. The separation of German and Eastern European sponsored charities was a natural expression of the different cultures of the two subcommunities, as well as the suspicion with which each regarded the other. This suspicion reflected in part the power and status differentials which existed between the two groups. It also reflected a broader uncertainty about the goals of the German Jewish philanthropic effort.

As suggested above, many German Jews viewed the Eastern European arrivals and their culture—including the religious traditionalism of some—as "alien." Some regarded even so basic a religious practice as Sabbath observance as inappropriate in the American context and a cause of poverty among the immigrants.[12] In general, settled American Jews viewed their own process of adjustment as a success, and wished the newer arrivals to emulate it. From the outset, charitable work had been defined to include not merely relief, but some form of education and training, if only for orphans. The goals of character improvement and cultural development had been part of the early endeavors to create Jewish institutions—Young Men's Hebrew Associations, e.g.—which would supplement the synagogue and provide a more "modern" environment for Jewish social activity. Thus, it is hardly surprising that a thrust to "Americanize" the immigrants became a major component of organized philanthropy. Yet, it would be incorrect to characterize the leadership of the German Jewish community as simply assimilationist. Rather, they sought to affirm and to inculcate a positive Jewish identity which would, at the same time, be distinctively and wholeheartedly American.

We can, therefore, find evidence from the first decade of the twentieth century of a tension and a resoltion of that tension which have characterized American Jewish civil religion up to the present day. In conceptual terms, the tension is that which Charles Liebman identified as that of the "ambivalent American Jew": between full integration into American society and survival of a distinctive Jewish group.[13] For the leaders of the philanthropic establishment in the early years of this century, the tension was expressed in debates over the extent to which the institutions they sponsored for immigrant Jews should seek to support the Jewish identities of those who used them. The record makes reasonably clear that Jewish education was not a priority for most charitable donors during this period. At the first National Conference of Jewish Charities in 1900, Morris Loeb reported that "hospitals and asylums had the largest numbers of supporters, temporary relief considerably less, education institutions (omitting Sabbath schools), the least of all."[14] Yet a considerable communal investment was made in settlement houses, Y's, and institutions like New York's famous Educational Alliance which offered diverse educational programs. Here, as Morris and Freund note, the issue of Jewish purposes and content became crystallized. "From the beginning, the Jewish settlement agency confronted its supporters with a dilemma as to its purpose: Was its function to Americanize Jews (and what did this entail?) or to preserve their Jewishness?"[15]

The initial view had clearly favored Americanization as the goal, but this approach proved inadequate. One leader, A. H. Fromenson, noted in 1904 that Eastern European Jews often viewed the settlement agencies with antipathy, and suggested that the problem lay in the lack of Jewishness in these institutions and their failure to embody Jewish ethics and ideals. Without such an element, he contended, the "regenerative work" being attempted could not fully succeed. "Restore Jewishness to the Jew in the institutions that are meant for his moral uplifting."[16] A few years later, Louis Marshall, perhaps the foremost Jewish leader of the first decades of the twentieth century, added his call for "a distinctively Jewish tendency in the conduct of Jewish educational institutions."[17] The response to this thrust was positive if not dramatic. Some YMHA leaders sought to promote "positive Judaism" by introducing religious education into their programs, and in general, the mission of the center/settlement agency was recast as a dual one: "to find a place for the immigrants in the general American scene, and also to create a distinctly Jewish place in it."[18]

The question, as posed by Jacob Billikopf in a 1915 speech, became "what machinery can be best adapted to the fulfillment of our dual obligation—the Americanization of the Jew and the Judaization of the immigrant?" Billikopf proposed a linking of the Talmud Torah (Jewish school) to the settlement. Thereby, he suggested, the strains and ex-cesses of adjustment could be eased, Jewish moral values conserved, and good citizenship insured.[19]

In this discussion critical elements of the nascent civil religion begin to become visible. The potential tension between integration into American life and Jewish group survival is acknowledged, but denied. By defining Judaism as a force for "character building" and a stimulus to good citizenship, the nurturance of Jewish values becomes an American virtue. From the inception of B'nai B'rith onward, the identification of Judaism with applied morality has been a primary Jewish civil religious stategy for vindicating both its embrace of America and its support of Jewish group perpetuation. Judaism is affirmed as functional in the American environment, but it must, in turn, be transmitted and lived out in institutional settings beyond the synagogue if its message is to re-ceive full validation.

The promotion of Jewish values was not the primary emphasis of the developing philanthropic system. Debate over the appropriateness of involvement in this arena—indeed over the need for sectarian social services altogether—would continue for several decades among leaders of the Jewish charitable field. But by the end of the first decade of the twentieth century the themes which would later become central to the mature American Jewish civil religion of the 1970s and 1980s had begun to be articulated. First was the theme of unity: of philanthropy as a basis for overcoming distinctions of origin, denomination, and ideology, and achieving unified Jewish action. Second, the theme of responsibility: of the obligation of Jews to aid other Jews as a primary expression of the meaning of Jewishness. Third, the theme of Jewish-American symbiosis: that Americanness produces a more elevated Judaism, and Jewishness a better quality of American citizenship. What emerged in this period was, then, precisely what is required for a civil religion to develop and take hold—a group seeking to express itself as a moral community, and needing to do so through institutions outside those of traditional reli-gion.

## Toward World-Wide Responsibility

In the next decade, the American Jewish community moved toward greater unity, heightened responsibility, and intensified self-consciousness. The primary stimulus was World War I, which thrust American Jewry into a new prominence on the world Jewish scene. Concern for the fate of Jews abroad had, since the mid-nineteenth cen-tury, served as a spur to efforts toward greater communal unity. Indeed, virtually the only arena where American Jews had achieved anything approximating unified national action was in responding to threats to Jews in other lands. The Damascus blood libel of 1840, the abduction and baptism of Edward Mortara in Italy in 1858, and the pogroms in Russia in the last decades of the nineteenth century each stimulated initiatives toward concerted action and coordinating institutions. The subsequent wave of pogroms in Russia in 1903–05 also provoked the first serious fundraising effort among American Jews for the relief of foreign victims. Out of the involvement of men like Jacob Schiff, the investment banker, in this fundraising—and the political activities which accompanied it—grew the idea for a permanent mechanism to represent American Jewry in defense of Jewish rights around the globe: an American Jewish Committee.[20]

The Committee, established in 1906, was clearly an institution of the German Jewish establishment. It spoke for American Jewry in the tradition of the *shtadlan,* and had no pretensions toward democratic representation of the Jewish masses. Indeed, it feared and opposed efforts to establish representative bodies as the means to unify American Jewry. World War I brought new issues to the fore, however, which demanded additional communal initiatives. The first of these issues was the massive problem of providing material relief to the Jews caught in the war zones, expecially in Eastern Europe. It is noteworthy that no segment of American Jewry denied a responsibility to provide assistance. Fundraising campaigns were undertaken not only among the German establishment, but by Orthodox Jews and socialists as well. Despite the sharp ideological antagonisms among these three groups, philanthropy (and a shared sense of responsibility for fellow Jews) proved a sufficiently potent unifying force to spur the creation of a single mechanism for disbursal of these funds: the American Jewish Joint Distribution Committee. The establishment of the JDC in 1914 is a landmark in American Jewish history and an important step toward the broadly based polity which is the institutional locus of the civil religion today.

The JDC represented practical confirmation of the concept that philanthropy could bring together essentially all American Jews in a way that no religious (or secular) ideology or other institution could. But the challenges to American Jewry during this period went beyond coordinated fundraising. World War I placed new political responsibilities on American Jews as well, with German, French, and British Jewry no longer able to act in concert as the natural leaders of world Jewry. American Zionists felt this responsibility especially acutely. Within the United States, Zionism had been a struggling movement prior to the outbreak of the war. With the exception of a few noteworthy individuals (Judah Magnes, Stephen Wise), Zionism was anathema to the German Jewish establishment. Its espousal of Jewish nationality threatened the Jewish leaders' commitment to full integration into American society and nationality. But Zionism had appeal (if not enormous organizational support) among the masses of Eastern European Jews, whose concept of Jewishness was more ethnically rooted than that of their German Jewish counterparts. The war pushed American Zionism to the forefront of the world movement. At the same time, the movement as a whole received a major boost from the issuance of the Balfour Declaration which, for the first time, gave its platform recognized legitimacy. Therefore, the war provided an unprecedented opportunity for American Zionists to establish legitimacy on the American Jewish scene.

That it succeeded in doing so is due above all to the work of two men: Louis D. Brandeis and Stephen M. Wise. Brandeis provided the Zionist movement with not only effective leadership at a critical period (and leadership by an "establishment" Jew at that), but the classic formulation of its ideological rationale in the American context. Zionism, in his view, was an extension and application of Judaism's and America's own ideals of liberty and social justice. A good Jew must be a Zionist, he argued, out of commitment to these values and a sense of solidarity with Jews struggling to escape suffering and persecution, and to enjoy the fruits of liberty. But such a good Jew would also be a better American because of this commitment. Thus, Brandeis reasoned, there was no conflict between Zionism and Americanism; indeed, the two were mutually reinforcing.[21] In this fashion, Brandeis made Zionism and Zionists if not popular, at least acceptable partners to many in the German Jewish establishment. Further, while not abandoning Zionism's political goals, Brandeis and his followers emphasized a strategy of development of Palestine through prudent, businesslike investment which appealed to the non-Zionist philanthropists. As settlement in Palestine showed more promise as at least a partial solution to the problems of Eastern European Jewry, even anti-Zionist stalwarts like Jacob Schiff (who had once averred that "the more thoroughly our people become dispersed among the nations, the nearer the great Jewish problem will be brought to a satisfactory solution")[22] began to acknowledge that the concept of a Jewish national home in Palestine was not without merit. Zionism had, he conceded after the war, helped to develop "greatly needed self-consciousness" among Jews, and he urged American Jewry to "forget its differences" and find a solution for the "Jewish Question, of which I verily believe Palestine has become the cornerstone."[23]

The "price" which Brandeis was quite prepared to pay ideologically for the possibility of such unity—"domesticating" Zionism as an American movement—was also acceptable organizationally to Stephen Wise, the popular leader of the largely Eastern European, pro-Zionist forces who sought to create a representative Congress of American Jewry to speak on its behalf on the world scene. Wise was opposed by the American Jewish Committee establishment, but eventually the pressure of the masses proved irresistible, and a Congress was convened. The positions formulated by the Congress supported a Jewish national home and minority rights for Eastern European Jews. Perhaps more important, however, was the choice of the man to head the delegation which would bring these positions to the Peace Conference in Paris: Louis Marshall, leader of the American Jewish Committee, and symbol of the German Jewish establishment.[24]

Brandeis's redefinition of the Zionist message and Wise's efforts to draw German Jews into a practical, if not ideological, alliance with Jewish nationalists hardly resolved all the conflicts between the several camps in the Jewish community. Zionists continued their own fundraising alongside that of the Joint Distribution Committee. Non-Zionists (not only the Committee, but B'nai B'rith as well) resisted Wise's attempts to make the American Jewish Congress a permanent body. Nevertheless, the overall impact of World War I and the challenges it brought forward was strongly in the direction of promoting communal unity.

On the national scene, not only the JDC, but also the Jewish Welfare Board (formed to provide chaplaincy services for Jewish soldiers), gave practical expression to this developing unity. In the local arena, federations continued their growth and expansion during the decade under the same banner of unity. After several abortive efforts, and inspired by the success of the wartime appeals for overseas relief in reaching the Jewish masses, philanthropic leaders in New York City finally achieved a federation of its charities in 1917. These leaders had come to believe that "philanthropy promised New York City Jews an unexpectd bonus from their charity: a sense of identity and a basis for community."[25] The emphasis on fundraising campaigns as the cornerstone of communal unity grew more pronounced. Boston's 1916–17 campaign slogan—"A United Israel for Charity," proclaimed in English, Hebrew, and Yiddish[26]—typified both the conceptual underpinnings and the practical efforts toward ever greater inclusiveness which began to transform the federations from leagues of charities into the bases of a Jewish polity. The federation movement was proving itself to be a successful vehicle for mobilizing the Jewish community for common—albeit still limited —goals. At the end of the decade there were federations in at least fifty communities, raising and expending more than $6,000,000.[27]

By 1919, Felix Warburg, son-in-law of Jacob Schiff and heir to his mantle as American Jewry's leading philanthropist, could claim before the National Conference of Jewish Charities that philanthropy had "wiped out" class antagonisms among Jews and predict that increased Jewish giving would "have as great effect on American life as upon Jewish life."[28] He was far from alone in his enthusiasm over the achievements of the previous several decades. Henry Rosenfelt, in a 1924 book entitled *This Thing of Giving*, offered this assessment of the impact of the wartime experience:

The touch of common danger made all kin. In the pools of war-blood all Jewish hyphens have been washed away. Jews today are closer together than ever before. . . . We are no longer orthodox and reform, conservative and radical—all are becoming united, bound together by that ancient formula, "I am a Jew!" And for this we owe our brethren across the sea an eternal obligation which outweighs our help to them, as fidelity to faith casts the scales of Israel against even the gold of unselfish charity.[29]

What Rosenfelt was witnessing was the emergence of a civil religion rooted in the sentiments and responses characterizing Jewish philanthropy. As the historian Oscar Handlin has noted, "from the point of view of the people who lived through that period, philanthropy was important not only for what it actually accomplished, but because it was the means by which they engaged in communal endeavors. Philanthropy supplied them with the signs by which they recognized one another."[30] Philanthropy drew upon and reinforced a feeling of Jewish solidarity at a primal level, one which transcended differences of ideology, nationality, and religious practice. It was identity-constructing both for the individual who engaged in it, and for the community which was created by it. It provided a vocabulary and a setting in which those who differed profoundly on "ultimate" issues could nevertheless reach common cause. Thus, philanthropy gradually came to express the meaning of "Jewishness." What is more, it defined a mode of Jewish identity and behavior which was thoroughly compatible with American values, in which group solidarity became the basis for the exercise of moral responsibility. Out of these building blocks, the American Jewish civil religion was being constructed.

### The 1920s: Conflict and Consolidation

The pressures of the war had propelled American Jewish philanthropy and its institutions to increasing prominence in shaping the character of American Jewish life as a whole. Nevertheless, the unity which its partisans proudly proclaimed was by no means achieved in fact. Genuine disagreements still existed between proponents of different ideological visions of Jewish life. Over the next decade, struggles between these camps continued, even as the momentum toward institutional consolidation and expansion of the philanthropic system propelled it toward centrality within the American Jewish polity.

At its heart, the ideological conflict of the 1920s (which was not resolved definitively until after World War II) was over the bases and character of organized Jewish group life in America. It expressed itself, as Morris and Freund have described it, in the search for an emotional and logical foundation for Jewish philanthropic activities:

At one extreme was the view that the Jewish future lay in a full assimilation with American life and the abandonment of separatist organizations
other than the synagogue. Very close to this was the view that Jews must
adapt themselves culturally and wholeheartedly to the American tradition, but should maintain some tenuous identity which was never well-
defined. At the other extreme was the view that Jewish group survival in
American was essential, and to this task all social and welfare agencies
and philanthropic enterprises should lend their continuous efforts.[31]

The debate among these groups placed the ambivalence of the the
American Jew at center stage. It is noteworthy that the arena for this
struggle was not primarily the synagogue, but the philanthropic and social welfare system. Particularism of belief and private religious practice
was not at issue. America could easily accept Jewish churches (with
their attendant variations of ritual and dogma). The question was
whether Jews should or could maintain a group identity beyond the religious sphere. It was already clear that the primary instrument to achieve
such an identity would have to be the network of fundraising and social
service agencies, which provided the only conceivable basis at the time
for unified communal endeavor. To play this role, however, the philanthropic leadership would have to resolve several key issues: What was
the "mission" of Jewish fundraising and social agencies? On what basis
should support be sought? What was the legitimate scope of activities in
this field? Could the support of all segments of the Jewish populace be
enlisted, and if so, what changes in direction might be required? Could
the system accommodate both survivalists and assimilationists, nationalists and antinationalists?

Participants and observers of the struggles of the period understood
that the American Jewish community was at a turning point. Morris
Waldman, one of the foremost professional leaders of the federation
movement during the period, assessed the new situation in a 1925 address to what was by then called the National Conference of Jewish Social Services. The war, he noted, had affected Jewish social work
profoundly by widening its horizons and extending its interests to the
international realm. Further, the rise of new Eastern European leadership had brought new attitudes into the social welfare system, and with
them new tensions over such issues as support for Jewish education. The
community, Waldman recognized, had achieved unity where material
relief programs were concerned, but now, "in those directions where
differences of point of view toward the philosphy of Jewish life are involved, much more difficulty is experienced." The difficulty lay in the
fact that the community was divided between two elements with con-
trasting "traditions as to the Jew's position in the world and his relation
to the community at large." Can these two elements of the same "race
and religion" be united? asked Waldman. The answer, he suggested,
would depend in part on what the scope of Jewish communal life would

be. Increasingly, he felt, that scope would be "spiritual or cultural." Recent developments, he stated, had "resulted in a broadening and deepening of our communal interests embracing Jewish life abroad, including Palestine, and a recognition of Jewish education as the most vital element in the preservation of the Jewish people." Yet it was precisely these new concerns pushing their way onto the agenda of the philanthropic system which much of the older establishment found difficult to accept, since they carried with them a clear commitment to Jewish national identity and cultural distinctiveness. Facing this dilemma, Waldman could envision only some vague new type of "double-barreled" federation, reconciling the two tendencies in Jewish social service.[32]

Like many of his contemporaries in the prosperous and relatively stable 1920s, Waldman overestimated the extent to which Jewish social welfare would be able to leave behind the tasks of material relief. But his portrayal of the debate over the direction which federations should take cuts to the heart of the struggle which would be played out over the next two decades in a variety of concrete ways and settings.

No party in the debates of the period was advocating a program of Jewish separatism in America. All accepted the validity of the goal of full Jewish integration into the mainstream of American life. Rather, the debate was over the terms of such integration, and whether the process was compatible with Jewish group survival. Often, the practical disputes carry echoes of academic debates over alternative models of assimilation.[33] It is little exaggeration to say that the "melting pot" met "cultural pluralism" in the halls where Jewish social service professionals and philanthropic leaders debated the future of "sectarian" agencies and the program of welfare institutions.

The emerging agenda for Jewish philanthropy in the 1920s was thus a hybrid of traditional concerns and a new self-consciousness about the need to make Jewish group survival an explicit goal. Not all accepted that goal—some viewed it as undesirable, some as unattainable. But gradually group perpetuation came to be a recognized factor to be considered in all discussions of communal policy and institutional programs. In some measure, the leaders of the social welfare system had no choice but to accept this reorientation. Their own commitment to the ideal of "Jewish unity" dictated an accommodation to the views of the Eastern European Jewish masses for whom perpetuating ethnic communality and culture was important. Perhaps more significantly, the very successes of the system in developing Jewish self-awareness and a sense of mutual responsibility through philanthropy, made the advocacy of voluntary self-liquidation of that Jewish consciousness and the institutional network it had spawned (as assimilationism would ultimately have meant) virtually self-contradictory.

The proponents of a new agenda were able to translate Brandeis's argument on behalf of Zionism into a broader assertion that heightened Jewish consciousness would, in fact, enhance the Jew's position in American life. Thus, community center leaders like Harry Glucksman came to define the mission of their agencies as "build[ing] up an active, articulate Jewish communal life as an integral part of the general community," and "strengthening [the community's] Jewish consciousness as a constructive force in American life." Without in any way abandoning its historic goal "to aid in the adjustment of Jewish life in America," the community center was now to be, as well, "an effective instrument for the perpetuation of Jewish life in this country."[34]

The adoption of group continuity as an explicit goal of the social service fundraising network complicated the consideration of several issues which Jewish philanthropic leaders faced during this period. One, for example, was how federations should relate to the spread of Community Chests. In many instances these chests had developed in imitation of the Jewish federations themselves, extending the principle of joint fundraising and coordination of services to the general community. By the early 1920s federations in a number of localities—mostly smaller, but in a few large cities as well—had opted to join the chest campaigns and give up their own fundraising. Federations in other cities were hesitant about taking this step, and the Conference of Jewish Social Service was sufficiently uncertain about what direction to recommend that it sponsored a national study to evaluate the pros and cons of chest affiliation.[35]

The study team, Maurice Hexter and Samuel Goldsmith, two of the foremost communal service professionals of the era, first noted the growing—but as yet incomplete—inclusiveness of the Federations themselves. On the issue of Federation-Chest relationships, Hexter's report took a cautious position. It concluded that Jewish agencies apparently fared well financially, and that Jews played an active role in campaign leadership and budgeting decisions in the Community Chests. Yet, Hexter expressed strong personal reservations about the "ultimate effect of such alliance."[36]

Hexter's concerns were shared by a number of other leaders throughout the next decade or so, and seem to have revolved around several key issues: (1) Would the Jewish community be perceived as receiving more from the chest than Jews were contributing to it, or Jewish agencies seen as seeking more funds in order to support levels of service greater than those available to non-Jews? (2) Would Community Chest involvement drain the Jewish community of needed leadership? (3) Would chest support for Jewish agencies weaken the interest and involvement of Jews with those agencies? (4) Would the Community Chest approach undermine the rationale for separate Jewish agencies altogether?[37] These questions were clearly both practical and ideological, and they reveal again the underlying ambivalence about the ultimate rationale for and future of Jewish communal organization in America which was characteristic of the period.

In general, the momentum during the 1920s and early 1930s was to ward Community Chest affiliation. A 1929 survey concluded that Jewish agencies had received equitable treatment by the chests, and also offered a rationale for inclusion which expresses well the universalistic ethos which was an important component of the Jewish social welfare system's philosophy: "The accompanying advantages of joinder with the chest, in promoting a working fellowship on a common humanitarian task and in securing the widespread participation of the public, are important considerations because of the stimulus towards the development of a progressive community program which is of benefit to all groups."[38] By the late 1930s, in cities which had both Jewish federations and Community Chests, the rate of affiliation was 65 percent.[39]

This movement toward greater Jewish organizational involvement in nonsectarian fundraising and social service was not, as we have seen, taken without discussion. Neither, for a majority of its proponents, was it aimed at the eventual liquidation of Jewish communal organization, even for philanthropic purposes. Indeed, it was during the 1920s, that the Jewish survivalists began to develop a platform which would come to dominate communal ideology and form a central tenet of the civil religion in future decades. The core of their position was the proposition that in adjusting to American society Jews need not and should not abandon the special concerns which made even their charitable work unique. One manifestation of that uniqueness was the unity which was both manifested and fostered by Jewish fundraising and social service. Jewish philanthropy was more than good works; it was an expression of Jewish identity and group cohesion. The chairman of the 1925 Chicago United Drive, whose campaign slogan was "Are You a Jew?", characterized the drive as a test of Jewish identity, a "drive for Jews to carry the burden of Jews."[40] Even the delivery of Jewish casework services— carried out with an uncharacteristic involvement of community groups in planning agency programs—was seen as reflecting

> the strong cohesion of the Jewish community, notwithstanding its superficial national, economic, and social stratifications. Jewish charity is not simply charity; Jewish welfare work is not simply scientific casework; it is an expression of a strong feeling not only of group solidarity, but of social responsibilities.[41]

Advocates of a broad view of the purposes of Jewish communal organization during the 1920s were thus able to point to the successes of Jewish fundraising as a sign of the commitment of Jews to group self-perpetuation, even when the ideological articulation of this commitment was still vague. Writing in 1925, Hyman Kaplan proclaimed that a great social force has been built up by Jewry during the past thirty years, which has expressed itself by a contribution of many millions of dollars annually to local philanthropies, and by active volunteer service of thousands of men and women. This *will* to give of time and money for a common cause has been a vital bond, making for community consciousness and concerted action. We are in a period of transition, and the formulation of programs to conserve basic values must depend upon the initiative and vision of our leaders.[42]

Jewish philanthropy, asserted Morris Waldman, was an expression of and mechanism for the "group will-to-live." Though Jews might still be "floundering . . . , groping in our attempts to adjust our community interests to the general interests," and thus lacking a "philosophy of Jewish life in America," there was, he concluded, a place for group perpetuation in the American ideal of brotherhood. Hence, whether federations participated in Community Chests or not, Jewish communal organization to pursue group interests—whether Palastine or Jewish education—would have to persist.[43]

This is precisely what occurred. Jewish involvement in nonsectarian fundraising and social service was thus integrative, but not assimilatory in its impact. Jews discovered that there were areas of evident communitywide concern which transcended a narrow definition of "charity," and which demanded communal fundraising efforts even where Community Chests provided the support for social service agencies. Thus were born Jewish Welfare Funds, the major institutional innovation of the 1920s. These were organizations, generally created under federation auspices, designed to provide central fundraising and allocation of community funds for national and overseas agencies, and for local services—e.g., Jewish education—which had a clearly "sectarian" character. The establishment and gradual spread of Welfare Funds was a clear signal that the underlying premise of the Jewish federation—that the community could and must unite its efforts in domains of Jewish activity where collective welfare and human needs were at stake—had taken firm root in what remained, in many ways, a divided community.

Such divisions indeed still existed. That between the Zionists and non-Zionists, expressed institutionally in the competitive fundraising of the United Palestine Appeal and the Joint Distribution Committee, was often acute. Unified campaigns at the national level in the early 1920s, and again in 1930 and 1934–35, were not successful in bridging the gap permanently (or in raising the anticipated funds).[44] Partisans of the respective causes often fought for Welfare Fund allocations as well. Yet, most striking during this period are precisely the repeated efforts, despite failure, to achieve what Felix Warburg, in announcing the 1930 national Allied Jewish Campaign, envisioned: "a lasting and permanent unity in American Israel."[45] Eventually, these efforts were to bear fruit, and the capacity of federations and Welfare Funds to establish themselves as dominant organizations on the local scene was perhaps the critical factor in compelling national unity. It is, however, the ideal, and the arena in which it was vested—philanthropy—which is again most telling. Philanthropy was proving once more to be the solvent which could soften ideological antagonisms and the cement which could bind the community, not simply because it presented itself as "non-ideological," but because it tapped a dimension of Jewish consciousness which was more fundamental—and would prove more enduring—than the divisions of the day. Samuel Kohs celebrated Jewish Welfare Funds in 1927 as vehicles for "uniting and integrating the divided groups in a Jewish community," but even more as mechanisms for "reawakening a hibernating Jewish self-consciousness, Jewish morale and conscience."[46] Indeed, the central theme of the 1920s and 1930s in American Jewish life may be that reawakening and the development of an institutional framework—a polity—through which it could find appropriate expression and by which it could be nurtured.[47] The federation-Jewish Welfare Fund system was not the sole candidate to play this role, but because it reached most directly those areas where a unified Jewish morale and conscience were to be found, it proved the victorious one.

This ascendance was both fostered and evidenced by the federation's ever-increasing penetration of the Jewish community. As federation leaders began to recognize that the instrumentality they directed was a polity as much as a charity, the impulse toward greater inclusiveness and representativeness—meaning incorporation of the agencies, concerns, and talented individuals of Eastern European Jewry—became more explicit. Federation leaders began to speak with the rhetoric of American political institutions, calling for a "wider franchise" and "greater democratization" in order to draw in organizations remaining outside its boundaries.[48] "There can be no place in the vocabulary of federation," one president argued in 1928, "once it serves as the articulate will of the united Jewish community, for such words as German, Russian, Polish, American, Orthodox, Reform, etc. Federation must concern itself with the cross-section needs and desires of the entire Jewish community."[49]

Following this path meant accepting an expanded definition of the purposes of Jewish communal organization in America and of the potential role of federation within it. In the broadest view, as articulated in 1930 by John Slawson, later to become a preeminent professional leader as head of the American Jewish Committee, the common purpose of all Jewish communal endeavor in the United States was "raising Jewish life to as high a functioning plane as possible." This required, he recognized, a variety of approaches: social work, religious activity, cultural programs. Slawson placed primary emphasis on what he called the "Jewish aspect." "The injection of Jewish values into Jewish communal life . . . with Jewish education as the principal mechanism . . . is . . . necessary if our work is to have a central purpose, compatible with the actual stuff out of which our activities are composed." Necessary, too, was a heightened interest in world Jewry. "Being at one with the sixteen millions of Jews throughout the world is for the Jewish individual a contribution to his ethnic personality." How were these bold aspirations to be pursued? Slawson suggested the federation as the most likely instrument. As the agency which already embodied a common purpose, and a democratic, integrated, and Jewish approach to communal concerns, federation must now become more than a palliative. It must serve as an expression of Jewish ethnic life in America and occupy itself with the broad range of Jewish activities.[50]

### Years of Challenge and Crisis

Time and circumstances worked to fulfill Slawson's vision of the purposes of Jewish communal organization and the role of federation. But that fulfillment was neither immediate, nor without controversy. The next fifteen years constituted an awesome challenge, both for the communal system and for the philosophy of Jewish life which it was evolving. At the outset of the 1930s knowledgeable observers expressed concern over the capacity of the federation system to deal with the range of activities—cultural, educational, and overseas, all in some measure controversial—which seemed to be replacing local philanthropy as foci of concern.[51] In fact, the challenges turned out to be far more extensive: a depression which made economic relief again a primary concern, and raised new questions about the relationship of the organized Jewish community to an activist government sponsoring a social near-revolution; the growing oppression of German Jewry which heightened pressures for unified action by American Jews even as it exacerbated fundamental ideological disputes; resurgent anti-Semitism in America that threatened to disturb the delicate equilibrium of adjustment and group survival which American Jewry had managed to maintain; and finally, a world war which demanded full Jewish mobilization behind the American war effort, even as six million fellow Jews were being systematically exterminated.

It is not our purpose to evaluate the effectiveness of the Jewish community in meeting these challenges. Rather, we must focus on two questions: (1) were the fundamental outlines of the organizational system evolved over the previous decades altered during this period? and, (2) how did the animating ideology of the polity change in response to the tumultuous events through which the Jewish community was living? The answer to the first question, whether, as some anticipated and others urged, a major structural reconfiguration of the community took place during this decade and a half, is "no." The federation system—

including Welfare Funds, local agencies, and national and overseas organizations—survived largely intact, though not unchallenged. The major institutional innovations which did take place ultimately reinforced the polity structure as it had developed. Certainly, the innovations—primarily the creation of Jewish Community Councils in some localities, the development of a national Council of Jewish Federations and Welfare Funds, and the establishment (finally) of a United Jewish Appeal carrying out combined fundraising for the Joint Distribution Committee and the United Palestine Appeal—represented extensions of the fundamental concept of unified communal endeavor, which the federations had championed.

In the ideological realm, the results of the decade and a half between the onset of the Depression and the end of the war were more complex, but perhaps even more conclusive. Slowly but surely, the various species of assimilationism, the several endeavors to restrict the concerns of communal organizations to noncontroversial philanthropy, were pushed to the margins of the community. A survivalist, but still profoundly integrationist, vision of American Jewish life moved to center stage. The program of the polity was reaffirmed and expanded as American Jews began to demonstrate that their communal instruments could indeed be used to foster both group consciousness and social responsibility.

This process was, to be sure, a gradual one and the product of continuous reappraisal by federation leaders of both the character of Jewish group life in America and the role of the federation system in guiding its development. The intensified pressure on the federations which accompanied the onset of economic depression spurred the creation of a new national instrumentality to help coordinate planning and to provide a forum for consideration of the multiplying problems faced by the local communities: the Council of Jewish Federations and Welfare Funds (CJFWF). Rapidly, the Council and its annual meeting (or General Assembly) became the prime gathering point for Jewish communal leadership as they grappled with these problems. By the early 1930s, federations had become, in Ben Selekman's words, "by and large the most influential organization in American Jewish life."[52] The Council's deliberations thereby became indicative of how that influence was to be used in shaping the course of the community's further development.

The dominant struggles during the Council's early years were between those who saw in the new challenges of the era a basis for retrenchment or caution, and those who wished to proceed boldly with the expansion of the federation agenda and an explicit commitment to survivalist ends. The debate was not new, though the specific circumstances often were. One key issue was the extent to which federations should be involved in supporting Jewish cultural and educational activities. Those who opposed such support cited both pragmatic and philosophical reasons. In pragmatic terms, the key considerations were the reluctance of major donors to endorse such expenditures and the urgent need to devote resources to traditional social welfare and economic assistance. Philosophically, some leaders continued to argue that cultural and educational programs were essentially "private" in character, linked as they often were with specific religious or ideological positions. Therefore, they did not belong in the federation, but rather "should be supported primarily by those who are particularly interested in this phase of Jewish communal endeavor."[53] Jewish education raised especially difficult questions for federations precisely because any attempt to define its content "strikes fundamentally at what should be the ultimate cultural adjustment of the Jewish community in the United States."[54] Thus, some prominent leaders like Joseph Proskauer, then president of New York's Federation for the Support of Jewish Philanthropic Societies and later of the American Jewish Committee, urged in the name of unity that all controversial issues be eschewed, and that the Council and the federations deal only with "those problems which have to do with the amelioration of the condition of our less fortunate, our under-privileged brethren."[55]

Such a narrow view of federation concerns was, however, increasingly difficult to sustain. By this period, the survivalists were (at least in national debates) on the ascendance, even challenging the right of those whom they accused of indifference to group continuity to claim leadership positions.[56] A series of reports and addresses in the early 1930s endorsed federation support for educational and cultural programs, albeit with some caution, and, characteristically, within a context in which strengthened Jewish knowledge and commitment was affirmed as functional in the American environment. In 1933, for example, a statement of federation objectives endorsed at the Council's General Assembly included (following provision of family, medical, children's, and elderly services) these two goals:

> To see that provision is made for the educational, recreational, and cultural needs of the Jewish population, both young and adult, to give to Jews the opportunity of freely developing, out of their traditions, their cultural and creative possibilities, and thereby to make a contribution to the cultural content of American life.
>
> To see that facilities are made available, according to modern pedagogical standards, to meet the needs of the Jewish child for education in the history, traditions, language and religion of the Jewish people.[57]

Jewish education was regarded as a legitimate social need meriting federation attention at least in part because it was perceived as "a force making for the development of character and good citizenship."[58] This linking of heightened Jewish consciousness with more successful adjustment to the American environment was one of the major conceptual tools of the proponents of Jewish survivalism. During the 1930s, with its upsurge of anti-Semitism, the theme of group continuity was given a new dimension as well. Supporters of inclusion of Jewish educational and cultural programs within federation provenance had their pragmatic arguments—primarily that such programs were totally dependent on Jewish support, unlike social welfare endeavors where governmental and nonsectarian funds were available. But the heart of their argument was an appeal to Jewish self-respect and dignity. Jewish survival was now a cause, and the rhetoric of support for those programs which were seen as promoting such survival took on a new tone.

Thus, the question of federation support for Jewish education began to assume the character of a litmus test. Will the General Assembly, one delegate asked in 1934, be placed "before the Jewish world as standing for Jewish survival, or [are] we going to be associated with those people who are either indifferent, or perhaps subtly opposed, or not concerned about it, or at times not quite possessed of the courage to come and say so openly?"[59] The following speaker was even bolder in his challenge:

> Sooner or later, it seems to me, there will have to come into being a body that will talk for the Jewish people, that will concern itself with the life, and the lives of the strong portion. Whether that should come out of the Federation or not, your decision today may determine. But such a body must come, and a primary purpose of such a body will be to bring up our children Jewishly and to strengthen the spirit within, and it will have to be a body whose psychology comes from the urge from within and not from the fear as to what the 'goy' will say about the things we are doing.[60]

Most among the top levels of federation leadership were not prepared to go so far in appearing to turn away from concern for the position of the Jewish community in American society. But the conviction that federations were called upon to strengthen those agencies charged with transmitting the Jewish heritage was being expressed with increasing vigor by both professional and lay leaders of the movement. Solomon Lowenstein, director of New York's federation, spoke at the 1935 National Conference on Jewish Welfare of the likely public takeover of much heretofore private health and welfare activity. For Jewish agencies, that would leave two primary arenas of action: programs of "character-building" and of religious education. That federations should embrace the latter as well as the former area he had no doubt:

> If we are to maintain our Jewish group intact, if we believe in the survival of the Jewish group as part of the American community, if we do not wish to see lost in our present generation all that the Jewish people have struggled for during centuries of dispersion and oppression, we must develop these institutions into agencies of which we can be proud and which can pass on that tradition of Jewish life which our fathers have died to save.[61]

This statement is striking even more for its rhetorical tone than for its content. The issue of whether Jewish group survival is an appropriate goal for American Jewry is not raised as one for rational debate (though there were still those among the communal leadership who had their doubts on this question). Rather, the audience is induced to see such survival—and federation responsibility for creating the necessary instrumentalities to insure it—as an act of faith with the martyrs of the Jewish past.

This sentiment—that Jewish survival is a goal beyond question, not a matter for philosophical discussion—became increasingly prominent in the rhetoric of communal leaders during this period. With Jews under assault both at home and abroad, turning away from Jewishness was seen almost as an act of cowardice, of betrayal. "We would be a poor kind of people," the director of the Jewish Charities of Chicago argued,

> a non-descript and fruitless people, if we could not find security among ourselves, and if we did not so strengthen our inner-life and so organize our group-life that we would have some dignity, some characteristic nobility, and some purposeful achievement to our credit.[62]

As it would for many American Jews after the Holocaust, anti-Semitism itself seemed to provide a rationale for a more self-assertive Jewishness. The fact of Jewish insecurity was seen by an increasing segment of communal leadership as an important rationale for insuring that individual Jews be made fully aware of the positive value and values of Jewish identity. "Growing numbers," stated Sidney Hollander (later to serve as CJFWF president) in 1936,

> are coming to the belief that Federations should accept a greater measure of responsibility for Jewish cultural and educational activities. In the face of widespread and growing anti-semitism, our young people must be fortified with the pride that comes only from an understanding of our history and heritage. We cannot let them be afraid to be Jews. They must meet whatever lies ahead courageously and unashamed.[63]

Jewish education, as another leader put it a year later, is a way to help Jews face a frequently antagonistic environment behind the bulwark of "the rich and positive meanings of our inheritance, re-evaluated and integrated with our modern life."[64]

This heightened concern on the part of some community leaders for Jewish consciousness was not purely reactive. Neither did it imply a desire to turn wholly inward. Rather, these leaders were groping for a renewed self-understanding of who American Jews were and what their responsibilities were during what all recognized as a period of trial. Federation leaders were by no means prepared to abandon the vision and values which had proven so successful in building the movement and mobilizing Jewish energies on its behalf. Morris Waldman undoubtedly spoke for many in warning that "the agitation which aggravates the Jewish problem today" must not be permitted to "throw us back into a ghetto of unhealthy Jew-consciousness and estrangement from our non-Jewish neighbors."[65] Support of Jewish education and culture did not supplant traditional philanthropic work as federations' chief priority.[66] The vast majority of leaders remained wholeheartedly committed to full Jewish participation in American society and culture.

For some, the "survivalist" turn was entirely unwelcome. Documents of the period testify to a pronounced "assimilationist" tendency among a segment of both the lay and professional communal leadership. One such leader on the national scene, George Backer, a vice-president of the Joint Distribution Committee, openly avowed assimilation as a not unworthy goal. Except for religious institutions, he believed, "Jewish institutions must eventually look forward to the time when they may disappear." Such was the inevitable outgrowth of America's progress toward the democratic ideal. "It is of course possible for a man to believe that Judaism is a way of life . . . ;but the person making this decision is not attempting to further the American experiment in democracy and must be considered as having dismissed American culture as a desirable possibility."[67]

Few leaders accepted Backer's premise that the American ideal negated the validity of Jewish group life beyond the religious sphere. But nearly all were concerned that such group activity not be perceived as in any way removing Jews from the mainstream of American life. William Shroder, the founding president of CJFWF, put the matter in these terms: "Jews are in the web and woof of American living. Their Jewishness is an additional, not a separate interest. Their loyalty to America, its ideals and its traditions is enhanced by their inheritance as Jews. There is no conflict; there is in truth a cumulative urge."[68] This conviction, amounting at times to a virtual indentification of Americanness and Jewishness, was articulated repeatedly throughout the 1930s and the war period which followed. "It is unthinkable to me," stated Samuel Rosenman, a judge and communal leader, at the 1937 General Assembly, "that there should be the slightest inconsistency in the statement that a man is a good American and a good Jew." Though there was no place in American life "for a separate nationalism or civilization," there was certainly room for "free religious and cultural expression by all minority groups."[69]

Although the compatibility of Jewish group survival and full participation in American social life was almost universally accepted, there was more uncertainty about what this principle implied for Jewish behavior and the activities of communal organizations. Some emphasized what might be termed the "integrationist" implications. Rosenman, for example, urged that Jews rid themselves of all remaining clannishness in their thinking and conduct, at the same time as they fought for the principles that protected the rights of all minorities.[70] Others, in the tradition of Brandeis, took the proposition as a warrant for intensifying Jewish commitment and communal activism, in the conviction that this would enable Jews to fulfill their responsibilities to America more fully.

This notion of a Jewish contribution to American life which would grow out of enhanced Jewishness and the work of Jewish communal agencies also began to receive more prominent articulation among communal leaders at this time. Rosenman himself linked his call for intensified involvement in the social struggles of the day to Jewish values: "Allegiance to the principles of social justice has been the heritage of the Jewish people from the time of its prophets," he contended, and went on to suggest that the Jewish experience of persecution had enriched this commitment.[71] The widespread evaluation of the Depression and New Deal as a watershed period in America's own quest for a more just society meshed well with liberal Judaism's characteristic emphasis on the social teachings of the prophets. Together, they produced a heightened sense of Jewish mission among the leaders of ostensibly secular Jewish communal organizations. In urging Jewish leaders not to compromise the principles of democracy, Morris Waldman, for example, cited not only the ultimate security these principles provided, but also "the ideals of the prophets, the conservation of which is both our high destiny and our *true* justification for existence as a people."[72] In a similar vein, I. M. Rubinow, general secretary of B'nai B'rith, told delegates to the 1936 General Assembly that they should be proud that the new social insurance programs of the New Deal owed something to Jewish prophetic ideals. Organized Jewry, he contended, could perform a "sacred task" by supporting social security, especially in light of "our own sacred conception of social justice."[73]

This linking of Jewish values to the work of communal agencies and the activities of its leaders represented an extension of the long-established notion that American Jewish philanthropy was but the latest expression of the traditional Jewish commitment to *tzedakah* (charity). Since the term *tzedakah* means more than charity—"social justice," indeed, accurately reflects the sense of "rightness" and "obligatoriness" attached to the Hebrew concept—the step from equating *tzedakah* with the philanthropic work of the community, to equating the Jewish value of social justice with support for New Deal initiatives was not, for many leaders, a radical one. More important than the validity of this equation, is the emerging sense it bespeaks that the Jewish community qua Jewish community had an important contribution to make to American life, and that Jewish tradition had helped to shape America's values.

In this spirit, Jewish communal organizations could see their own work as upholding both Jewish and American ideals. Joseph Willen, a pioneering federation professional leader in New York, suggested that Jewish leaders could take pride in their "speaking for and safeguarding certain basic and permanent values in our American life," especially the concept of "individual responsibility in meeting human need." At the same time, they were also assuming their responsibilities as Jews, whose "tradition of Jewish fellow-feeling and generosity is among our proudest boasts."[74] The Jewish people, another leader contended at the 1938 General Assembly, possessed a "great civilizing tradition," which could be brought to their fellow men as a "cultural contribution for the enrichment of all peoples." By instilling Jewish youth with this conviction, they could take their place with pride in American society, rejecting Jewish separatism, but accepting their distinctiveness as a "distinction of merit, gilded by the rich and heroic past of their people."[75]

The frequent evocation of pride in the Jewish past and of a Jewish mission in the present in statements like these may well have been in part a defensive reaction to the anti-Semitism of the period. But in substance, they added an important note of transcendent purposiveness to the work of the federations and their leadership. At times, the significance attached to these endeavors rhetorically was enormous. Here, for example, is the text of an appeal made by the president of Boston's Combined Jewish Appeal in 1938 as part of its report to its contributors:

> Surely, in these tragically dark days no one need stress the importance of supporting Jewish charities. Just because the world has become so brutalized and inhuman it is all the more incumbent upon us as Jews to keep lofty all the symbols and sentiments of humanitarianism, of kindliness, of concern of one human being for another. What are our hospital, family and child welfare, neighborhood center, Jewish education and health camp services but the embodiment of all the age-old precepts and experiences of our people in caring for the poor and oppressed, for strangers and refugees, for the hungry and sick . . . The Jewish philanthropies is a trust . . . placed in our hands. Let us preserve and strengthen it so that we, in our way, will help the virtues and decencies of civilization come to life and thrive again.[76]

Jewish philanthropic leaders may well have believed that the work that they were engaged in was profoundly meaningful from the very beginning of the growth of the communal system. But the direct articulation of this belief—the explicit effort to legitimate their activities in near-transcendent terms—was not nearly as common in earlier periods. This rhetorical shift surely reflects the extraordinary situation which the leaders of the 1930s faced. No small part of this situation was the growing crisis in Germany and Europe, which, as had happened so often in the past, called forth a deep sense of universal Jewish solidarity. David Heyman, president of the Bureau of Jewish Social Research, a forerunner and later a part of the CJFWF, spoke of this renewed awareness at the 1934 General Assembly:

> Recent world events and impending changes have brought us to sharp

realization that we are participants in a single destiny and that the political, social, and economic forces are likely to affect all of us as though we were parts of a single organism. . . . World events have precipitated a larger solidarity: they have erased factional differences; they have overwhelmingly convinced us of the need for joint programs and common action.[77]

Heyman was somewhat premature in his expectation of unified action —it was not until 1938 that federation leaders were able to push the overseas agencies into a long-lasting (though initially often tenuous) fundraising partnership—but the identification of American Jewish leadership with the traumas of Jewry abroad was more intense than ever before. The 1936 General Assembly passed a resolution calling "the present catastrophe . . . the most terrible calamity that has befallen the Jewish people within the memory of living man," and appealing for maximum gifts to both the Joint Distribution Committee and the United Palestine Appeal "for the sake of the victims of this awful tragedy and for our own self-respect and character."[78]

Federation leaders struggled throughout the period with the dual problems of enlisting support for overseas relief and mediating the still simmering disputes between the non-Zionist and Zionist camps identified with the JDC and UPA respectively. Support for the Jewish community in Palestine was not per se a controversial issue. But the political content of Zionism and its emphasis on emigration to Palestine as the only solution for the Jewish problem in Europe continued to make it anathema to many major donors. Some professional leaders were, on the other hand, becoming bolder in their public endorsement of Zionism within federation circles, citing, for example, "the inspiriting and unifying force" which many Jews felt in contemplating "the possibilities of developing in the world a free and untrammeled State where social justice, where a planned life and a free culture, may blossom again."[79]

The establishment of a United Jewish Appeal, linking the Joint Distribution Committee and United Palestine Appeal, in the wake of the trauma of *Kristallnacht* in 1938—largely through the efforts of CJFWF—was, therefore, both a major substantive and symbolic achievement. Though disputes were to break out repeatedly between the partners concerning how the funds collected were to be allocated, local Welfare Fund leaders would not permit the alliance to be permanently destroyed. Each time a break-up occurred the UJA was reconstituted within months. The United Jewish Appeal successfully adopted the rhetoric which had already become characteristic among the communal leadership. It campaigned first to alleviate despair and tragedy, then to celebrate Jewish courage and independence, and during the war it secured the endorsement of non-Jews as well by labeling a contribution to the UJA as a contribution to democracy.[80]

Once more, as it had during World War I, fundraising and the practical work of relief and rescue provided a basis for unity where ideological and organizational differences made unity on other levels difficult.[81] The impulse toward unity was not, however, confined to the traditional philanthropic domain. Just as federation leaders pushed to coordinate overseas activities and fundraising, so too they began to urge heightened cooperation among the major national community relations agencies who approached the Welfare Funds for financial support.

The resurgence of anti-Semitism in the 1930s had produced a renewed concern on the part of American Jews for securing their place in American society. The response was on two levels. One was a strengthening of the national "defense" organizations—the American Jewish Committee, the American Jewish Congress, the Anti-Defamation League of B'nai B'rith, and the newly formed Jewish Labor Committee. Federation leaders began to question whether the independent, and at times conflicting policies and programs of these agencies could not be better coordinated. The effort to promote such coordination resulted eventually in the establishment by CJFWF in 1944 of the National Community Relations Advisory Council, designed to bring the major national agencies together within some type of formal consultative framework. The struggle for cooperation in the community relations field proved a long and difficult one, with results that could best be described as mixed. Nevertheless, the sustained involvement of federation leaders in this venture provides further confirmation that the concept of unity had become an overarching value for these leaders and a recurrent organizational thrust.

The second major institutional response to the threats to Jewish security during the 1930s involved federations even more directly. As we noted earlier, Jewish communal organization in America has always struggled with the twin ideals of inclusiveness and democracy. In the face of the pressures confronting the Jewish community in the 1930s, the call for a representative, community-wide vehicle for grappling with issues common to all Jews echoed with new vigor. The form which emerged in several communities was a Jewish Community Council, designed to bring together on a voluntary basis representatives of every major group in community life. The council concept revived the long-standing debate over the wisdom and feasibility of establishing a single authoritative instrument for setting community policy or resolving communal disputes. Ultimately, the councils did not become American *kehillot*. They did, however, become effective vehicles for furthering communal unity in a number of cities.

Although some saw the councils as rivals and potential successors to the federations and Welfare Funds as the primary foci for community organization, the two institutions more often developed a working relationship which did not threaten federation primacy. Eventually, the federation and council merged in many communities; in others, the council was absorbed as a functional component of the federation; in still others, the council (whether preexisting or created at federation initiative) became part of the agency system with federation funding.

Again, it is not the institutional fate of the Community Councils which is important, but what they—and the interest which federations took in their development—say about the maturation of the organized Jewish community as a polity. From the late 1930s onward, General Assembly sessions were devoted to the council concept and experience. A CJFWF report presented at the 1938 General Assembly cited Community Councils as an expression of growing communal unity based on intensified fellow-feeling and an awareness that Jews face problems which affect all, and which no single agency can deal with. "The rise of Hitler, the persecution of Jews in other European lands, and the dangers of anti-semitism in America, have made it more clear that the destiny of all Jews is bound together." The principle behind the councils was that "Jewish responsibilities should be borne by all Jews." The report noted that councils in different communities embraced a wide diversity of functions, ranging from serving as a communal discussion forum, to combating discrimination and coordinating anti-Nazi activities, to trying to arbitrate internal disputes within the community.[82]

Both federation and Community Council leaders expressed enthusiasm about the potential of the new institution. One cited its lineage from biblical and talmudic times, and William Shroder encouraged its development as "a thoroughly democratic type of organization," albeit not one which should claim to speak with "authority." The president of the Detroit council was perhaps the most ambitious in his claims. The Jewish Community Council, he stated, constituted a survival program for Jewish life which could unite even those whom philanthropy divides (presumably donors and recipients, or proponents of different causes). The goal of the council was to

> give stability and equilibrium to Jewish life, condition it against demoralization of assaults, both from within and without, and so establish the basis for Jewish living as to enable us to make our noblest possible contribution to the totality of American life, of which we form a constituent part.[83]

Expectations that the council would revolutionize local Jewish organizational life were not realized. Even one of its strongest proponents still referred to it as "experimental" in 1944.[84] Yet, the *principle* which the councils sought to embody—communal responsibility for those problems which "involve the *fate* of the community, its dignity, its social standards, its intellectual and cultural existence, and its relationships, as a community, to the world around it"[85]—was adopted by federations and their leadership regardless of how council structures fared in the various localities. In this way, the Community Council movement, like the Welfare Funds of a decade earlier, helped to fashion the shape of what would become a mature American Jewish polity.

As federation leaders surveyed the achievements of the depression and war years, their evaluations were often sober. They continued to espouse and celebrate unity, while accepting ideological differences within the community as a virtual given. Writing in 1938, Harry Lurie, executive director of CJFWF, balanced his acknowledgement of the general movement toward greater activity and organizational coordination with a strong caution that "sharply divergent ultimate aims and principles are . . . still acting as a brake on progress." The cleavage between the Zionists/nationalists and their ideological opponents, labeled "with the supposedly derogatory term of 'assimilationists,'" prevented, in Lurie's view, the development of more encompassing forms of community organization. Yet, despite the antagonisms, the trend was toward greater cooperation, spurred on by "the urge to respond to Jewish problems, to assist in the relief of Jews overseas, to aid in the upbuilding of Palestine, to deal with the problems of group protection and Jewish adjustment." Whether the centripetal forces pulling Jews together, or the centrifugal ones pushing them apart, would eventually win out was still uncertain in Lurie's mind.[86]

By 1941, William Shroder was prepared to go a step further. Over the previous decade, he stated, federations had tried to demonstrate that "persons with diametrically opposed ideals and desires can work together and live together, and bring into fruition what is best for the group as a whole." America truly was a nation of minorities, a "jewel of many facets," and to contribute its share a minority had to organize. Jews had discovered too, that they possessed a "unity [and] an interresponsibility that we cannot escape, even if we wanted to." Despite the clashes of fundamental thinking which marked the leaders' deliberations even then, Shroder concluded, the communities had "passed their test."[87]

Three years later, Shroder's successor, Sidney Hollander, echoed the same theme. "The continuing evidences of community achievement and community solidarity seems to me the most heartening thing we find in Jewish life in America today," he told the delegates to the General Assembly. Federations, Welfare Funds and Community Councils were showing "that responsibilities can be met . . . with no sacrifice of any man's ideals or the yielding of any man's principles. You have found the formula wherein Zionists and non-Zionists, orthodox and reform, Jews of the East and Jews of the West, can work together in common purpose."[88]

The federation system had indeed found such a formula. It is not clear, however, whether even these top national leaders, so concerned about the historic antagonisms within the Jewish community, fully understood what had happened. By the end of the war, the work of the federations had come to express a fundamental consensus of American Jews concerning who and why they were. They were Jews who felt a strong sense of solidarity with other Jews, especially those in need. They were proud of their heritage and its ideals, and wished to see these preserved. They were fired with a sense of mutual responsibility and a desire to make a contribution to the world around them. And they were grateful and proud Americans, taking advantage of its opportunities to express their own culture while helping to weave alongside others the fabric of democracy and social justice.

Even as history would shortly render some of the burning disputes of the day moot, American Jews were deciding that nearly all their disagreements were ultimately less significant that what they could agree on. The federation agenda had grown to reflect that agreement. Thus, though the differences which Lurie, Shroder, and Hollander pointed to were certainly real, they were eventually transcended far more easily than these leaders envisioned. Theoretical disputes over the future of Palestine, the national character of the Jewish people, or the appropriate model for minority group adjustment to American society, paled before the concrete work of maintaining vital services, raising the funds for overseas programs, helping refugees, and promoting intergroup cooperation. More importantly, the work—not the debates—reflected the true Jewish faith of those who devoted themselves to it, a faith in the destiny of the Jewish people and the potential for its realization in America. In the postwar world, that faith, freed from its entanglements with the disputes of another era, would blossom into a full-fledged civil religion.

### The Articulation of a Faith: 1945–1967

American Jewry faced the postwar world with a sense of continuing responsibility, but also with an understandable desire to put behind it the years of trial and trauma. Faced with an immediate crisis of unprecedented proportions—hundreds of thousands of Jewish refugees—the Jewish community responded with unprecedented feats of fundraising: $100,000,00 in 1946, $150,000,00 in 1947, over $200,000,00 in 1948.[89] The United Jewish Appeal billed these as years of "survival" and of "destiny,"[90] and they were unlike any which Jews had known in modern memory. The combination of anxiety and exhilaration which attended the rebirth of a Jewish state overwhelmed all but the most recalcitrant anti-Zionists. Israel became not only a focus for fundraising, but a source of prideful identification for virtually all of American Jewry.

The real test of what had been achieved in the American Jewish community over the previous decades came after the excitement had faded and the river of history had returned to its banks. How would the federation system and its leaders respond to the return to relative "normalcy"? Would the sense of purposefulness and the feeling of unity endure as fundraising totals began to decline? Had the challenges of the Depression, the war, the rescue of the refugees, and the rebuilding of a homeland produced a new level of Jewish consciousness, or were they merely an interlude in a long process of assimilation?

During the decade and a half which ended with the conclusion of World War II, federation leaders had developed a largely implicit, at times explicit, worldview and ethos which legitimated their expanding endeavors. In the face of competing philosophies of Jewish life, they had evolved a functional institutional ideology. But that ideology contained the seeds of something far grander, a full-fledged meaning system which accorded the work of the community organizations transcendent, and not merely proximate, significance. It fell to the leaders of the Jewish polity in the 1950s and 1960s to give that meaning system clear articulation and thereby answer the question of what direction the American Jewish community would take as it reached toward full maturity.

One debate which no longer raged among the leadership was over the extent of federation responsibility for helping to set this direction. The themes of the 1949 and 1950 General Assemblies—"Building the Model Jewish Community" and "Agenda for American Jewry–1950"—spoke eloquently of the breadth of horizons of the movement and its leadership. The responsibilities of the community organizations were phrased in encompassing terms: "for a progressive development of Jewish community life in America, . . . for the rehabilitation and resettlement of the survivors of the greatest catastrophe which has ever befallen the Jewish people, and to help build a firm foundation for a free and democratic Israel."[91] All needs, suggested CJFWF president, Stanley Myers, were part of a single agenda. "Community health, like individual health is indivisible. . . . In the final analysis, in its living reality, every responsibility is a local one—whether the people in need are overseas, or in some other city in America, or in our own backyard." Federations had moved to the forefront of American Jewish life to meet these global responsibilities. "We have built up a pattern of organization that is unique in the world, and unique in our history. Its achievements are magnificent."[92]

This bold assertion of the federation's universal scope of responsibility—and its capabilities—was matched with a growing awareness that the character of the communal activities it coordinated was changing as well. Federations and their agencies were becoming less vehicles for noblesse oblige philanthropy than instruments of Jewish self-expression and development for the community as a whole. "Instead of one-half of us financing and administering programs for the other half, Jewish agencies more and more represent the community serving itself, with the beneficiaries and contributors constituting the same group."[93] What the

Philadelphia Federation of Jewish Agencies said of itself in 1965 expressed what had happened in virtually every community:

> The Federation of 1964–65 . . . is drastically different from the Federation of twenty years ago. This is dramatically illustrated by the shift in meaning of the word "welfare." Until about a generation ago, welfare service was something the well-to-do provided for the poor. Nowadays welfare services is something that all of us provide for ourselves. . . .
>
> This means that Federation and its agencies are directly involved in the daily life and vital concerns of most of the people of the Jewish community. Their role is no longer limited to acting for the community in matters of philanthropic service to the minority. . . . They are now instrumentalities of the total community in acting for the welfare of its entire populace.[94]

This shift, however, was not merely a matter of redefining the donor and client groups. Rather, the entire communal organizational structure was self-consciously taking on a new meaning and role in American Jewish life. What was said in a 1953 CJFWF report with regard to family services could be applied to virtually any component of the system's activities:

> The symbolic significance that the family agency has for the client . . . applies also to the board member, the volunteer and the professional. To many of them the agency serves as a medium for attaching themselves to the Jewish tradition and Jewish community; as a means of giving expression to their religious sentiment and Jewish creativity; as a practical method of functioning as a Jew on behalf of other Jews and keeping related in an active way to the mainstream of Jewish life.[95]

The polity and its activities were increasingly being seen as the expression of a particular way of being Jewish—one both deeply rooted in the Jewish tradition and uniquely suited to the conditions of American life. Federations, proclaimed CJFWF president, Stanley Myers, in 1950,

> have worked because they represent the finest fusion of Jewish idealism and American experience. Centuries of Jewish religious and social values and of American political democracy have merged to make possible—in fact to create—our Jewish communal organizations. They are the living expressions of the great and noble Jewish aspirations for social justice, the expressions of our concern for the well-being of our fellow men, for the dignity of the human spirit, our concern for the helpless, for the aged, for the sick, for our children, for the sanctity of family life. They are the living expressions of our historic dedication to learning and culture and decency in personal life and human relations.

Our Jewish communal organizations, he concluded, represent "the soul and conscience of American Jewry."[96]

In this statement, federation has become, in effect, religion. The rhetoric of this period—both in substance and in tone—ever more strongly reinforced this emerging self-understanding. All of the functional responsibilities which the polity had assumed—from support of Israel, to social services, to the strengthening of Jewish education and culture, to promoting Jewish involvement in American life—now received validation and signification in terms of the conviction that Jewish communal organization expressed the essential meaning of Jewishness during this historic hour. When Myers looked at the agenda facing Federations and American Jewry—support of America and its ideals, the preservation of Israel, the quest for social justice—he saw at stake "the validity of our existence as a religious and cultural group." Social justice, he insisted, "is our historic heritage, immortalized by our ancient prophets. Without it our Jewishness has no meaning."[97]

During the ensuing years, federation leaders would return repeatedly to this theme, reformulating the underlying assertion that the American Jewish polity had become a fundamental expression not just of fellow-feeling or charitable obligation, but of the essence of Judaism itself. Here, for example, is how Philip Bernstein, the preeminent federation professional leader of the postwar period, put the matter:

> Jewish communal service [is] a service distinctly rooted in a religious code in which the obligations of social justice, of man's humanity to man, are central to a way of life. Underlying that service are values and motivations which have become pervasive in the mores of a people—whether as individuals they are observant of Jewish ritual or not.
>
> It is a religion of action—social action, not a creed of belief alone. . . . It is a religion centered in the infinite sanctity of each individual, his life, his spirit, his dignity—in which the highest level of social service has been the prevention of human need. . . .
>
> If our goals are broader and greater, as they must be, our standards are also higher. This is entirely consistent with the Jewish traditions and aspirations which our services express, with the leadership role they must fill.[98]

Much of this rhetoric can be understood as part of a quest for self-justification by federation leaders. During the 1950s synagogues enjoyed a period of significant institutional growth as Jews moved to the suburbs, and America as a whole experienced a "religious revival." With campaign results stagnant, with Israel losing some of its appeal as a focal point of active concern, one can read the efforts of communal leaders to identify their work with the religious tradition as a defensive response. Yet, such a view would mistake context for content. Polity leaders were indeed "in quest of purpose," as the title of Irving Kane's 1960 presidential address to the CJFWF General Assembly put it.[99] Their decision to articulate that purpose in terms of the religious rootedness and spiritual significance of their work was no less far-reaching in its import for the American Jewish community because it may have emerged out of a sense of institutional disquiet.

The leaders of the polity during this period were virtually concerned with demonstrating that their enterprise was Jewishly meaningful. They found that meaning in what they believed were the traditional fundamental values of their communal endeavor. Kane, for example, accepted the proposition that "in America, Jews will ultimately survive as a religious community, or not at all," that Jewish faith had not only enabled the Jewish people to survive, but that it continued to validate all that they did as Jews. But he insisted as well that

> what are sometimes referred to as secular activities, because they are not directly under synagogue auspices, are not only necessary but they, too, are Torah, for they were born of and are informed and infused by our religious faith. Judaism as a religion has always been a social force—it is the application of timeless principles to timely problems.[100]

This claim was reiterated over the next years by volunteer and professional leaders alike. Louis Stern, who succeeded Kane as CJFWF president, again raised the question of purpose in his address to the 1963 General Assembly. He too answered that such purpose could only be found in "the service of Jewish religious ideals." "Judaism is theology, doctrine, custom, ritual and ceremony which specify and dramatize our ideals; it is equally social service, social justice and every humanitarian endeavor which is guided by these ideals."[101] Thus, federations and their agencies were part of the fabric of Judaism. "What we want to bring about," argued Hyman Safran, president of Detroit's Jewish Welfare Fund, "is an amalgamation of the concepts of mitzvah and Torah. Mitzvoth are the good deeds or the philanthropies we perform; Torah is our Jewish awareness, education, and conscious identification." Safran cited the biblical phrase *"na'aseh v'nishma"* ("we will do and we will hear") as the model for Jewish responsibility. "A complete citizen of our Jewish community knows the commandment 'Honor thy father and thy mother' and practices it when he helps provide a service or a home for the aged. He knows the requirement that we 'rescue the captive' and he fulfills it by contributing generously for immigration and resettlement." Thus, federation is the meeting ground of the "know-why" and the "know-how" of Judaism, "the mitzvah with the Torah." It is the "instrument for the living application of our age-old values."[102]

The philanthropic system had, as we have seen, always pointed to *tzedakah* as the traditional Jewish foundation of its work. Now, however, the claim of religious significance for its work was being restated with new boldness, scope, and intensity. When, for example, two leading professionals, Irving Greenberg and David Zeff, addressed the recurrent question of the Jewish significance of the family case-work agency in 1965, they did so in terms which went beyond even what the CJFWF statement a dozen years earlier had ventured. The family agency should indeed, they asserted, be seen as a "symbol of Jewish identification." Its values, "concern with each human being, the sacredness of life, the value of earthly existence, the inexplicable reasons for misery, the claims that we have, each upon the other, are imbedded in our historic Judaic foundation." In fact, they claimed, if the synagogue is the prime expression of the pillars of *tefilah* (prayer) and *torah* (sacred learning) in contemporary Jewish life, then the family agency should regard itself as the expression of *tzedakah* and *chesed* (loving-kindness). However, if it wishes to make this claim, it must do so with religious seriousness, even while functioning in a secular context. "We believe that Chesed is interwoven with our religion, our Torah, our history and our belief in the meaning of the Brith (covenant), and must become part of the framework if not the essence of social service to Jewish people." Jewish concern flows from a God-focused perspective on human issues; agencies which want to embody this concern must, therefore, "begin relating themselves to a spiritual, Judaic consideration."[103]

Certainly, not all leaders sought to go this far in "spiritualizing" and "Judaizing" the work of the ostensibly "secular" polity. But the legitimation of their activities as a fundamental expression of Judaism was almost universally endorsed. A vocabulary of mission, of challenge, of historic opportunity, increasingly pervaded the rhetoric of polity leaders during the postwar period. The communal enterprise not only expressed Jewish values, it became a source of meaning in life, the meaning that flows from being united with others in an unquestionably great task. Out of the many strands of responsibility which the federation-framed communal system had assumed—for Israel, for Jewish continuity in America, for assisting those in need, for building American society—grew a vision of transcendent purposiveness which in turn infused each of the specific arenas of endeavor with new significance.

We should not be surprised that American Jewish leaders emerged from a period of world war, of unimaginable tragedy for the Jewish people, and of unprecedented achievement with a heightened feeling for the historical significance of their day and of their efforts. "We are partners in a tremendous historic adventure," CJFWF president, Julian Freeman, told General Assembly delegates in 1950. "We are partners in a great enterprise—dedicated to the saving of lives—the regeneration of human beings and our dedicated assistance to the rebuilding of a state —the dynamic development of our American Jewish life."[104] Speaking at the same assembly, Jerome Curtis offered an even more expansive vision: A mature American Jewish community could "become one of the outstanding landmarks in the long history of organized Jewish communities and will make possible the development here of another truly Golden Age in Jewish life."[105]

The sense of possibility and of urgency which was to characterize this entire period flowed in part from the bitter contrast of the present with the recent past. If the leaders of the day came, as Joseph Schwartz, director of the JDC and later of the UJA, suggested, to see themselves as part of a "dedicated decade, a generation with a mission," it was indeed as a response to the helplessness of the Hitler years. Jews took an "almost collective vow that if, and when, the time ever came when we could do something about the daily horrors we then experienced, we would do it."[106] And so they did. Ten years later, Herbert Friedman, UJA's top professional leader, summarized the experience of the decade by citing what he called the American Jewish community's perennial campaign slogan: "We have dedicated ourselves in this generation to answering Hitler back in two ways: by rescuing a people wherever they are, and by building a land which was the choicest dream of our fathers and will be of our sons."[107]

As the massive fundraising of the late 1940s had demonstrated, and the continued concern and support of the American Jewish community in succeeding decades reiterated, the reestablishment of the State of Israel indeed served to crystallize the sense of American Jewish leaders that they lived in a watershed period of Jewish history. We should not exaggerate the importance of Israel in the American Jewish consciousness in the period prior to 1967.[108] Still, there can be no question that assistance to the struggling state was regarded as a prime responsibility, and that Israel itself was a source of pride. The state was seen as a "bulwark of democracy," the "salvation of . . . refugees . . . (seeking) freedom and security," and a "haven for the oppressed."[109] If this sounds like a portrait of America as well, that was no accident. American Jewish leaders could identify with Israel because, as they had since Brandeis's days, they saw in it a reflection of their own American-bred ideals.

Because Israel was, in addition, bound up with Jewry's historic past, and with the recent devastation of European Jewry, its existence took on an almost mystical aura for some leaders. "No acheivement of modern Jewry is crowned with greater glory," stated Irving Kane, "than the life-saving work of rescue and rehabilitation and the miracle of resettling a million souls on the ancient, sacred soil of Israel."[110] As more American Jewish leaders began to visit Israel, its impact on these leaders grew. "If only it were possible to recapture the dewy, virginal impressions of that first contact with the land and the people," wrote Sidney Vincent, one of the "statesmen" professionals of the federation movement, recalling the visit of Cleveland leaders in 1959.

> Yes, yes, I kept saying to myself, it's really so! Here all the weary cliches come to vigorous life; all the campaign slogans get recharged with immediate meaning. . . . Suddenly, as the lights of Jerusalem came into view, sparkling from the very top of the last hill, the line of the old ghetto song of faith flashed into my mind: "Mir zeinen doh!" ("We are here!")[111]

Though for many Jews, the outpouring of support for Israel during the crisis and triumph of 1967 seemed to emerge from the blue, for those at the core of the polity it represented an identification already present, waiting to be reenergized. Two years before the Six-Day War, Max Fisher, perhaps American Jewry's most eminent volunteer leader during the post-war period, gave eloquent testimony to Israel's meaning and the challenge it represented. He recalled the time twenty years earlier when American Jews had raised $100 million for Jewish survival, still oppressed by the feeling that perhaps no one else cared about the displaced, the entrapped Jews of Moslem lands, and the struggle in Palestine. American Jews had declared that catastrophe must never happen again, that they would change the world for homeless Jews. Now, Fisher went, on

> we face the obligation and the great challenge to help Israel show the world, as America once showed it, that "from the wretched refuse of teeming shores" we Jews can build a new, modern and truly successful society. . . . We are a Chosen Generation. In our time we have seen the lowest point in Jewish history in over twenty centuries. In our time we also have seen the greatest revival of the Jewish people on record. And we helped, and must continue to make that revival possible.[112]

Here, surely, was something worth living for, a mission to help snatch light from darkness. In his plea, Fisher evoked a myth which was to become central to the American Jewish civil religion in the years to come.[113] For many leaders, the challenge which was implicit in that myth—the challenge to insure Jewish revival in the wake of attempts to destroy the people and its culture—pointed in another direction as well: to the long-standing question of whether American Jewry could develop a rich indigenous Jewish culture. The destruction of European Jewry heightened the sense of responsiblity: if American Jews did not keep Jewish learning and culture alive, who would?

Many leaders shared Irving Kane's conviction that Israel could "and will deepen the content of our lives, our communal purpose," but that American Jewry could not "live culturally and spiritually as a parasite on a body six thousasnd miles away."[114] The challenge of deepening Jewish culture in America, like that of rebuilding Israel, stimulated feelings of both great possibility and great urgency. Characteristically, the issue was often presented in the terms leaders were not prepared to understand best: survival. "Once we faced anti-semitism, talked of survival and expended millions of dollars to survive," Edwin Wolf, a Philadelphia Jewish leader and president of the National Foundation for Jewish Culture, reminded participants at the 1962 General Assembly. "We have given hundreds of millions of dollars to enable Israel to survive. Now we must face our own survival in terms of an indigenous Jewish culture. What is it worth?"[115]

Two years later, William Goldfarb, a young leader from Cleveland, posed the same question in greater detail. Survival, he asserted, was no longer a debatable issue in the Jewish community. But American Jewry would not survive "unless it identifies itself with Jews and with Judaism in time and in space." External forces had pushed Jews into Jewish awareness, but now identification must come from internal forces. Such commitment, Goldfarb asserted, requires Jewish education to instill knowledge and feelings, an understanding of the values of Jewish ethics, and the ability to pose and answer the questions of why and how to be Jewish. "We American Jews," he concluded,

> have achieved affluence and comfort and freedom and equality and status and a high degree of efficiency in communal organization. It would be tragic indeed to have attained all this and then to sacrifice the inner content of our Jewishness and with it our ability to survive. It would be tragic both for us and for America.[116]

The specter which Goldfarb held out of a community unable to survive because it had lost touch with the why and how of being Jewish, was one which the polity leadership struggled with throughout this period of accelerated adjustment. Support for Jewish culture was presented not only as a weapon in the struggle for survival, but as an historic affirmation as well. Increasing attention to such issues was, argued one federation professional leader, "a wholesome indication of the fact that the Jewish community had moved out of the shadow of destruction and was emerging again into the light of a rich cultural life essential for any meaningful civilization."[117]

The prescription to put more resources and commitment into Jewish education and culture was widely endorsed by federation leaders in principle, if not always adhered to in practice.[118] By the mid 1960s the issue of Jewish identification and commitment—especially of young Jews—was a fixture of concern at General Assemblies. There was broad agreement that reform of the Jewish educational system was needed, so that Jewish youth would appreciate the roots and purposes of Judaism, the why of Jewish distinctiveness, and the importance of carrying on and carrying out its teaching. Yet many of the speeches testify to the gap between rhetoric and reality. The call for action fell perhaps not on deaf ears, but certainly on as yet largely ineffectual hands.[119]

Here again, our primary concern is not to evaluate the success of the polity's endeavors in this domain, but to note that survivalist concerns had produced a clear commitment to the concept of educational and cultural development as a primary responsibility of the system. The hesitations and objections of the 1930s were long past, rendered insupportable by the federation system's new understanding of itself as a religious force. Still, in defining itself as an instrument for Jewish continuity, the polity did not abandon its traditional role as a vehicle for

Jewish involvement in and contribution to the larger society. Indeed, the same sensibility of historic mission was brought to bear in reaffirming this component of the polity's activism as well.

Federation leaders never wavered in their conviction that the Jewish values which were becoming increasingly prominent in the federation system's self-legitimation were one with America's own social values. "What we strive for as Jews is identical with what we strive for as Americans," stated Julian Freeman in 1951. "The values we have been working for are part and parcel of the values Americans hold so dear."[120] Because of this essential identity, it was possible for a community leader to assert that "our Jewish community is part of American democracy . . . not only when we work to fulfill local needs, but equally when we strive . . . to assist in strengthening the State of Israel."[121]

Thus, even as the Jewish polity became more rooted in its own religious value system, and more committed to its perpetuation, its leaders never doubted their responsibility and capacity to contribute "to the entire cultural, political, and historical development of the countries and hemisphere of which we form a part," and indeed "to a world of tolerance, of progress and peace."[122] Here, the definition of the essence of Judaism as a religion of action and the self-assumed Jewish mission to contribute to society and civilization came together. In a speech to the 1957 General Assembly, Irving Kane applauded the so-called religious revival, if that meant a revival of what he believed religion demanded: "a ceaseless concern—a divine discontent, if you please—with the great problems of our times." The special Jewish concern for social justice and public welfare, rooted in traditional Jewish attitudes, should, he urged, be projected in turn "upon the still emerging American conceptions of communal responsibility."[123]

It was this sensibility, with its echoes of similar statements by Jewish leaders in the 1930s, which propelled the leadership of the Jewish community into active support of civil rights and the War on Poverty in the 1960s. The resolution of the 1963 General Assembly on civil rights was in many ways typical in its themes:

> The ideal of individual dignity and worth is rooted in Jewish tradition and stems from a profound commitment to democratic freedoms reinforced by centuries of Jewish experience and history.
>
> Our history as a people gives us a special understanding of the struggle of the Negroes and other minority groups for full civil rights and liberties, and places every Jewish organization under obligation to advance the cause of equality by all means appropriate to it as a sectarian agency.[124]

In similar fashion, Phil Bernstein suggested that the community was prepared to lead in the War on Poverty "as part of our deep religious commitment, as part of our unique commitment to the eradication of poverty, our commitment as a Jewish group and not just as a number of Jewish individuals."[125]

From time to time, debate broke out anew over whether the Jewish community was devoting too much energy to social action, or on the contrary, had become too preoccupied with its own survival. But the conflict was by and large a muted one; both survival and participation in the larger society were so firmly established as values that most leaders could not entertain the possibility of a clash between the two. Interestingly, a new twist was even added to their reconciliation. If the future of the Jewish community indeed depended on youth's adoption of Jewish values as meaningful for their own lives, was it not in fact necessary to demonstrate the significance of these values for dealing with the most pressing issues of the day? "If Judaism had no answers," warned Louis Stern, "if ritual and customs were all we had to offer, we would indeed be in difficulty." To survive, we must translate "the ethical concepts which are the heart of Judaism" into language and action that young people can understand.[126] It was for precisely this task that the Jewishly conscious polity now felt itself equipped.

What the federation-framed polity achieved in the roughly two decades from the end of World War II to the Six Day War was not a revolution but a consolidation. Out of the themes bequeathed to it by its predecessors and the unique trials and triumphs which it witnessed and experienced, it fashioned a working faith for its activist cadres and countless other American Jews who shared its vision and values. The polity became self-consciously a religious one, not in terms of the theological or ritual norms of the denominational structures, but in terms of its own definition of what Jewishness and Judaism must be about in the modern world.

If piety is fundamentally "the attempt to leave the world a better place for our having lived in it" (as one rabbi had defined it), then, Louis Stern told the delegates to the 1962 General Assembly, "this is an assemblage of pious men and women." Federation, he continued, is

> the expression of the collective conscience of the community. That conscience is as deep, as profound, and as timeless as our Judaic ideals which, transmitted over three thousand years of history, have kept us alive as a people and continue to be our enduring mission, encompassing the multitude of responsibilities which begin in each of our cities, extend across the continent, and circle the globe.[127]

One of Stern's successors as CJFWF president, Irving Blum, offered a similar vision of federation's role and mission: "Federation," he claimed, "represents all of Judaism in its dedication to faith in man—in this world, and faith in our time." It is the common denominator for all Jews. And in meeting the challenge to this generation, the fulfillment of the prophetic mission, "Federation—its organizations, its people, its ideas

—is the living embodiment of four thousand years of commitment to the highest moral and ethical ideals."[128]

This vision is what emboldened the leaders of the American Jewish polity to believe that its endeavors could provide transcendent meaning. The polity was, first, the expression and embodiment of the central values of Judaism. But beyond this, it was an audacious attempt to affect the course of history itself on behalf of those values. For those engaged in its work, the polity was, therefore, a way to link one's individual destiny with that of the Jewish people, and of mankind.

With this, the American Jewish polity had become the focus and the bearer of a religious faith, what we have called American Jewry's civil religion. In the next chapters we will examine that religion as it functions today. We will explore its tenets, its myths and rituals, and, finally, its significance for the lives of American Jews and for the future of Judaism.

# III

# THE CIVIL JEWISH FAITH

### "Am Yisrael Chai!" The Jewish People Lives

On a Sunday afternoon in March 1982, nearly two thousand American Jews, most in their late twenties and thirties, gathered in the ballroom of the Washington Hilton hotel for the opening session of the third bi-annual Washington Conference organized by the men's and women's Young Leadership Cabinets of the United Jewish Appeal.[1] The attendees were exemplars of the American Jewish success story. The vast majority were affluent, successful in their business or professional careers, sophisticated, and polished. They had come to Washington as concerned and potentially influential American citizens to listen to prominent politicians, lobby their representatives on Capitol Hill, and attend an exhausting series of political education seminars and strategy sessions.

But they had come for another reason as well: to express their identity and faith as Jews. Most of the participants were activists not only in American politics, but in the American Jewish polity as well. The fact that they were gathered under the banner of the United Jewish Appeal —probably the most visible symbol of that polity—was no coincidence, because the Jewish commitment they had come to manifest was first and foremost a commitment to the polity's civil religion.

The conference was opened by Edward Robin, chairman of the Young Leadership Cabinet. He spoke not of specific political issues, but of the meaning of the event itself. "The first time a Jew was ever called upon," Robin began, "Abraham answered simply 'Hineni—I am here.' So we— a new generation of American Jews—are here. But why? for what purpose?" The answer, Robin proposed, was that they had gathered in response to a challenge: "Can our generation of American Jews break through the cycle of security, comfort, and reluctance, and forge a genuine impact on the future of our people? We must. We are here to learn to make that difference."

This desire to affect the future was in turn linked to an appropriation of the Jewish past:

We are here because of our tradition. We are the people of the Book—

we are enjoined to be a light unto the nations, to set an example. We have a tradition that values the individual and the sanctity of life. Yes, through our tradition we have ingrained in us a responsibility to society and to our community without parallel.

And we are here because of our history. A history which puts Jews in the forefront of every decent human movement and on the cutting edge of every crisis. . . . Each of us lives in a post-Auschwitz world where we must exist each day with the knowledge of what man can do to man—and particularly to us. Yet we do this while avoiding the abyss of despair, fearfulness, and insecurity.

In the struggle against such despair, Robin went on to suggest, the American Jew can draw on a reservoir of strength: the State of Israel—"declared before many of us were born; unmeasurable in the sense of creativity, pride and accomplishment it has given to Jews everywhere; our bedrock of the present, our hope of the future, our centrality." Yet it is not to Israel alone that an American Jew can look to see what can be done. "Here, in the *goldene medine*," Robin continued,

under the constant threats of assimilation and loss of identity, we face the question of whether the Jewish people can retain its uniqueness in a free society. In the face of this challenge, we have created the greatest philanthropic movement in history and have begun to build for ourselves a creative Jewish existence of learning and observance, concern and love.

The ultimate challenge, Robin concluded, is "to believe in the future," and to forge a connection to that future through "participation in Jewish life."

When our children and grandchildren gather in years to come, let them say that each of us responded Hineni—that we made a difference. If we act now, we—you and I—can take part in a future for the Jewish people even brighter than our glorious past. And the Jewish people can live forever. That's why we are here. Am Yisrael Chai![2]

Ed Robin's speech that afternoon was eloquent, but not unique in its sentiments. Indeed, its impact lay precisely in the fact that it expressed dramatically and incisively the worldview and ethos which so many in the audience—and so many other contemporary American Jewish communal activists—shared. In its vision of Jews forging their own destiny, in its values of responsibility to community and society and the maintenance of Jewish distinctiveness, in its evocation of Israel and the Holocaust, of Jewish tradition and America as the *goldene medine*, Robin's address is a virtual catechism for the civil religious faith of the American Jewish polity. Ed Robin spoke, therefore, not simply as an organizational leader, but as a prophet/priest of that civil religion. His words crystallize the beliefs and evoke the symbols which bind American Jews together as a moral community and which give transcendent purpose to the activities of its network of communal institutions.

The American Jewish civil religion which Robin's words invoke is, as detailed in the previous chapter, the product of an evolutionary process which has woven together strands from American Jewish folk religion and from the elite ideologies affirmed by important segments of American Jewry's institutional leadership. Its tenets reflect this process and the successful synthesis of diverse sentiments into an encompassing worldview and ethos. The social values of this civil Judaism bespeak its origins in the philanthropic ethos of the communal establishment. Its grounding in a firm sense of Jewish peoplehood reflects the intensity of ethnic sentiment among the masses of Eastern European Jews who migrated to America during the last century. The civil religion's commitment to Jewish continuity constitutes a clear response to the threats to Jewish survival which have become manifest in recent decades. And its affirmation of America as a setting for Jewish success and achievement expresses a nearly universal American Jewish conviction that here they are no longer in exile, but part of a pluralistic society which offers unprecedented opportunities for both integration and Jewish self-expression.

These themes were firmly established as part of the civil religion by the middle of the 1960s. It was during the years following Israel's Six Day War in 1967, however, that civil Judaism truly came of age as a force in the American Jewish religious consciousness. The late 1960s and the decades which have followed have been a period of Jewish renewal in North America. Despite frequently cited manifestations of assimilation on the part of some Jews (e.g., rising rates of intermarriage), the American Jewish community experienced as well a new wave of energy. Across a broad variety of fronts—in the development of new religious institutions, in the burgeoning of Jewish Studies in American universities, in growing political activism—Jews became more self-confident in their Jewishness and more creative in its expression.

Nineteen sixty-seven will surely be remembered as a watershed year in Jewish history. The impact of the events of that year on the State of Israel has obviously been enormous. Its impact on American Jewish life was only slightly less monumental. The traumatic days of May and June 1967, when Israel first seemed threatened by a new Holocaust, only to win a magnificent, almost miraculous victory culminating in the reunification of Jerusalem, galvanized American Jewry and launched a chain of response which eventually acquired a momentum independent of its original impetus. The Six Day War was not alone responsible for the intensification of Jewish activity in America which followed. The seeds had begun to be planted even before the war. Indigenous factors—the general mood of social activism, the reawakened ethnic consciousness of many groups, the discomfort of some Jews with the direction of the civil rights movements, and later a broadly renewed interest in religion and spirituality —all played a role in sustaining the resurgence. But 1967 marked a clear turning point, and especially so for the federation-framed polity and its civil religion.

The most dramatic manifestation of the growing centrality of the polity in American Jewish life in the period following the Six Day War is the tremendous increase in the funds raised by federations and the UJA. In 1967 and again in the wake of the Yom Kippur War of 1973, American Jews gave unprecedently, both in numbers and in amount. Moreover, the primacy of the federation/UJA campaign was accepted by virtually every institution on the American Jewish scene. Though giving fell back when the immediate crises had waned, new plateaus were established, and from the post-1973 plateau annual contributions have risen again to surpass $600,000,000.

Even more important, however, is the extent to which the UFA/federation movement and its leadership have emerged clearly as a preeminent force in Jewish communal life in the post-1967 period. It is perhaps the link to Israel through fundraising which made this rise to preeminence possible. But Israel has hardly been the entire focus of the polity's efforts or the sole source of its expanded influence. The impact of polity institutions has come to be felt in every sphere of Jewish activity. The federations and UJA have become a focal point for Jewish identification, and a rallying point for those seeking to strengthen Jewish life in all its dimensions. The Jewish polity has ridden the broad wave of intensifying Jewishness in North America; it has also helped to feed and to steer its currents.

The "Judaization" of the federation/UJA structure which has given it credibility as a "central address" for American Jewry came as a result of both pressure from without and a process of self-discovery from within. The self-discovery had been taking place for several decades as the polity moved ever more firmly toward a survivalist agenda. Its climax was the 1967 war, during which thousands of American Jews, including many who had been active leaders in the community, discovered a depth of Jewish concern and commitment in themselves they had not previously recognized was there. The push to translate that heightened Jewish consciousness into an intensified programmatic thrust came often from activist Jewish youth. They turned to the federations and demanded that verbal professions of concern for Jewish survival be matched by a greatly augmented financial and programmatic commitment to Jewish education as the best guarantor of Jewish continuity.

The 1969 CJF General Assembly in Boston, which witnessed a major demonstration by Jewish students and a stirring, challenging speech by one of their number to a plenary session of the assembly,[3] has gone down in federation lore as a second major turning point in the "Judaization" process. It was a critical moment, less in terms of immediate practical results, than for what it and the federation response to it symbolized. The federations did not repudiate "their children" (as the demonstrators referred to themselves and were, by and large, felt by the delegates to be); they embraced them. If the gradiose dreams of both demonstrators and delegates of a federation-led revolution in American Jewish life proved unrealistic, the conviction which both shared—that the federation system would have to take on the challenge of building and preserving an authentic Jewish culture in America—endured and was confirmed over the next decade and more. The federations thus came to see themselves as responsible for the fate and future of both Jews and Judaism with an intensity and earnestness that had not existed only a few years earlier.

As a result of the event of 1967 and the years immediately following, the federation/UJA system became the heart of the American Jewish community as a public enterprise. The newly reinforced and deepened ethos and worldview of that polity—what we have defined as its civil religion—came in turn to be central to the community's self-definition and self-awareness. Since 1967, the themes articulated in Ed Robin's speech to the young leaders gathered in Washington have formed the tenets of an ascendant faith, one which today permeates the rhetoric of a vast institutional network and the consciousness of thousands of communal activists.

The tenets of this American Jewish civil religion are neither radical nor unprecedented. Many represent modern restatements of classical Jewish values and perspectives. Civil Judaism selects and adapts traditional religious concepts for use in a setting—American Jewish communal life—which has been heavily affected by the process of secularization. Through this process of selective adaptation, the civil religion is able to offer American Jews a modern faith rooted in popular Jewish sentiment, yet resonant with Jewish tradition. It embraces those Jewish commitments which unite the community, while leaving room for diverse private Jewish convictions in domains lying beyond its scope of concern.

In order to understand both the substance and coherence of the American Jewish civil religion, it is important to examine its central tenets—the themes which form the core of Robin's message—in some detail. This is what we shall do in the sections which follow. Any attempt to reduce a complex living faith to a set of propositions or tenets of belief runs the risk of distortion. Yet, the power of the American Jewish civil religion lies in large measure in the simplicity and straightforwardness of its central affirmations. Civil Judaism affirms seven major tenets:

1. The unity of the Jewish people
2. Mutual responsibility
3. Jewish survival in a threatening world
4. The centrality of the State of Israel

5. The enduring value of Jewish tradition
6. *Tzedakah:* philanthropy and social justice
7. Americanness as a virtue

Together, these tenets define the American Jewish civil religion's essential worldview and ethos. As statements of faith, they legitimate the work of the American Jewish polity and serve to unite and inspire its citizens.

## The Unity of the Jewish People

For traditional Judaism, Jews constitute *am echad* (one people) by virtue of both their descent from the patriarchal family, Abraham, Isaac, and Jacob, and the covenant at Mt. Sinai which established them as God's people. The unity of Israel is more than a simple statement of fact; it is one element in a complex of interwoven ideas which define the fundamental character of the Jewish people and their place in the world.

In the American Jewish civil religion as well, the claim that all Jews are part of one people is central, and more than a factual statement. It constitutes the core of civil Judaism's response to the modern challenge to Jewish life, a reaffirmation of the very possibility of a Jewish civil religion and of that religion's raison d'être. Modernity, we have suggested, constitutes a fundamental threat, both practically and ideologically, to Jewish unity. Jews are divided by religious conviction (or the lack thereof), by nationality, by a host of social and cultural characteristics including language and lifestyle. Nevertheless, civil Judaism insists, at a deeper level Jews remain, despite all, one people, sharing a common and distinctive destiny. "We are a single world-wide Jewish people whose fate is inextricably tied together no matter where we live."[4] "All of the Jewish people are bound together—by religion, by history, by tradition, by common values, by a common destiny."[5] Out of this assertion of essential Jewish unity, civil Judaism constructs its worldview and ethos.

Over the last decade and a half this fundamental element of the civil Jewish worldview has been crystallized in what may be the most powerful watchword of Jewish faith in this era: the United Jewish Appeal campaign slogan "We are one." Like all potent religious formulae, this ostensibly simple statement is rich in condensed and multivocal meaning. Its potency is manifest in the response which it has engendered among American Jews. As a fundraising slogan, it served for more than a decade as the master theme of highly successful campaigns. It worked because it captured as no other phrase could the emotional content of Jewishness in a period dominated by the memory of the Holocaust and the reality of the State of Israel. "We are one" evokes not only identification with other Jews, but an existential solidarity in the face of the world which renders Jewish existence self-evidently meaningful. It is a statement of collective and personal identity, of an indomitable Jewish presence: we are here, and we are one.

This assertion of Jewish unity is also an effective legitimation of the organizational principle of the Jewish polity, and especially of instrumentalities such as the Jewish federations and United Jewish Appeal which seek universal Jewish participation in their endeavors. As Philip Bernstein has expressed it: "Federations have been based on the maxim of unity. . . . [They] are living expressions of the words of the Psalmists: 'Behold how good and beautiful it is for brethren to dwell together in unity.' "[6] In seeking to unify the community, to build a communal consensus behind their work, federations are, by their own self-understanding, not attempting to impose something artificial and purely self-interested. Rather, they are the vehicles, civil Judaism asserts, for the realization of an underlying principle, that of Jewish unity, which is central to the Jewish tradition. In a Jewish world whose divisions often evoke confusion, frustration, and disillusionment, federations keep alive the essential meaning of Jewish community.

"We are one" is, therefore, more than an organizational slogan; it epitomizes an encompassing, multidimensional Jewish integrity which is reemerging in the contemporary era in and through the Jewish polity. The broadening of the federation agenda which has marked its evolution has enabled it to pull together the various threads of modern Jewish life into single program for Jewish continuity in the contemporary world. That program, as one leader described it,

> represents a convergence of the two forces that were traditionally separate—the objective reality that presses in on us from the outside, and the subjective thrust of our own goals, our own aspirations, our own values. . . . The fate of Jews and Judaism have become totally intertwined as we move into a new level of integration of concerns. No longer are we split personalities. We can truly say "we are one" and express by it an inner harmony that can serve as a solid base for our communal work.[7]

A holistic Jewish commitment is both an explicit goal and a by-product of the activities of the Jewish polity. Acknowledgement of the unity of all Jews implies the acceptance of an encompassing communal agenda. By directing Jews toward an active concern with the full range of issues affecting Jewry, and by seeking to embody in this concern the values of the Jewish tradition, federations exemplify the bases of Jewish unity in the contemporary world. In turn, through their personal involvement in the work of the polity, individual Jews can come to feel their ties to their fellow Jews more intimately and directly. What the civil religion teaches as a proposition, the Jewish polity makes manifest—that all Jews are part of one family, one community.

This unity binds Jewry together across both space and time. We are one today, and we are one with our ancestors:

In the final analysis there is one partnership—no, one brotherhood and sisterhood—one peoplehood, with common religious principles and common spiritual values. The Torah that was given at Sinai is the Torah we use today. We are still the people of the Covenant, the children of Abraham, Isaac and Jacob: the oldest continuously surviving heritage on the face of the earth.[8]

The affirmation of unity means not only identification with the entirety of the Jewish heritage; it is a vital requisite for the perpetutation of that heritage. Jewish unity, expressed in the commitment to Jewish community, is a signal to the world that Jews will not abandon their self-definition as a distinctive people. It is a basis of strength in the struggle for self-perpetuation.

At the very heart of the mystery of Jewish survival throughout the ages, in magnificent denial of the normal laws of history that decree the death sentence on peoples that lose their homeland, is the idea of community . . . the sense of a profoundly shared destiny, a shared purpose, a shared history and customs, a shared responsibility.[9]

Unity—a unity rooted in a common heritage and sustained through common action—is what preserves Jewish life. "'We are One' is our shield and our answer to those who have sought through the long years to impose on us *their* motto—you are alone."[10]

In asserting the unity of the Jewish people, civil Judaism makes a statement which is at once historical and ethical. Jewish unity is founded on what is taken to be an historical fact: that Jews share a common past. But it is clearly seen to be based in addition on something more significant: a common set of values. The unity of the Jewish people is not merely an interdependence of fate. It is the basis and expression of a shared commitment. It "is the touchstone that can firm our resolve and lift our hearts and minds to undertake to do that which must be done."[11]

Civil Judaism identifies the commitment implicit in the proclamation of Jewish unity with the values of Judaism's religious tradition. Affirming one's identification with the Jewish people is, therefore, an affirmation of these values as well. Jewish community is the vehicle through which the abstract principle of Jewish unity and the values which that unity enshrines are made manifest in contemporary Jewish life. In the endeavors of the Jewish polity, American Jews are forging a link in a "chain of Jewish unity—of Jewish courage and Jewish response" which is "the heart of our peoplehood."[12] "We are one" affirms not only the unity, but the purposiveness of Jewish existence.

Ultimately, then, the assertion of Jewish unity leads to the assertion of a special Jewish destiny. "We are one" because a shared Jewish history and a common Jewish condition in the world are pregnant with meaning. Because "we are one," each Jew must participate in the realization of that meaning through the work of Jewish community. What the Jewish destiny is, is often left vague or unstated by civil religious spokespersons. But that Jews are a singular, as well as single, people is not to be doubted. Jewish unity is both the end and the foundation of the civil Jewish faith, the core of its worldview and the generative force behind its ethos.

## Mutual Responsibility

For civil Judaism, the assertion of Jewish unity is virtually inseparable from a corollary proposition: that Jews are responsible for one another. The injunction of the classical tradition *"kol Yisrael areivin zeh bazeh"* (all Jews are responsible, one for the other) is a cardinal norm of the civil religion as well. The rhetoric of the Jewish polity resounds with pleas for the Jews of America to attend to the physical and spiritual needs of all Jews, everywhere. "For us," asserts a UJA fundraising brochure, "there can be no rest . . . We hear the cries and see the need. We must respond quickly. For in our hands we hold the tools to mold this moment in history. As Jews we recognize no boundaries on the map of human need . . . we are responsible, one for another."[13]

The ethos of the Jewish polity is shaped by this assertion of Jewish mutual responsibility. The principle legitimates the concrete work of the polity and its institutions. "When we say 'All Jews are responsible for one another' we are not speaking in abstract terms, but in terms of genuine responsibility and genuine action, implemented through our great Jewish institutions": the Jewish Welfare Federation, "meeting human needs of Jews from right next door," the Council of Jewish Federations, the Joint Distribution Committee, the United Jewish Appeal, and the United Israel Appeal.[14] The programs of these agencies—and the fundraising to sustain them—are the vehicles for fulfilling this Jewish precept. They are not merely organizational endeavors, even "good works." They are not the products of "a moment of compassion." They are expressions of the essential meaning of Jewishness. If required, "our support is . . . even for life."[15]

The parameters of mutual responsibility as defined by the Jewish civil religion are broad. Jews are responsible for one another's safety and security, for physical and economic well-being. Regardless of where they live and what they believe, Jews are entitled to the supportive concern of their American brethren. They are entitled as well to the opportunity to be Jewish. All Jews must be given the means to acquire, express, and transmit their Jewish identity. Hence, the polity has come to accept responsibility for the spiritual, as well as physical, well-being of Jews throughout the world.

Responsibility is exercised communally, but must be felt individually. Jews are not only responsible *for* one another; they are responsible *to* one another. For the civil religion, caring and sharing are obligations owed to other Jews. But they are even more. The ethos which civil Judaism prescribes retains an element of the noblesse oblige sensibility of an earlier generation of philanthropists, but it rests on a more fundamental assertion of the personal significance of the exercise of responsibility. "Each person's destiny and fulfillment are tied to the well-being of his community. He has basic obligations to the community."[16] A Jew cannot truly fulfill himself as a human being without assuming his place within the community of responsibility. Responsibility is an obligation for the Jew, but it is also a privilege. It is a "chosen responsibility."[17]

Thus, the exercise of responsibility takes on a transcendent as well as a pragmatic dimension. The Jew's chosen responsibility is "to renew life time and time again . . . to release the human potential—to protect personal dignity—and to assure man's freedom." The exercise of responsibility is a way of controlling Jewish destiny. Hence, it is a "sacred obligation."[18] As the active expression of Jewish unity, mutual responsibility insures Jewish continuity. "We have survived as Jews because when we have been asked over the centuries if we were our brother's keeper, we have always answered yes."[19] Civil Judaism asks that Jews continue to answer yes. "Around the corner, around the world, wherever we live on this planet, each Jew is responsible, one to another."[20] In a Jewish world of manifest diversity, the Jewish civil religion insists on a global bond of mutual sustenance and support. In this insistence it stands on firm traditional Jewish ground, but it also gives the commitment it seeks global significance. By actualizing the principle of mutual responsibility through his participation in the massive, world-wide endeavors of the Jewish polity, the contemporary Jew becomes part of a network of action whose impact extends far beyond his immediate sphere of influence. He can indeed affect Jewish destiny in every corner of the world. He can reaffirm his solidarity with that destiny, and hence insure that his own life takes on meaning within its embrace.

## Jewish Survival in a Threatening World

Responsibility is the cornerstone of the civil Jewish ethos. It is an encompassing obligation, which is at once a source of pride and of challenge. It mediates between the cardinal tenet of civil Judaism's world view—the unity of the Jewish people—and its central aspiration: the continuity of Jewish life. Through the exercise of mutual responsiblity, Jews demonstrate their unity and insure the conditions under which Jews and Judaism can survive.

Insuring that survival has become the polity's and the civil religion's consuming passion. It is difficult to find a single major speech by a polity leader or a single document explicating the concerns and activities of its agencies which does not place Jewish continuity in a position of the highest priority. Jewish survival is what the Jewish polity is about. Commitment to Jewish survival is an unqualified demand of its civil religion.

The backdrop against which this preoccupation has taken hold is a perception of the world in which Jews live as inherently inimical to Jewish continuity. In their analysis of the contemporary Israeli civil religion, Liebman and Don-Yehiya emphasize the prominence of the theme of Jewish isolation and endangerment as embodied in the traditional assertions that "Esau hates Jacob," that Israel is a "people which dwells alone."[21] The American Jewish civil religion is perhaps less vigorous than the Israeli in its depiction of a uniformly hostile environment, but it is no less convinced that Jewish survival is persistently endangered in the modern world. It has adopted as its own the perspective which the Jewish philosopher Simon Rawidowicz identified in his classic essay "Israel: The Ever-Dying People": Jewish life stands "on the verge of ceasing to be, of disappearing."[22] Like the many other generations of Jews who have felt similarly, the leaders of the polity who fear that the end may be near have transformed this concern into a survivalist weapon. For the Jews of the past, Rawidowicz suggests, a formulaic anticipation of the end strengthened the ability to withstand the assaults which did come. For the contemporary Jews who perceive manifold threats to Jewish continuity on every front, the civil religion prescribes a different strategy: active efforts to forestall such dangers and insure the perpetuation of Jewish life.

When leaders of the Jewish polity speak of survival they mean, first and foremost, the physical survival of Jews and the Jewish people. Since the Holocaust, no leader of the Jewish polity is prepared to take even this level of continuity for granted. It is, in Max Fisher's words, "our paramount concern."[23] Wherever Jews are perceived to be in danger—and especially in Israel, which is seen as an embattled nation surrounded by implacable enemies—the American Jewish polity feels a responsibility to offer its support. A constant vigilance is maintained against manifestations of anti-Semitism, heightened by the conviction that the anti-Semite's ultimate aim is Jewish extinction. Such is the lesson of Jewish history, ancient and contemporary. "Throughout history," a UJA pamphlet reminds its readers,

> there have been many solutions to the "Jewish Problem." Jewish history has been a struggle to survive against everything: from economic and religious persecution to the horrors of the European ghettos and the Middle East mellahs, from the *Protocols of Zion* to the UN resolution condemning Zionism as "racism."[24]

The danger of extinction at the hands of enemies persists, but the civil religion points to another threat to Jewish survival as well: disappearance through assimilation. "Today we face twentieth century-style dangers, some coming out of age-old hatreds, and some the product of affluence and acceptance in today's enlightened society."[25] The institutions of the Jewish polity now accept an explicit responsibility not only for the protection of Jews, but for the nurturing of Jewish identity. "[S]trengthening Jewish commitment has become a prime concern in Jewish communal life."[26] It is not enough, polity leaders have repeatedly declared, merely to repel the enemies without. Rather, survival means enhancing the "quality of Jewish life"; it must be "creative survival," "meaningful survival." This can only come from intensifying the Jewish identity of Jews to withstand the lures of assimilation.

The polity's relatively recent focus on enhancing the Jewishness of Jews reflects a conviction that physical survival is intimately linked to spiritual and cultural survival, i.e., that ultimately Jews cannot endure without Judaism, without a set of values which renders their survival meaningful. Against immediate external threats it is enough to point to the enemy and rely on the instinctual urge to defend oneself. Against the more subtle but insidious forces of the modern world which undermine the Jewishness of Jews, it is vital to provide a rationale for remaining Jewish. One national leader of the American Jewish Committee (once the most prominent institution of the assimilation-minded German Jewish establishment) explained that organization's increasing involvement in matters relating to Jewish identity in these terms:

> Neither our efforts as a defense organization against the forces of anti-semitism, nor our efforts as a human rights organization in support of a liberal society, or even our labors on behalf of the safety and well-being of Israel, none of these, important and critical as they may be, is sufficient to secure the future of Judaism. Rather, it is the cultivation and transmission of our cultural, moral, and spiritual heritage that gives purpose, that gives direction and passion to all of the other activities in which institutionalized Jewry engages in the United States.[27]

Commitment to Jewish survival now validates virtually the entirety of the polity's agenda. It serves as the primary motivator in fundraising: "We give because the ordeals of the past have taught us how to survive a difficult present. The present reminds us that ancient hatreds still seek to deny the Jewish people their future."[28] In turn, the programs paid for with these funds "can ensure the survival of a high quality of Jewish life for generations to come."[29] Indeed, so pervasive has the rhetoric of "survival" become that the concept threatens to become cliché, a legitimation for everything from aid given to Jewish communities in distress to recreational programs in Jewish community centers. Yet, this broad legitimating canopy is vital as a means of integrating the disparate specific programs and projects which the various agencies of the polity sponsor. If all, in some fashion or another, contribute to Jewish survival, then all are indeed part of one community, with one overriding purpose.

The prominence of the theme of Jewish survival in the rhetoric of the civil religion reveals the extent to which contemporary Jews are still struggling with the fundamental challenges of modernity. The fact of Jewish persistence is itself a vital source of morale, a confirmation that the quest to survive against what often seem discouraging odds is indeed worthwhile. Civil Judaism celebrates Jewish survival even as it agonizes over it: "We survive. Victorious over 10,000 tragedies and dangers over the last 4,000 years—we still survive." Its anxiety is assuaged in its proclamations of confident determination:

> I know that we will continue to survive and grow strong; this great saga of the Jewish people will continue . . .
> We, and thousands like us, will have the resolve and the wit and the wisdom to pass this heritage on to our children—renewed and vigorous and alive in our modern world. Together we will have the faith, commitment, courage and vision that will be required to insure the strength and safety of the State of Israel and the creative continuity of the Jewish people.[30]

The challenge which civil Judaism, like all other modern ideologies of Judaism, faces is to convince those whom it addresses that this is a goal worth seeking and investing themselves in. Commitment to Jewish survival—any religious commitment—is rarely, of course, the product of a rational process of decision-making. It is part of a more encompassing process of identification, with a group, a way of life, a view of the world. Commitment to Jewish survival is inspired as much by events—historical and biographical—as it is by any argumentation. In fact, civil Judaism does not often speak at length about why Jewish survival is important; the validity of the goal is a given. When it does, however, it generally offers two linked responses to the question. One focuses on the contribution which Jews and Judaism have made and continue to make to the world. "Judaism is a positive force for man," one leader asserted,

> because we are struggling to teach man how to build a better world for all men—not by what we say, but by what we do. Therefore, I believe the survival of Judaism is the central issue in Jewish life, and because I believe that, I am concerned about the survival of Jews, who carry these ideals and this force.[31]

This statement is unusually straightforward, but the rationale which it offers for Jewish survival is implicit in much of the rhetoric of civil Judaism. Its evocation of a Jewish teaching mission is reminiscent of the initial efforts of German Reform and Neo-Orthodox religious leaders to respond to the challenge of validating Jewish survival a century and a half ago. In essence, this argument cites Jewish values and the impact which those values have had on history and society as the fundamental justification for concern for Jewish continuity.[32] The Jewish polity seeks to exemplify and realize these values in the contemporary world. Hence, it not only works *for* Jewish survival, its work *validates* Jewish survival. "The very elements in our tradition which motivate us to care for the poor, the elderly, the isolated, are the very values that we seek to perpetuate when we teach our Judaism."[33]

Civil Judaism offers a second response to the Jew asking why he or she should be personally committed to Jewish survival: Your own life takes on significance in the work of the Jewish people, and in your participation in that work. The Jewish community offers individuals an opportunity to render their lives meaningful. "If I were asked," one leader recounted to a gathering of his colleagues,

> to condense into one capsule the most rewarding achievement of my life, I would say it has been the participation with you in helping to save lives. It is written that he who saves the life of one man, it is as if he saved the whole world. I can't do this alone, nor can you, so we have the concept of community.[34]

The question, he suggested, is therefore not really whether the Jews will survive, but how individuals will survive as Jews. They will survive, civil Judaism avers, by helping other Jews, transmitting the heritage, living by Jewish values—sharing in the ethos of the Jewish polity, and thereby discovering the inherent meaning in their Jewishness.

Critical observers of the American Jewish civil religion, including some of its thoughtful adherents, have at times expressed concern that Jewish survival has become an end in itself for the Jewish polity. The critics have asked, to what end?, and have decried the absence of answers in much civil Jewish rhetoric. There is validity to this critique, but it also misses to some extent both the content and context of civil Judaism's conception of Jewish survival. In traditional Judaism, Torah and the people of Israel are inseparable. Israel is a people only by virtue of Torah, and the Torah is carried on earth by Israel. In its modernized idiom, civil Judaism makes the same assertion: The survival of the Jewish people is a consuming passion because the Jewish poeple plays a unique role in history as the bearer of Jewish values. In the work to insure the perpetuation of these values, the survival of the Jewish people and the Jewish community becomes a value in its own right, a crystallization of all that is being defended. Jewish survival is not, for the civil religion, survival for its own sake. It is a purposive continuity. But the purpose is intimately bound up with the very institutional vehicles working to insure that continuity. The endeavors of the Jewish polity are at once a path to survival and exemplifications of why and how that survival is meaningful in the contemporary world.

## The Centrality of Israel

Nowhere is the struggle and significance of Jewish survival more focused for civil Judaism than in the State of Israel. It has been said that American Judaism recognizes only one heresy which subjects the perpetrator to immediate excommunication: denial of support to the State of Israel. The role which Israel plays in the civil religion is indeed central, though complex. In practical terms, an enormous proportion of the energies of the institutions of the Jewish polity is devoted to work of one sort or another on behalf of the state and people of Israel. For many activists, Israel is the prime motivator and focus of their involvement. It remains the central theme and cause in communitywide fundraising campaigns. Jewish unity, mutual responsibility, and Jewish survival all come together in Israel; it is the symbolic center of the civil Jewish universe, the place where the lines of Jewish existence—of Jewish history and tradition, of the modern Jewish condition and the response to that condition—intersect.

Like all important religious symbols, Israel has multiple meanings for civil Judaism. It is "a spiritual homeland" for all Jews, "the focus for our sense of peoplehood, a fountainhead to nourish our Jewish pride and a place of refuge for Jews in crisis anywhere in the world."[35] Israel is the symbol and source of a renewed Jewish vitality:

> There is an Israel where for two thousand years there was no Israel. And everywhere, too, there is a vital Jewish people knowing each other and working together in unity and in fellowship. And it is all as if in our own time, in our own years, we had seen the Valley of the Dry Bones come to life once more.[36]

The rebirth of Israel "has changed all of our lives." It is "the blossoming of hope, the greening of the desert."[37] Israel exemplifies the fundamental values of Judaism. In Jerusalem, the very stones "speak of conscience and the integrity of life."[38] For the American Jewish civil religion, Israel is, in the phrase of sociologist Peter Berger, a "signal of transcendence,"[39] "a harbinger of new understanding of how history is intertwined with the mystery of life . . . a light unto the nations."[40]

Words such as these, coming from the lips of hard-headed businessmen and organizational leaders, bespeak the enormous religious significance with which Israel has been invested by American civil Judaism. But Israel is also a real place, with serious problems, and an uncertain future. The civil religion places Israel as well at the center of its picture of endangered Jewish survival and of its ethos of responsibility for Jews in need. Israel is under attack; its Arab foes remain implacable; the United Nations has become a forum for assaults on its legitimacy; anti-Zionism and anti-Semitism have become inseparable threats to Jews everywhere. When Israel is endangered, civil Judaism avers, all Jews are endangered.

Israel is also a home for Jews who must be housed, fed, and educated. The human needs of its citizens, especially the immigrants for whom it is the only refuge, demand a response from all Jews. Israeli society, a society which is to serve as a model of social justice and compassion, cannot be permitted to become rent by ethnic and social divisions. For this too, as for Israel's political defense, the especially privileged Jews of North America bear a special responsibility.

Civil Judaism thus presents two distinct, possibly even contradictory, images of Israel—as the focus and radiating source of Jewish spiritual energies and as the beleaguered exemplar of the Jewish condition of insecurity in the modern world. The two images are integrated, characteristically, at the level of action. In the prodigious endeavors of the polity in celebration and support of Israel, in the proclamation of Israel's transcendent significance and the struggle against all threats to the realization of that vision, Israel becomes a symbol in which the entire worldview and ethos of the civil religion are crystallized. The American Jewish obligation to help Israel survive and to promote the human betterment of its people is nothing less than a "sacred covenant."[41] In so acting, American Jews help to make possible—indeed to participate in —the fulfillment of the extraordinary historic role which Israel is assigned. Thereby, they act to insure their own historic significance as well.

The civil Jewish ideological investment in Israel is enormous, but, as many observers have pointed out, it is not the classic ideology of Zionism which animates the American Jewish polity. This does not mean that polity leaders are insincere when they speak of "the historic centrality of Israel in the American Jewish consciousness,"[42] or in Jewish life in general. Israel is preeminent as a focus of concern, and its role as the major factor in Jewish history today is readily acknowledged. But there is no Zionist theory of Diaspora insubstantiality undergirding this acknowledgement. Only recently has the American Jewish polity given any serious attention, for example, to the idea of *aliya* (immigration to Israel)—the central "commandment" of Zionist ideology—from the United States. For the civil religion, *aliya* is even today at best a worthy personal choice, neither of obligation nor even, necessarily, an ideal.

The civil religious alternative to the ideology of Zionism is the concept of "partnership."

> A partnership of equals, who seek practical ways to work with, and relate
> to, and understand, each other. A partnership that pools its talent, and
> strives to improve the quality of life of both partners, with a full and total
> commitment to the viability of Jewish life in Israel, and of Jewish life in
> North America.[43]

The meaningful existence of the Jewish people, the ability to live "with pride and hope and worth, with comfort and safety and meaning in our lives" demands a worldwide Jewish partnership. "The nation of Israel and the people of Israel—the Jewish people—depend on each other and need each other. It takes the combined strength of the Jews in the Diaspora and the Jews of Israel to insure the destiny of the Jewish people."[44]

The concept of Israeli–American Jewish partnership plays a critical role in enabling American Jews to affirm their unity with the people of Israel, their participation in its historic mission, and, at the same time, the integrity of their own Jewish lives. Israel's signficance is not depreciated; indeed its role as a "spiritual center" is affirmed. Former CJF president, Martin Citrin, for example, has asserted, "We must recognize that the future of the generations that follow us is inextricably linked to Israel as a source of deepening commitment to our own sense of Jewishness and spiritual identification." But, Israel is not the sole source of such commitment. "It is not and cannot be a substitute for our own increased commitment to creative Jewish continuity at all levels in our own communities."[45]

The conviction that American Jewish life has and must have an integrity of its own separates this position from that of Zionist ideologists like Ahad Ha'am who envisioned Israel as a spiritual center for an ongoing, but essentially uncreative, Diaspora.[46] The ultimate ideological implications of the civil Jewish position have been spelled out by Charles Zibbell, for many years associate executive vice-president of CJF, in a provocative article written after the Yom Kippur War of 1973. Zibbell spoke of the need for a new American Jewish self-understanding based on "the total obsolescence of both the concept and the term *Diaspora.*"

> The idea of *Diaspora* is not only dated; its impact is actually mischievous. It has served as a crutch for our own inaction. It has bred a lack of responsibility for enriching the quality of our own life here. It has led to a form of vicarious Jewish living on a global scale that borders on pathology. . . . [W]e need to recognize that we have a single Jewish community, with parts of it located in various places on this planet.[47]

The appropriate goal for Jewish communal endeavor is the strengthening of all Jewish communites—in Israel and wherever Jews live—as ends in their own right. In this endeavor, Israel and American Jewry can and must be partners, but on the basis of mutuality of understanding and common objectives.

American Jewish civil religion does not challenge the central symbolic role of Israel. Rather, it proposes to integrate that centrality into a yet broader framework of Jewish self-understanding in which the unity of the Jewish people is expressed through, but not exhausted by, the restored national homeland. For American Jews, the civil religious image of Israel and of American Jewry's relationship to it is carefully constructed so as to inspire rather than depress a self-affirming Jewish activism. By identifying with Israel as a second homeland and promised land, one which they help to sustain and from which they draw nourishment

—but in which they do not need to live—American Jews link themselves to the historic unity and destiny of the Jewish people. By insisting, however, that they relate to this homeland not as subordinates, but as full partners in that destiny—and by striving to prove that they are capable of building a viable Jewish community in America—they validate their own position in Jewish history.

## The Enduring Value of Jewish Tradition

American Jewish civil religion has always maintained a respectful, if selective, attitude toward the contents of the classical Judaic tradition. In its origins, the ideology which was to become a civil religion had little if any traditional religious substance beyond the value of charity. For many years, the polity defined and understood itself as "secular," in contrast to the synagogue sphere of Jewish life which was obviously "religious." But in the American Jewish context, even this use of the term "secular" meant primarily "non-denominational" rather than "anti-religious." The attitude of nascent civil Judaism toward traditional religious institutions, beliefs, and practices might be described as "benevolent neutrality." Ideological secularists—those who negated the value of the religious tradition or explicitly transvalued it into secular terms (e.g., Jewish socialists or the early Zionists who rebelled against Judaism)—never were a powerful force in the American Jewish polity and contributed little to its emerging civil religion.

The distance which the Jewish polity maintained from the religious tradition thus reflected more the narrowness of its self-defined agenda than any fundamental hostility to that tradition. Positive Jewish identification was regarded as a virtue, but the polity did not prescribe the form which identification should take, and it viewed the inculcation of such an identification as essentially a private responsibility. From this posture of benevolent neutrality, the polity moved slowly but steadily during the post-World War II period to one of active appropriation of and support for Jewish tradition. The Judaic heritage has come to be seen as central both to the polity's raison d'être and to the potential meaningfulness of Jewish life in the modern era. The polity no longer defines itself as "secular"; instead it proudly claims the mantle and the mandate of a continuator of the Judaic religious heritage.

The spokespersons of the civil religion seek to promote this identification by incorporating terms like "Torah" and "mitzvah"—terms drawn from the traditional vocabulary of Jewish religious life—and by citing classical texts and Jewish heroes in their characterizations of the polity's endeavors. What, one leader asked, is the real meaning of Project Renewal, the major social development program launched in the late 1970s to rehabilitate depressed neighborhoods in Israel? "It is Jewish Renewal," he answered.

> It goes directly to the heart of Judaism. . . . It is to give another Jew a
> chance—a chance to be independent, a chance to live a fuller and more
> beautiful Jewish life.
>
> This, ladies and gentlemen, is the highest tenet of our belief. . . . It
> affords me the opportunity to be a good Jew. It gives me a chance to per-
> form the Mitzvah that each of us is charged to perform.[48]

"Our giving," another leader insisted, "is not charity; it is an investment
in Jewish continuity. The Talmud says: 'As our Fathers planted for us, so
do we plant for our children.' This is our reward for giving. This is the
basic tenet of Jewish life: Mitzvah."[49] UJA activists, yet another leader
suggested, can look to Abraham as a model for their work. Abraham,
noted by the rabbis for his hospitality, is "the concerned Jew, the man
who feels that he is indeed his brother's keeper." Abraham exemplifies
as well "a principle that has been important to Judaism ever since: the
responsibility of the righteous few toward the rest of society, and the capacity of these few to save it from destruction by the sheer force of their
own merit and moral impact." It was Abraham who, in offering his son
Isaac to God, demonstrated that "the continuation of Jewish life seems
related to the willingness of Jews to sacrifice for survival." Today's leaders must follow in this tradition.

> We are again and again called upon for sacrificial level financial commit-
> ment. We are also reminded of the necessity to see the human side of our
> giving . . . the human factors in showing concern for the stranger, the
> wayfarer, and the alienated members of society. . . . Our support of the
> United Jewish Appeal represents the highest values of our Jewish heri-
> tage and tradition. By doing our share, we, in essence, become worthy
> descendants of Abraham.[50]

In seeking to legitimate its contemporary work in this fashion, as a direct translation of traditional Judaic obligation, the Jewish polity is implicitly affirming the viability of Jewish tradition as a source of meaning
in the modern world. That affirmation is made explicitly as well. The
civil religion is no longer "neutral" on the question of whether the Jewish religious tradition must endure for the Jewish people to survive.
There is "no Jewish future without Judaism."[51] The social welfare
agenda of the Jewish federation is not enough to sustain a meaningful
Jewish commitment. It is "but one expression of our Jewishness, satisfying, but not fulfilling all of our Jewish purpose and emotional need, and
we long for other expressions to recapture the romance and the passion
and the joy, the insights and the wisdom to which we are heirs and to
bring them into our daily lives."[52]

The Jewish polity has thus assumed a new role: as an advocate and
sponsor of Jewish study, religious observance, and other efforts to revitalize the impact of Jewish tradition on the lives of its citizens. Public
functions of the polity are now marked by the incorporation of tradi-

tional ritual forms: religious services, Sabbath celebration, blessings recited before and after meals. Polity institutions offer programs and
educational materials which focus on the study of classical Jewish texts,
Jewish philosophy, and Jewish history. These activities serve not merely
to accommodate the participation of more observant or educated segments of the community, but to express concretely the fundamental
transformation in self-understanding which the polity has undergone in
recent years. For the endeavors of the Jewish polity to endure, it recognizes, they must be firmly linked to the larger framework of meaning
which the Jewish tradition can provide. Since that tradition is itself too
little understood and appreciated by American Jews, the polity, in faithfulness to its own values and for self-preservation, must become its advocate, its sponsor, even its transmitter.

This affirmation by the civil religion of the enduring value and
importance of the Judaic religious tradition finds expression in programs
and policies, and in a more encompassing model of Jewish leadership.
Federations are devoting a continuously increasing proportion of the
funds they raise to support Jewish educational activities. Agencies in the
communities are shaping their own programs to reflect a greater emphasis on transmission of Jewish knowledge and values. Leaders are being
trained to view their communal activities as not only rooted in traditional Jewish values, but as only a part of the definition of what a
contemporary Jewish leader can and should be. "How are you to carry
forward the peculiar system of thought and action which comprises Jewish peoplehood?" asked a prominent federation executive addressing a
group of young leaders. "You may pray with your fellow Jews. You may
observe rituals and celebrate holy days. You may educate yourself and
your children. You may involve yourself in the concerns of the Jewish
people—at home, overseas, and in Israel."[53]

For civil Judaism, a measure of personal identification with and appropriation of the Jewish tradition is necessary for leaders to experience the
full import of the work they are engaged in. Activism must be wedded to
understanding, the *na'aseh* (we will do) of Judaism to its *nishma* (we will
apprehend). For its 1984 General Assembly the Council of Jewish Federations adopted the theme: "The Jewish Leader as a Learning Person,"
and devoted an entire morning to sessions emphasizing the relationship
between Jewish tradition and contemporary concerns. This affirmation
and aspiration of the civil religion—that Jewish tradition is central to
the work of the polity, and that leaders must come to understand it more
fully—was expressed boldly by Herschel Blumberg, outgoing chairman
of the United Jewish Appeal's Board of Trustees, at its 1984 Leadership
Conference: "Together," he urged the assembly of national leaders,

> we may become scrolls of psalms, volumes of verse, tomes of Talmudic
> lore. We may become a veritable library of Jewish praise, prayer and

perception. We need to study more and be inspired to live more with our holy texts. They are ours to possess. If we let them possess us, we will become finer human beings, more knowledgeable Jews and more secure in the great work we do.[54]

The civil religious embrace of the Jewish tradition does not mean that it has become a variety of traditional religion in its own right. Unlike the Jewish denominations which have developed over the past two centuries to mediate the passage of the Jewish tradition into the modern world, civil Judaism has no theory of that tradition and only the most rudimentary theology. Its spokespersons are generally unconcerned with the modern debates concerning the historical development of Jewish tradition, with issues of when and how it may be modified based on past precedent or current insight. Civil Judaism makes no pretense of serving as a full-fledged alternative to denominational Judaism, either functionally or substantively.

The civil religion does, nevertheless, have an approach to Jewish tradition which is clearly modernistic in spirit. Civil Judaism views Jewish tradition as timeless in its essential message. "The mortar of the teachings of the Torah and the requirements of tzedakah are the changeless binding between the bricks of our ever-changing social architecture." For the sake of continuity, to keep the timeless tradition timely, the Jewish people must be prepared to make changes. The challenge is to keep the forces of tradition and change in balance, "to breathe new energy into those thunderous biblical phrases from . . . Genesis and from Isaiah."[55]

Dwight Eisenhower has been credited with the classic American civil religious assertion that every American must have a faith, and that it doesn't matter which faith it is. Civil Judaism's approach to the Jewish tradition is similar. The tradition which it endorses is both "homogenized" and "pluralized." Civil Judaism focuses on the unobjectionable, primarily ethical, dimensions of the tradition. Of necessity, its "Jewish tradition" represents a kind of religious common denominator, general principles of moral behavior, generalized affirmation of a modicum of ritual. The civil religion does not dictate (or even strongly suggest) specific norms for personal Jewish observance. A Jew, it contends, should take Jewish tradition seriously, should look to it for values and for the enrichment of his or her life. But defining the scope and content of that tradition beyond those elements which are clearly functional in the communal context is a task in which civil Judaism has no stake or interest.

Like American civil religion, contemporary civil Judaism is supportive of denominational religion. It accepts and affirms the plurality of Jewish denominations; all enjoy equal legitimacy. The civil religion seeks to antagonize the adherents of none, to emphasize their commonalities and promote cooperation at a level where ideological disputes can be suspended. By and large it has been successful in this endeavor, one which reaches to the very core of a civil religion's social function. If civil Judaism had a more elaborate and sophisticated philosphy of Jewish tradition in its own right, it might well jeopardize this success. What is left unsaid can be filled in in various ways by the respective denominations.

Since its affirmation of pluralism and implicit modernism run counter to the principled stance of some traditionally observant Jews, civil Judaism will always enjoy an uneasy peace with those who cannot acknowledge the legitimacy of interpretations of Jewish tradition not rooted in fidelity to *halakhic* norms. Should it, on the other hand, concede to any such group the authority to serve as the sole authentic arbiter of the tradition's meaning and demands, it would alienate the principled modernists among its adherents. Civil Judaism has, therefore, despite the occasional tensions which flare up, opted for a strategy of "ad hocism" and individual choice. Tradition is respected wherever possible; but the rationale is social and functional, not theological.

The selectivity which the civil religion manifests in its appropriation of Jewish tradition thus reflects not a deliberate effort to carve out a new understanding of that tradition, but a need to hew closely to its fundamental role as integrator, legitimator, and motivator. The enduring value of Jewish tradition is central to civil Judaism's self-understanding and to its prescription for how the Jewish polity and its activists should conduct their affairs. Without that tradition, and without a determination to preserve it, the work of the polity would be both purposeless and pointless. The Jewish tradition stands behind all that the polity does; hence the transmission of that tradition—in whatever specific form it is crystallized—is one of the polity's most vital tasks.

### *Tzedakah:* Philanthropy and Social Justice

In the previous chapter, we traced the evolution of the contemporary American Jewish polity from its origins in a set of charitable agencies. The polity has never given up its self-definition as a philanthropic enterprise, even as other dimensions have been added to that self-understanding. The institutions of the polity view themselves as the lineal descendants of the charitable organizations of the traditional Jewish *kehillah.* They frame their contemporary mission in terms of the core value of *tzedakah,* seen as a thread running throughout Jewish life across time and space. "In some ways," Charles Zibbell has written, "the history of Tzedakah turns out to be a history of the spirit of the Jewish people." As the exponents of that value in the modern world, the institutions of the polity thus place themselves along the central path of Jewry's spiritual history as authentic inheritors and preservers of the Judaic tradition.

The traditional meaning of *tzedakah* encompasses both a narrower and a broader dimension. The narrower dimension equates *tzedakah* with philanthropy or charity in practical terms. *Tzedakah* is the giving of money to aid those in need. Jewish communities collected and maintained funds for this purpose; every Jew was expected to contribute. As noted earlier, however, the root meaning of the Hebrew term *tzedakah* is not akin to that of charity or philanthropy. *Tzedakah* is derived from a root which means "righteousness" or "justice." Hence, Jewish didactics has always emphasized that the specific act of contributing for the welfare of the poor is an obligatory act of justice, not a noblesse oblige expression of personal beneficence. *Tzedakah* is a collective communal responsibility, one aspect of the larger command to the Jewish people that they pursue justice as a society.

For the contemporary civil religion this dual meaning of the value of *tzedakah* is affirmed in a dual focus on Jewish philanthropy and on work for social justice as central elements of its prescribed ethos. Both are seen as necessary contemporary expressions of the traditional value— indeed, the two are viewed as virtually inseparable. "The purposes and motivations of Jewish Federations," stated Phil Bernstein,

> are rooted in the central Jewish religious maxims, principles and precepts of the Bible, defining the requirements of a just society, and the centrality of that requirement in the Jewish way of life.
>
> The motivations are found especially in the magnificent nineteenth chapter of Leviticus, the Ten Commandments, the Prophets such as Isaiah and Micah, the levels of charity defined by Maimonides, the requirements of Judaism not only for learning and prayer, but for acts of loving kindness.[57]

*Tzedakah* demands both that Jews take care of their own needy through human welfare programs and that they participate in the struggles to extend the principles of justice within the larger society.

Civil Judaism insists on the obligatory character of *tzedakah* for the individual Jew and for the community. It is the most basic and pervasive of the civil religion's few "commandments." "Charity and working for social justice—Tzedakah and Mitzvos—are not options for Jews. They have the force of articles of faith. They are duties and requirements."[58] To the extent that the Jewish polity is able to promote among Jews an acknowledgement that *tzedakah* is in fact an obligation in their lives, and that it is the authoritative instrument through which that obligation is to be fulfilled, the civil religion continues to provide a basis for Jewish unity on both a pragmatic and an ideological level. The claim which was made in the earliest days of organized American Jewish philanthropy is still made today: Though American Jews may be divided in many of their convictions, they can agree on one principle, that of *tzedakah*. What civil Judaism goes on to add is a critical extension, namely that that principle is itself the heart of Jewish religion. When Jews come together in and through the Jewish polity, they do so, therefore, not apart from or despite their religious convictions, but in affirmation of the central meaning of Judaism for the modern Jew.

The single most visible activity of the Jewish polity for the vast majority of American Jews is fundraising. The campaigns of the Jewish federations and the United Jewish Appeal—plus the independent fundraising endeavors of the hundreds of other national and local agencies which are part of the larger Jewish polity—are highly sophisticated financial and organizational enterprises. But at heart, the civil religion claims, they are nothing but the modern expression of the timeless injunction to give *tzedakah*. To contribute to these campaigns is thus not only a Jewish obligation, but a contribution to the preservation of Jewish values, hence, of Jewish life itself. Similarly, the manifold human welfare programs which the polity maintains are not merely services for those in need. They are fulfillments of the religious command to care for the poor, the stranger, the widow and the orphan. "To perform an act of *tzedakah*, to share resources and skills, is to make a commitment to Jewish well-being, to reaffirm Jewish values."[59] The philanthropic work of the Jewish polity is, therefore, itself a vehicle for Jewish continuity, a "transmitter of Jewish values, not through reading or listening, but through doing."[60]

The second component of the civil religion's definition of *tzedakah*—work on behalf of social justice—is also seen as rooted in Jewish tradition. "It has always been Jewish doctrine that social justice cannot be limited to Jews alone; Jews are dedicated to social justice for all mankind. 'Love the stranger as thyself,' the Bible taught."[61] "For us, social justice—Tzedakah in its full meaning—has always been indivisible—for all."[62] This insistence that Jewish religious values mandate concern with the welfare of the larger society validates the polity's involvement in causes beyond the boundaries of the Jewish community. It is not necessary to choose, civil Judaism asserts, between particularistic and universalistic concerns. The particular character of Judaism demands universal concern alongside commitment to the welfare of Jews. Thus, Jewish involvement—individual and communal—in the civil rights movement, in efforts to combat poverty, in seeking solutions to the urban crisis, in supporting government human services programs, is also an expression of Jewish commitment. Indeed, this involvement emphasizes that it is out of the matrix of Judaism that values such as human rights and social justice have emerged. "Those ethical principles which our tradition and our teaching gave to the world have come to be accepted as ideal by men of good will, and by and large have worked in perfect harmony with the group interest of the Jewish people."[63]

Since the last great wave of social activism in America in the 1960s, the rhetoric of Jewish pursuit of social justice has been somewhat muted within the polity. Greater attention has been paid to the tasks of Jewish self-preservation; the polity has, in the view of many observers, "turned inward." There has not, however, been any repudiation of the fundamental assertion that the Jewish value of *tzedakah* mandates concern for the welfare of society as a whole. Federations and Jewish communal agencies continue to be advocates for social welfare programs and to express broad concern for civil and human rights in society and in the world. Jews remain, CJF president, Martin Citrin, asserted at the 1983 General Assembly, participants with other Americans and Canadians in "a partnership of conscience and caring—for the poor, for the disenfranchised and for the disadvantaged."[64]

Despite the recent "turning inward," *tzedakah* as pursuit of social justice remains a cardinal tenet of the civil religion. Jews care not only for their own, but for all human beings, and they do so not as "universal men," but precisely as Jews, as the heirs and executors of the tradition which contributed these ideals to humanity in the first place. *Tzedakah* thus serves at once to validate Jewish participation in the larger society and to reinforce the consciousness among Jews that they bear a unique legacy which must be preserved. It legitimates Jewish commitment as a form of human concern, and human concern as a necessary expression of Jewish commitment. Through the practice of *tzedakah*—both as philanthropy and as social justice—the Jew reaffirms his fidelity to Jewish values and the efficacy and relevance of those values within the modern world.

The civil religious belief that Jews must be exemplary in their practice of *tzedakah* provides the polity with a sense of mission and duty which transcends self-perpetuation. Civil Judaism thereby responds to both the self-interested and the altruistic instincts of a population still concerned about its "place" in the world, and still seeking moral justification. As long as Jews remain a people committed to *tzedakah*, Jewish survival is not a chauvinistic conceit, but a requisite for the continued fulfillment of the Jewish role as an exemplar of human values.

## Americanness as a Virtue

Nothing in civil Judaism's strong advocacy of Jewish unity, mutual responsibility, and continuity is seen as calling into question either the possibility or the desirability of full participation by Jews in American society and culture. From its inception, the Jewish polity has promoted such participation as a virtue. America has been good to the Jews, making possible unprecedented achievement and success. In turn, Jews owe America not only their loyalty, but their active engagement in the process of America's self-realization. They can undertake this involvement because America does not seek to undermine their Jewishness in the process of calling forth their Americanness. More fundamentally, they can be fully American because the meanings of Jewishness and Americanness are so intimately related:

> We are blessed, as native American sons and daughters and as Jews, with a heritage of devotion to man's inherent birthright—justice and freedom for all. As Americans and Jews, our dual traditions parallel and complement the other, fusing our timeless Jewish ideals, ethics, and practices with the bold and vigorous spirit of our still young America.[65]

American Jews can serve as a living synthesis of these two traditions, bringing both to fuller realization and thereby serving both faithfully.

The underlying conviction of the civil religion is that Jewishness and Americanness are mutually reinforcing. "A good Jew is a good citizen and a good American—and we have much to bring and much to receive from our involvement in communal welfare."[66] By being better Jews, Jews will be better Americans, and vice versa. This implies a dual responsibility for the Jew: participating in American life, but also strengthening the fabric of Jewish life so that Jews will have something to contribute to the richness of American society. American Jews, Phil Bernstein asserted, can be "true to our country only as we are true to ourselves, only as we build a Jewish community whose living example of social justice and communal integrity is a source of strength and pride to all Americans."[67] America, civil Judaism believes, permits and desires this degree of self-preoccupation as a means of developing its own strength as a pluralistic society. At the height of the movement to involve the polity in efforts to renew Jewish identity, one prominent young leader asserted, "We *want* our children to conceive of themselves as Jews who *happen* to be Americans—not Americans who happen to be Jews." Yet, there was nothing truly radical in this assertion, as the rationale he offered for it made clear: "Only in this way," he went on, "can we make a contribution to America—to the creation of a pluralistic society—encouraging and accepting difference—enriched by the interaction of many groups, many cultures, many faiths—and secure a just and orderly society."[68]

For civil Judaism, participation in American society does represent a challenge of sorts. "We insist on being citizens of two worlds—of both the Jewish and the general community. And that poses constant problems."[69] But the dominant meaning of America for the civil religion is opportunity, an opportunity to demonstrate that Judaism and modernity are compatible. Civil Judaism expects Jews to take advantage of the opportunities which America provides, and to use them to better fulfill their Jewish responsibilities. Jews have earned the right to expect America to honor their concerns. In turn, American Jews are more than willing to shoulder their share of the responsibilities of American citizenship.

Since civil Judaism is modernistic in its approach to Jewish practice and belief, it does not perceive American social and cultural norms as substantial barriers to the expression of Jewishness. Social isolation is neither necessary nor desirable. If some Jews assimilate to the point of abandoning their Jewishness altogether, that is indeed a problem, but one for Jews to deal with by strengthening Jewish identity. It is not a rationale for withdrawing from the larger society. One the contrary, only by continuing to participate actively in every phase of American life, can Jews help America become what it was meant to be, and thereby fulfill their own particular mission of service and contribution.[70]

## A Pervasive Rhetoric

The seven tenets outlined above form the propositional core of the contemporary civil Jewish faith. In fashioning our portrait of this faith we have cited liberally from the speeches and writings of polity leaders. Yet even these citations do not fully demonstrate the pervasiveness of the themes of civil Judaism in the rhetoric of the Jewish polity. As part of the research for this book 135 speeches and publications emanating from a variety of polity institutions over the past fifteen years were subjected to a detailed content analysis.[71] The documents utilized cannot be construed as a scientific sample of all documents produced by all polity agencies during this period. Included, however, are different types of documents (speeches, annual reports, public relations literature, resolutions), from different agencies (local federations, national community relations and social service agencies, as well as a preponderance from the Council of Jewish Federations and the United Jewish Appeal), with both lay and professional authors.

The results of the content analysis are striking. Several motifs recur consistently. Israel is cited as an important focus of Jewish concern and activity in more than four-fifths of all the documents examined. Nearly three-fourths of the documents analyzed make some reference to Jewish insecurity/security: anti-Semitism, oppression, the struggle for Jewish rights, or some other close variant on this theme. Jewish unity or community is a motif in two-thirds of the documents, as is some variant on the theme of *tzedakah*, Jewish or human needs. Three-fourths of the speeches and publications examined refer to Jewish tradition, Jewish education, and/or the quality of Jewish life. Three-fifths of the documents speak explicitly of concern for Jewish continuity or survival. The motifs of Jewish "mission," "responsibility," or "service" appear in two-thirds of the documents, and nearly half contain some affirmation of America or reference to Jewish contributions to the larger world.

Of the more than fifty documents analyzed which emanated from CJF or from national federation movement leaders, only two contain no reference to at least one of the cardinal themes of Jewish unity/community,

Jewish survival, or Jewish insecurity/security. All of the other central themes of the civil religion—Israel, *tzedakah*, Jewish tradition, America—appear, in one form or another, in at least half the documents. A number of documents, especially the speeches of volunteer and professional leaders on "state" occasions from which we have cited so often, are virtual catechisms of civil Judaism, incorporating nearly all of its tenets.

For the three dozen documents analyzed which can be classified as UJA originated, the picture is equally clear. Not surprisingly, Israel is a theme in nearly all of these. But other key tenets of civil Judaism—Jewish unity, anti-Semitism and Jewish endangerment, survival, responsibility and mission, Jewish tradition and the quality of Jewish life, meeting human/Jewish needs and the value of *tzedakah*—also recur repeatedly throughout the speeches, reports, and campaign literature examined. The UJA version of the civil religion differs from that of the federation movement (the institutions are, in fact, intimately linked, with a heavily interlocking leadership) only in its relative deemphasis on the theme of America, a lacuna which is entirely understandable in light of UJA's explicit overseas focus.

A statistical content analysis of this sort can never substitute for a reading of the documents themselves. It can only suggest the extent to which the tenets of the civil religion pervade the polity's self-understanding and the legitimation of its endeavors. Moreover, it is inadequate to capture the coherence of civil Judaism as a meaning system. The themes we have noted rarely appear singly and in isolation from one another. Typically, they are wedded together into larger units, themselves pieces of a consistent worldview and a shared ethos which are at times so widely assumed as to not even require explicit articulation.

In the documents and speeches of the Jewish polity, American Jewish civil religion is rarely laid out in the propositional form we have given it. But the themes and tone of civil Judaism are woven throughout the polity's rhetoric. They are signposts which define the territory through which the leaders and institutions of the polity move in the conduct of their activities. The civil religion's tenets provide formulae with which leaders can express the bases and rationale of their commitment to the enterprise of communal activism, and the solidarity implicit in the endeavor itself. The civil religion reinforces the unity it celebrates by providing a common language for the polity. As in the case of all such language systems, the whole is far greater than the sum of its parts. Reference to one theme—Israel, or human needs, or Jewish survival—evokes, by the repeated weaving and reweaving of such themes together into larger units of perception and value, an entire ethos and worldview. Each theme points beyond itself to the whole; the whole, as a coherent vision of the meaning of Jewishness in the contemporary world, stands behind each unit, deepening its meaning, broadening its scope or reference.

At those unusual moments when an explicit articulation of the themes of civil Judaism is sought—as in the speech by Ed Robin cited at the outset of this chapter—the full import of civil Judaism as a religious belief system becomes most evident. The civil religion locates the work of the Jewish polity and its activists in a transcendent framework of meaning. It takes their perceptions of the world around them (at times confused and even self-contradictory), their values (derived from an understanding of Jewish tradition which is sometimes partial and inchoate), and their emotional commitments (often far deeper than their rationality can effectively explicate), and binds these into prescriptions for a way of life which is personally and collectively ennobling. Civil Judaism places Jewishness at the center of its picture of the world and makes the affirmation of that Jewishness the key to individual and communal self-realization. At its best, it embodies the power of the greatest faith systems: the power to define the reality we face as humans and to chart the path which will lead us to salvation in such a world.

## Religion without Theology

There is one notable element of traditional religion conspicuously missing from the picture of civil Judaism which we have drawn thus far: reference to God, or some form of transcendent reality. In noting this absence, we are not concerned with the definitional question: Can civil Judaism appropriately be termed "religious" if it lacks such reference?[72] Rather, our concern is interpretive: how shall we evaluate that silence?

We should note at the outset that the absence of reference to God in civil religious statements and documents is characteristic, though not absolute. One can find such references in occasional speeches (a few of which are cited in this chapter and elsewhere in the book). In most of these instances, God is invoked in a routinized, almost deistic, fashion— a deity who stands behind the world and Jewish tradition, but plays little or no active role in the working out of the contemporary destiny of either. What is most striking even where reference is made, and especially in the vast majority of instances where it is not, is the thoroughly insignificant role which any God-concept plays in the civil religion. This is particularly noteworthy in light of the historic association of Judaism with the biblical monotheistic conception of the "living God." For the civil religion, Judaism is very much a matter of concern; God is not.

This does not, however, imply that civil Judaism is atheistic. The existence of God is never questioned, much less denied. Civil Judaism offers no explicitly secular ideology of Judaism. Rather, the civil religion is by and large simply silent on the matter. This silence is not surprising for several reasons. First, it reflects the historical origins of the polity as a network of secular, i.e., nonreligious, agencies. Although the secular-religious boundary in American Jewish life has grown increasingly fuzzy in recent years, there remains a strong sense that theological concerns are the domain of religious institutions—i.e., the synagogues and rabbinate. The agencies of the once secular polity are neither expected nor desired to manifest theological positions. They are expected to be respectful of traditional religion (as we have seen). Hence, by indireciton, in the affirmation of Jewish values and of the importance of Judaism in sustaining Jewish life, the civil religion makes room for a serious theistic and theological commitment, but it lacks such in its own right.

This historically rooted reluctance remains functional. The watchword of civil Judaism is unity. Theology, except at the most rudimentary formulaic level (where even atheists and agnostics can be accepting of God-language as metaphorical), is inherently divisive in contemporary Jewish life. Not only does the polity embrace believers and (relative) non-believers, it seeks to include Jews with highly diverse theological standpoints. By remaining silent on the nature or role of God in human life and Jewish destiny, civil Judaism avoids antagonizing any of these Jews. It also avoids having to deal with potentially difficult, even embarrassing, theological issues: e.g., assurance of the validity of the oft-cited "prophetic values" of Judaism, or the central role of the Jewish people in human history. Such assertions, vital, we have seen, to the civil religion, are perhaps better left as incoherent statements of faith rather than being subject to theological examination. It is, then, not so much God who is missing from civil Judaism as it is any serious theological discussion. Civil Judaism is atheological—not atheistic—religion.

Still, the absence of any significant reference to the deity in civil religious rhetoric is not merely a reflection of history or a functional adaptation. It bespeaks as well the essential character of civil religion in general and raises questions about that character. Civil religion, as we noted in chapter 1, inevitably places the collectivity, be it nation or group, at the center of its meaning system. While this redrawing of the traditional religious universe certainly allows for a serious theistic component, placing the collectivity "under God," it also, as Marty points out, permits the nation or group itself to assume a transcendental character.[73] In traditional Judaism the Jewish people indeed has such a character: it is a religious entity, a "kingdom of priests and a holy nation." But it derives its unique character, its destiny, and its mission from its relationship to the one transcendent God. It is this relational component, the covenantal basis of Jewish existence, which both empowers and sets limits upon the Jewish people's self-expression in history.

Civil Judaism is a religion of Jewish destiny. It takes with utmost seriousness both the assertion of a special Jewish role in history and the recognition that, in the modern world, Jews have recovered the power to defend themselves and to pursue that role actively. Jewish destiny, the civil religion preaches, is in Jewish hands. The Jewish reentry into history, one of the hallmarks of Jewish modernity, is the starting point for civil Judaism's understanding of the contemporary Jewish experience, as well as its (perhaps somewhat distorted) reading of the Jewish past. The dramatic impact of this sense of Jewish autonomy and capacity to set its course in the world has, for the civil religion, in effect overwhelmed the question of the ultimate source of the destiny which Jews now vigorously pursue.

Again, this analysis should not be seen as implying that civil Judaism advocates a collective Jewish self-deification. In operational if not theological terms, civil Judaism continues to regard the Jewish people as under the authority of norms which transcend their own impulses or aspirations. Jewish tradition stands as a source of values which contemporary Jews must seek to uphold. Thus, even if what lies behind the tradition itself is unclear, the concept of responsibility and the potential for judgment of the people and the community in terms of that responsibility—i.e., a potentially prophetic dimension—remain. In the absence of a serious civil religious theology, however, "responsibility" and "judgment" must necessarily be slippery concepts, left vague and ill-defined. Often it is history or the people itself who are invoked as the source of accountability. Civil Judaism is thus clearly a religion of horizontal transcendence, of covenantal responsibility stretched across space and time. But its lack of theological content undermines an active affirmation of vertical transcendence. In turn, the capacity of the civil religion to anchor its faith in Jewish destiny in a reality beyond history itself becomes problematic.

The theological inarticulateness of civil Judaism is noteworthy, but not unique for civil religions. This is one reason why "public theology," more elaborate and explicit efforts to explicate the theological import and bases of civil religious tenets, often develops alongside civil religion itself. In the American tradition, the arena of public theology, where clergy and occasionally statesmen have struggled to clarify the religious meaning of American nationhood which the civil religion invokes, has been an important source of themes and understandings which have filtered into the civil religion itself. Jewish "public theology" deserves an analysis of its own. Clearly, the issues and concerns of civil Judaism have been addressed by dozens of American Jewish religious leaders—rabbis and scholars—in greater depth and with greater nuance than the civil religion is itself able to muster. The institutions of the polity have not shut themselves off from this work; indeed, rabbis and other Jewish thinkers have been addressing major gatherings from the outset of the polity's development. In recent years, the receptivity of polity leaders to essays in public theology and to discussion of religious issues in gen-

eral, as well as the readiness of some religious thinkers to speak explicitly to this audience, have both markedly increased. It remains difficult,
however, to find among the characteristic articulations of the civil religion itself more than occasional echoes of the public theologizing which
has taken place under polity auspices. Civil Judaism remains largely an
unself-conscious religious ideology, little disposed to self-examination
and elaboration of either its theological premises or their implications.

Lacking this theological concern, civil Judaism moves unsystematic-
ally between and among Marty's several types of civil religion. It is alter-
nately priestly and prophetic; it speaks of a Jewish people which is at
once self-transcending and under the guidance and command of a transcendent deity. The theological incoherence of civil Judaism helps it to
appeal to a Jewish populace which is itself often uncertain of its religiosity. But that appeal is purchased at a price. The civil religion is a faith
which tries to speak two languages: one of traditional Judaic religiosity,
one of the modern secular world. How to do both is a challenge which
has not yet been fully met, and one we shall return to in the final chapter.


### A Faith for the American Jew

Our account of the development and tenets of civil Judaism in the last
two chapters has inevitably linked the description of a faith with that of
a body of the faithful: the leadership of the American Jewish polity. Civil
Judaism is, as we have seen, a powerful institutional ideology. It sacralizes the work of the Jewish polity by recasting organizational programs
and interests into expressions of and vehicles for the realization of collective purposes which far transcend the substance of those programs.
But the impact of civil Judaism is not limited to the institutions and leaders of the polity alone. We would contend that civil Judaism provides
the cement which binds together not only organizations, but American
Jewry as a community. The worldview and ethos of the civil religion are
not merely functional for the institutions of the Jewish polity, but persuasive to large numbers of Jews for whom they substantially define
what it means to be an American Jew today.

There is, to be sure, no definitive evidence to demonstrate that this is
in fact the case. In the next chapter we shall cite some empirical data
which indicate that the tenets of the civil religion do inform the personal
belief systems of polity activists themselves. No comparable large-scale
studies have been done of the American Jewish populace as a whole. We
would suggest, nevertheless, that the faith we have described is widely
shared among American Jews. Charles Liebman, for example, identifies
six principles which he claims "arous[e] the deepest loyalties and passions of American Jews":

1. That there is nothing incompatible in being a good Jew and a good American
2. That separation of church and state is an essential for protecting Jews and Judaism in America
3. That Jews constitute one indivisible people and that denominational differences must not be permitted to threaten this essential unity
4. That problems of theology are somewhat irrelevant, and that insuring the physical and spiritual survival of the Jewish people is more important than theological disputation
5. That Jewish rituals are valuable forms of Jewish self-expression and help unify the family, but that individuals must be free to select and adapt Jewish practices to conform with modern norms
6. That every Jew must work for the survival of Israel, but need not live there

These principles lie at the heart of what Liebman terms the American Jewish "folk religion," a religion which is nowhere formally articulated, but which he regards as the popular substructure of American Jewish belief and practice.[74]

Virtually all accounts of contemporary American Jewish life agree on the universality and intensity of support for Israel among American Jews, on the prominence of philanthropy and solidarity with their brethren in need in defining the norms of Jewish behavior, and on the enthusiasm of American Jewry's embrace of America. A number of observers in recent years have noted how prone American Jews are to detect threats to Jewish security and survival. Researchers and commentators have pointed to the paradoxical American Jewish attitude toward religious tradition: though relatively few maintain extensive patterns of regular observance, most continue to undertake some level of religious practice and to define themselves Jewishly in religious terms.

That the tenets of Americans Jewish "folk religion" are strikingly similar to those which we have identified as central to the civil religion should not be surprising. Civil religion, as the expression of a group's identity and purposiveness as a moral community, must be rooted in popular sentiments. As it becomes attached to specific institutional structures, it takes on some of the characteristics of more formalized "elite" ideologies. As the ideology of those social institutions which seek to be most encompassing, however (and which are often prepared to abjure intellectual rigor and consistency in order to maintain broad popular support), civil religion is likely to remain more firmly anchored in the folk religion than other species of elite religious ideology. This, we suggest, is the case with civil Judaism. Although there are several elite formulations of American Jewish folk religion (Reconstructionism, e.g., is another attempt to restate the folk religion in systematic terms), civil Judaism is probably the most broadly affirmed. Whatever it may lack in theological depth, the civil religion makes up for in the incisiveness of its grasp of the central concerns and essential sentiments of a large mass of American Jewry.

We are, therefore, led to consider civil Judaism in a broader context, not merely as an institutional meaning system, but as a response of American Jews to the larger questions of modern Jewish life. The appeal of the civil religion lies in the response which it embodies to the fundamental and persistent question of whether Jews—individually and collectively—may indeed be fully engaged in the modern world, yet retain their integrity and purposivenss as Jews.

In answering this question, civil Judaism suggests answers as well to each of the questions framed in chapter 1. To the question of what it means to be Jewish, civil Judaism responds: to be part of a people with a proud tradition and enduring values, values which can be embodied in the life of the modern Jew and the modern Jewish community. To the question of how to be Jewish, the civil religion answers: by exemplifying those values, by insuring that all Jews have the ability to do so as well, and by seeking to insure that those values are transmitted and preserved. To the question, how do we maintain our unity, civil Judaism proposes: through voluntary community, through loyalty to Israel, through the recognition that Jewish unity transcends nationality and opinion. To the question of how to relate to non-Jewish society, the civil religion avers: as both a part, and apart. Participation is to be embraced, but distinctiveness is to be maintained. Where either opportunity is denied the Jew, it must be secured. Where both are possible, both must be affirmed. And to the question, why—why strive to maintain this balance of distinctiveness and integration—civil Judaism offers its boldest answer: because that is how modern Jewry fulfills its mission and its destiny.

Civil Judaism, like the Jewish ideologies outlined in chapter 1, is an attempt to synthesize tradition and modernity. The Emancipation and Enlightenment asked Jews to make a choice: the modern world or traditional Jewish life. Jews have ever since struggled to avoid the full implications of that demand. In one fashion or another they have sought to embrace both by redefining the terms of one or the other. To the extent that those redefinitions have been acceptable—to the Jews themselves and to the non-Jewish world—modern Jewish ideologies have been able to hold back the most radical implications of modernity's challenge. Civil Judaism stands in this line of succession. It tells American Jews that they can and must be both modern and traditional—at least within the definitions which it gives to each of these terms.

But if civil Judaism is only one among these ideological responses to modernity, what accounts for its unique capacity (thus far) to enlist an unprecedentedly broad range of Jews behind its vision of how and why to be Jewish in the modern world? One answer, we would suggest, lies in the specific way it deals with the very tension implicit in its embrace of both modernity and Judaism. Civil Judaism addresses itself to Jews who seek both full participation in contemporary society and the persistence of a collective Jewish life. According to Charles Liebman, this dual aspiration bespeaks a fundamental ambivalence which stands at the core of the American Jewish condition. In Liebman's view this ambivalence constitutes American Jewry's Achilles heel. Ultimately, he argues, the two pulls are indeed in contradiction. The conditions necessary to realize adequately one goal render fulfillment of the other impossible. American Jews will have to choose between the steps that can truly insure Jewish survival—accepting the authoritative character of traditional Jewish law, making *aliya*—or their desire to be like other Americans.[75]

Liebman describes an "objective" tension between these two aspirations, what might be termed a *sociological* ambivalence. This tension can be the source of *psychological* ambivalence as well—a feeling of inner dividedness, an uncertainty of ultimate identity. In a sense, therefore, civil Judaism, with its explicit affirmation of both Jewish group survival and full social integraton as values, would seem to be an open invitation to ambivalence—certainly in sociological terms and perhaps psychologically as well. Yet civil Judaism obviously does not acknowledge such ambivalence as debilitating, either collectively or individually. In one respect, it simply denies that the tension Liebman posits really exists. The two goals are not incompatible. In a deeper sense, however, civil Judaism can be seen as a complex ideological mechanism for dealing with ambivalence by integrating it into its understanding of the contemporary American Jewish condition and validating it as appropriate and necessary.

From this perspective, civil Judaism's intense anxiety about the prospects of Jewish survival in America, its struggle against assimilaton, is a signal that its denial of ambivalence is not to be taken entirely at face value. The civil religion knows that the goals of Jewish group survival and social integration are indeed in tension. Civil Judaism's worldview and ethos in fact incorporate a host of assertions which are potentially contradictory: Jews are under siege, their survival constantly endangered. But Jews have an unprecedented opportunity to shape their own destiny and to affect history—especially in America. Jews constitute one distinctive people. But individual Jews may legitimately adopt many different Jewish lifestyles and theologies, and need not separate themselves socially or culturally from the non-Jews among whom they live. Israel is the homeland of the Jewish people. But American Jews may find Jewish fulfillment and exercise their Jewish responsibility living where they do. Jewish tradition must be cultivated and treasured as the source of the values which Jews must pursue today. But those values are shared by American society as a whole. Jews must focus their energies on winning and sustaining the well-being of other Jews, since no one else will. But Jews must be exemplary citizens, working for the good of society and all its dispossessed from their own position of privilege. Civil Judaism is in this respect a religion of thorough-going ambivalence, of paradox and inconsistency.

The key question is what we are to make of these ostensibly mutually contradictory assertions. Do they bespeak an ideology irrevocably torn between the embrace of the larger world and the securing of the Jewish place within that world? Or, as we would suggest, do they reflect a response to modernity which works primarily not at the level of logic, but by validating and significating the very ambiguities which are inherent in the contemporary Jewish situation and consciousness? Civil Judaism recognizes the tensions between integration and survival, but not the impossibility of sustaining those tensions. What may be logically incompatible, is existentially supportable. Indeed, the endeavor which civil Judaism advocates—the attempt to do justice to both poles of the modern Jewish tension—gives the civil religion a type of heroic grandeur.

Civil Judaism tells American Jews that they cannot extricate themselves from their dilemmas by abandoning one dimension of their aspirations. Instead, it urges that they seize both poles—Jewish survival and social integration—firmly, trusting that if they are truly prepared to embrace both, the tension will give way to a higher synthesis. This synthesis is embodied in the characteristic civil Jewish vision of an assertive Jewish community making its contribution to a pluralistic American society. Civil Judaism's faith transforms a problem into a virtue. What is a tension at one level is a fulfillment at another.

Civil Judaism thus renders the duality of its goals supportable by defining the tension between them as the appropriate condition for the modern American Jew. If that Jew indeed feels ambivalent, the civil religion offers a form of comfort: Ambivalence is the sign that one has in fact grasped the meaning of being a Jew in this era. The sociological ambivalence of American Jewry (its collective pursuit of what Liebman claims to be incompatible goals) is pronounced by civil Judaism to be at the very core of the Jewish mission and task in the modern world. The psychological ambivalence of the individual Jew can be transcended by accepting that mission, joining in the fulfillment of that task.

This "solution" to American Jewish ambivalence may present practical problems for both Jews and American society. Not every Jew can or wants to sustain the tension in order to achieve the synthesis. Nor is American society necessarily as uniformly supportive of Jewish particularity or as receptive to Jewish participation as the pluralist model implies. At a minimum, however, civil Judaism defines a response to Liebman's ambivalence which permits American Jews to believe that this tension can be transcended. Its message is thus one of both challenge and reassurance—challenge to face the ambivalence directly, reassurance that the confrontation will not be in vain.

Civil Judaism is not, of course unique among American Jewish ideologies in affirming that Jewish survival and social integration are both possible. Virtually all varieties of American Judaism share this affirmation, though they define the terms under which this dual ideal can be achieved differently. Civil Judaism's particular contribution and achievement lies in its marking out a sphere of Jewish activity—the public agenda of the Jewish polity—where particularist/survivalist goals can be pursued and validated in American terms, and where universalist/integrative programs can be undertaken and legitimated in terms of Jewish values. The civil religion's model of Jewish identity, individual and communal, is inherently synthesizing: "By being a better Jew, you will be a better American; by being a better American, you will be a better Jew." Whether this is in fact true of every type of Jewish and American self-expression is debatable. But in the sphere which civil Judaism had made its own, philanthropy and social activism, the statement has sufficient face validity to make its articulation as a general principle plausible.

Even those elements of the polity's agenda which emphasize its Jewish survivalist aspirations actually serve to reinforce the civil religion's claim that good Jewishness and good Americanness can and do reinforce one another. In a doctoral dissertation being written at the University of California, Ellen Lasser LeVee suggests, e.g., that intense concern for anti-Semitism and for Israel helps American Jews mediate the goals of group survival and full social integration in several ways. At one level, civil Judaism's emphasis on countering anti-Semitism (of which there is relatively little in the United States) and on supporting Israel (which is done primarily through financial and political activity, not through emigration) enables the American Jew to feel that (s)he is contributing to Jewish survival without materially affecting his/her lifestyle or position in American society. Survivalism in this key poses little or no threat to integration.[76]

The polity's preoccupation with threats to Jewish security in America and in Israel effects a mediation between the survivalist and integrationist aspirations in more subtle ways as well. In building his case for American Jewish ambivalence, Charles Liebman notes that American Jews are constantly on the alert against any possible manifestation of discrimination against them as Jews. They demand that society never permit their Jewishness be a factor in the way they are treated. Yet, they continue to oppose intermarriage and in numerous other ways to manifest a profound group consciousness. In Liebman's view, these inconsistencies are clear evidence of their incapacity to choose between survival or integration, or even to see them as alternatives.[77]

Yet, are American Jews in fact wrong in this refusal to choose or to regard survival and integration as incompatible alternatives? Anti-Semitism, as American Jews experience it, is indeed as much (or more) an attack on their achieved position in American society as it is on their survival. It is also perceived as a violation of the fundamental ground rules of American society itself. Thus, when the Jewish community fights anti-Semitism it is, at least within its own terms, fighting both a survivalist *and* an integrationist battle. By seeking to root out discrimination against them, Jews *are* being better Americans; and by defending their right to full integration as Americans, they are securing their Jewish future. Liebman is correct: American Jews do not see integration and survival as alternatives, but rather as complementary achievements, which not only can, but must be pursued simultaneously. The work of the Jewish polity enables them to do so.

The civil religion's quintessential symbol of anti-Semitism, the Holocaust, confirms this proposition. The Nazi assault on German Jewry began as an attempt to dis-integrate them from German society; it ended by seeking all Jewry's physical annihilation. Yet, the Holocaust is proof too that no measure of presumed integration will protect Jews against those who seek their destruction. Hence, unless integrationist aspirations are pursued within a self-consciously survivalist framework, they are not merely unworthy, but dangerously self-delusive. The message of the Holocaust is that integration and survival *must* be seen as complementary paths. America, where a Holocaust has not happened, is proof (thus far) that the two paths can be trod simultaneously. The Holocaust is the perpetual reminder why.

Support for Israel helps to further civil Judaism's mediation of the survivalist/integrationist tension in a similar fashion. Israel is a symbol of Jewish continuity. It is also, however, a fundamental expression of the modern Jewish aspiration to participate fully in the larger social-political order. Though no activist in the American Jewish polity would dismiss the military threat to Israel's survival (and that of its Jewish populace) as insignificant, it is Israel's legitimacy as a member nation of the world community which is today under the most direct assault. Anti-Zionism, like the more classical forms of anti-Semitism, is a threat to Jewish *integration* as much as to Jewish survival. To defend Israel today one must defend its right to be "a nation like all the nations."

Although American Jewish leaders obviously do not accept Jewish nationhood as the only framework within which Jews can integrate into the modern world, Israel's existence as a nation state is a substantive and symbolic statement of the highest importance to American Jews: Israel means that Jews have a place in the world, one which cannot be made contingent on the strictures and definitions of others. Its existence demonstrates that Jews need not give up their determination to survive as a united and distinctive people in order to claim their rights of participation.

Here again, integration and survival are seen to be not ultimately in conflict, but rather to represent complementary thrusts for Jewry in the modern world. American Jews (rightly or wrongly) apply the same lesson to themselves. What they seek is recognition of their right to live as a distinctive group within American society without disabilities, just as Israel seeks to be "a nation like all the nations" at the same time as it remains the singular Jewish State. This not the inability to choose between survival and integration; it is the insistence that the two really do sustain one another.

Liebman is perhaps correct in claiming that American Jewry is deluding itself in maintaining this proposition. But since, in their minds, Israel represents a consummation of America's own values of democracy and justice, American Jews feel no anxiety that their passionate support of its security in the world makes them any less American and resent anyone who so regards them. In this way too, pursuit of the polity's survivalist agenda in fact reinforces the American Jew's sense of integration as well. Israel, like anti-Semitism and the Holocaust, all of which might be regarded as warnings to American Jewry that reconciliation of their integrationist and survivalist aspirations is inevitably tenuous or even chimerical, is instead appropriated in a way which seemingly demonstrates just the opposite: that the pursuit of integration together with survival is not only possible, but essential. Each thrust undergirds the other; good Jewishness and good Americanness indeed go together.

The plausibility of this critical assertion is further enhanced by another characteristic of civil Judaism: the congruence between its central motifs and those of America's own civil religion. At the heart of American civil religion lies a self-perception of America as "God's new Israel." The dominant symbolic and theological key for the American experience is provided by the Hebrew Bible. America is a promised land of liberty and destiny, a moral beacon, a "light unto the nations." From the pilgrims through contemporary presidents, Americans have understood themselves as a new chosen people, playing a salvific role in human history.[78]

Civil Judaism, as we have seen, depicts the Jewish historical experience in essentially similar terms. It could hardly do otherwise without abandoning entirely its links to the Jewish tradition. This means that "Judaic" America and American Jewry are, in David Altshuler's words, "covenantal siblings," viewing themselves through the same prism, speaking a common language of self-understanding.[79] They share a fundamental orientation to the world: activist, moralistic, messianic, at once highly particularistic and universal. Echoes resonate continually back and forth between the two civil religions, the American and the Jewish, and the echoes ring most loudly in the ears of American Jews.

The question for American Jews is whether they hear a dissonant or a harmonious chord in these echoes. (Siblings may, after all, be bitter rivals.) The congruence between American and Jewish civil religion may appear to mandate a choice: the "old" Israel or the "new." Indeed for past generations that choice often seemed unavoidable. They were prepared to subsume or subordinate their identification with Jewish destiny to their new found identity as Americans. The "Jewishness" of America's civil religion smoothed the way for assimilation. Judaism became merely a particular form of the national religion, and was reshaped and adjusted to fit this mold.[80]

But the Jewish civil religion did not, as we have seen, remain simply "an ideology of acculturation," as Deborah Dash Moore describes it.[81] Jews drew strength from the familial resemblance they recognized in America's religious self-understanding to reassert their particular destiny as Jews. Even as they continued eagerly to embrace the American civil religion, they put forward ever more boldly their claim to an enduring integrity and mission for the "old Israel" alongside the "new." Contemporary civil Judaism finds in the congruence between its comprehension of the meaning of Jewish peoplehood and the American civil religion's understanding of American nationhood not the necessity for a bitter choice or a submerging of Jewishness in the melting pot of the "new Israel," but precisely the opposite. The common vision of Jewish and American civil religion serves as testimony to the reality of the higher synthesis which civil Judaism preaches and pursues. It is the authorization for American Jews to pursue their dual destiny in confidence that they are truly members of the American family, and that America is a brother inheritor of the legacy which their Jewish ancestors first forged millennia ago.[82] Through the simultaneous affirmation of both civil religions American Jews establish their true belongingness in American life (even if their ancestors arrived but a few generations ago), but also their special place in that experience. America is, after all, created in their image, and in pursuing the civil Jewish version of Jewish destiny they are merely reinforcing the terms of America's own self-understanding.

Civil Judaism's efforts to confront and transcend the fundamental tension between Jewish survival and social integration which has plagued the modern Jew could not have achieved the measure of success which they have were it not for a final factor to which we alluded above: the existence of the Jewish polity itself as a powerful "plausibility structure" for the civil religion's faith tenets. The sociologist of religion Peter Berger argues that any socially constructed worldview—and religion is preeminently the sponsor and legitimator of such "worlds"—depends for its plausibility on the maintenance of a social "base," of specific social processes which continually reconstruct that "world" in reality. The stronger the plausibility structure, the less need there is for elaborate intellectual legitimation of the worldview in question, and vice versa.[83]

The Jewish community served as a powerful plausibility structure for traditional Judaism. Everything which went on in the *kehillah*—indeed, its very existence—made the truth claims of Judaism more self-evident. It is for this reason that the modern disintegration and dissolution of the traditional Jewish community constituted such a profound crisis for Jewish belief as well as social structure.

Almost uniquely among modern Jewish ideologies (at least in the United States), civil Judaism can point to a massive plausibility structure to support its Jewish belief claims. The Jewish polity is impressive in its size and scope. It can direct assistance to Jews virtually anywhere in the world. Its leaders meet with presidents and prime ministers. Its appeals for funds reach into nearly every American Jewish home. It is affecting Jewish history. Hence, the absence of an articulated theology, of persuasive intelletual validations of its worldview and ethos, which we noted above, is not a fatal debility for the civil religion. It persuades by the sheer force of the polity's own energy. Civil Judaism's claims of Jewish unity, endangerment, responsibility, and destiny are rendered believeable because they are being lived, not only in the North American Jewish polity, but in the unprecedented plausibility structure, the State of Israel, with which the polity is so closely bound up. Thus, the civil religion provides legitimation for the Jewish polity, but it is at the same time sustained as a belief system by that polity. Its depiction of the Jewish condition, complete with ambiguities, is supportable because the institutions of the Jewish polity face that condition and visibly surmount it.

Today, the civil Jewish faith finds preeminent expression just where we would be led to expect it: in the young activists of the American Jewish polity, those to whom Ed Robin addressed himself in the speech which opened this chapter. In the next chapter we will extend our description and interpretation of civil Judaism by drawing a portrait of these activists and of the role which the civil religion plays in their Jewishness and in their vision of American Jewish life.

# IV

# THE CIVIL JEWISH ACTIVISTS —A PORTRAIT

### Institutional Meaning System or Personal Faith?

In the previous two chapters we have drawn a detailed portrait of civil Judaism and its evolution as an institutional meaning system for the American Jewish polity. We suggested as well that this meaning system is something more: a faith which helps large numbers of American Jews to affirm and significate their Jewishness within a framework of American modernity. The evidence we could cite for the latter proposition was only impressionistic; no study conclusively enshrines civil Judaism as American Jewry's "common faith." Yet, that evidence is sufficiently suggestive to justify a closer examination of the claim and of the role which civil Jewish faith plays in the lives of individual Jews.

The questions of whether and how civil religious beliefs shape and/or are reflected in the values and behaviors of individuals as well as collective institutions have been the source of considerable scholarly debate, both theoretical and empirical. In the American context, attempts to demonstrate that significant segments of the public do in fact hold beliefs which can be termed "civil religious" have been somewhat supportive, but hardly conclusive.[1] They have clearly not deflected the challenge emanating from those, like Peter Berger and Richard Fenn, who see the spheres of public and private religion becoming increasingly distinct in the modern secularized world. According to this view, religious convictions expressed in the private spheres of one's life (usually in the familial context) have no substantial linkage to public religious rhetoric (civil religion). Private religious conceptions play little role in shaping societal institutional structures (one of the consequences of religious pluralism), while civil religion does not inform in any significant way personal meaning systems.[2]

If this perspective is indeed correct and applicable to the Jewish arena, then civil Judaism, no matter how prominent in the speeches of polity leaders, is simply an exercise in public rhetoric. As public rhetoric, it would still deserve our attention and analysis, but its import as a modern religious ideology would be dramatically reduced. Even in terms of the fulfillment of its prime functions as civil religion—integration, legitimation, and mobilization—its impact would inevitably be substantially weakened. If the fundamental conceptions of civil Judaism are not carried into the personal religious sensibilities of American Jews, then its capacity to bind American Jewry into a true moral community is undermined.

It is, therefore, important in our analysis of American Jewish civil religion to return to the empirical question: to what extent have the propositions of civil Judaism become part of the personal values and beliefs of those Jews whom the polity seeks to mobilize and to integrate? We cannot answer this question for American Jewry in general beyond the evidence offered in the previous chapter. But we will, in this chapter, seek to demonstrate that civil Judaism is an important component of personal belief for at least one important segment of the Jewish populace whose commitment the civil religion must have: active participants within the polity itself.[3]

## The Leadership Study

The specific evidence we wish to examine is derived from studies of participants in federation and UJA sponsored Leadership Development (LD) programs which were conducted from 1978 to 1980. The primary aim of the studies (all using a similar multisection, closed-ended questionnaire) was to explore the role of the institutional civil Jewish meaning system in the personal Jewish belief/value systems of these LD participants. This involved efforts to determine whether civil Jewish attitudes and orientations were in fact widely and strongly affirmed by these individuals, and how these attitudes were related to other dimensions of the individuals' Jewish beliefs and behaviors.

The study participants fall into three groups: individuals who attended Leadership Development sessions at the 1978 General Assembly of the Council of Jewish Federations (the "GA Group," 97 respondents); members of federation LD groups in several local communities and participants in two regional Young Leadership retreats (the "Communities Group," 212 respondents); and members of the men's Young Leadership Cabinet of the United Jewish Appeal (the "Cabinet Group," 134 respondents). None of the three groups (nor all together) constitutes a statistically valid sample of all participants in federation or UJA sponsored leadership development programs, much less of American Jews as a whole. Nevertheless, the study population does constitute a broadly representative group on a number of social and Jewish variables, and hence a reasonable "initial test case" for examining civil Judaism's role in personal beliefs.[4]

## The Survey Participants

All three of the groups surveyed were composed largely of young middle- and upper-middle-class individuals. The median age for all of the groups was in the mid-thirties. Over 95% of the respondents were American born, and over 85% were married and living with their spouse. Eighty-six percent of the Cabinet, 82% of the GA Group, and 72% of the Communities Group reported at least one child living at home. Close to 90% were college graduates, and the vast majority of those employed worked in business or one of the professions. Well over 80% of all those surveyed had incomes of over $25,000 a year, and close to half reported incomes greater that $50,000. In terms of political views, somewhat more than half described themselves as moderates, a little more than a quarter as liberal, and less than 20% as conservative. The Cabinet Group was all male, the GA Group nearly equally divided between men and women, and the Communities Group had approximately a 3:2 female/male ratio.

All of the survey respondents were asked a number of questions about their Jewish backgrounds, dealing with familial Jewish identification and practices while they were growing up, Jewish educational experiences, and childhood involvement in Jewish groups and activities. Nearly all of the respondents were born Jewish. Over 90% reported that their families had belonged to a synagogue at some point during their childhood. About two-thirds of the respondents indicated that their families regarded themselves as religious, and of these the largest number in all three groups came from Conservative backgrounds. Nearly nine in ten of the respondents received some form of Jewish education, but only about a third considered that education to be either excellent or good. Approximately two-thirds belonged to a Jewish youth group at some point, and half attended a summer camp with Jewish educational, religious, or cultural programming.

The families in which these respondents grew up generally maintained at least some elements of Jewish ritual observance. More than 90% of those surveyed reported attending a seder on Passover. Close to that percentage attended synagogue on the high holidays and lit Hanukkah candles. More than half of the families lit Sabbath candles, and nearly half did not eat pork or shellfish at home.[5] About a third of the GA Group and Communities Group, and more than half of the Cabinet Group, reported that *tzedakah* was collected in their homes. More than three-quarters of the respondents recalled that their parents donated money to Jewish philanthropies or causes while they were growing up.

Taken as a whole, approximately three-fifths of these LD participants described their upbringing as "strongly Jewish" and another 30% as "somewhat Jewish." While they survey responses do not tell us all that we might like to know about the qualitative dimensions of the Jewish background which these individuals bring to their adult activism, they do indicate that a sizable majority come from families with significant levels of Jewish practice. The proportion of those describing their upbringing as strongly Jewish is well above that reported for individuals of comparable age in the National Jewish Population Study conducted in the early 1970s.[6] On the other hand, there is no indication that a substantial segment of the respondents had Jewish backgrounds which were out of the mainstream for American Jews. In this respect too, they are a broadly representative group, not of all Jews, but of that portion of American Jewry which has been socialized toward a positive Jewish commitment within the American context.

### Jewish Activity and Behavior

The most notable, though hardly surprising, characteristic of the LD participants surveyed for this study was their high level of Jewish activity. As Table 1 indicates, the vast majority of respondents in all three groups were engaged in a wide range of communally-oriented activities.

**TABLE 1—Participation in Jewish Activities (Percentage Engaged)**

| *Group* <br> Activity or Behavior | *GA* | *Communities* | *Cabinet* |
|---|---|---|---|
| Synagogue membership | 95 | 86 | 93 |
| Membership in other Jewish organizations | 97 | 92 | 98 |
| Officer or board member | 88 | 75 | 93 |
| Subscribe to Jewish newspaper or periodical | 94 | 83 | 96 |
| Engaged in formal Jewish studies in past year | 49 | 40 | 37 |
| Contributed to federation campaign in past year | 98 | 93 | 100 |
| Solicited for campaign in past year | 91 | 61 | 96 |
| Engaged in political activity on behalf of Israel or Soviet Jewry in past year | 88 | 62 | 81 |

This communal activism was indeed broad in scope, embracing for most respondents the spheres of religious, cultural, and political activity in addition to those more specifically focused on the work of federations and UJA. Compared to the Jewish population as a whole, the degree of involvement of the LD participants even in synagogue life is substantially greater. There are, it would appear, certain minima which are acknowledged virtually universally among these individuals as obligatory expressions of Jewish commitment. Beyond these minima, however, there are substantial variations within the groups in, for example, such matters as regular attendance at religious services or participation in formal Jewish learning.

The same pattern may be found when we examine the respondents' ritual observance as recorded in Table 2.

TABLE 2—Religious Observances (Percent Currently Practicing)

| Group<br>RITUAL OR OBSERVANCE | GA | Communities | Cabinet |
|---|---|---|---|
| Lighting Sabbath candles | 88 | 71 | 83 |
| Reciting kiddush on Sabbath | 80 | 56 | 75 |
| Not riding on Sabbath | 2 | 6 | 5 |
| Attending a Passover seder | 100 | 95 | 98 |
| Not eating bread during Passover | 89 | 81 | 79 |
| Using special dishes during Passover | 46 | 33 | 36 |
| Fasting on Yom Kippur | 88 | 85 | 87 |
| Fasting on Tisha B'av | 6 | 9 | 7 |
| Lighting Hanukkah candles | 100 | 95 | 96 |
| Exchanging gifts during Hanukkah | 97 | 90 | 91 |
| Building a sukkah | 37 | 23 | 34 |
| Attending synagogue on the high holidays | 99 | 98 | 97 |
| Attending synagogue on most Sabbaths | 28 | 33 | 30 |
| Praying daily | 8 | 11 | 11 |
| Keeping two sets of dishes for meat and dairy meals | 36 | 31 | 30 |
| Not eating pork or shellfish at home | 46 | 49 | 43 |
| Not eating non-Kosher meat outside the home | 12 | 12 | 10 |
| Having a mezuzah on the door of the home | 98 | 92 | 94 |
| Collecting tzedakah at home | 52 | 46 | 53 |

Again, the LD participants as a group maintained a level of ritual observance substantially greater than that of a random sample of their peers. Of the nineteen practices listed, nine were observed by a sizable majority of all three groups, and the average number of rituals observed by an individual respondent was more than ten. Under 10% of the respondents observed fewer than seven of the listed practices. We find, therefore, once more a de facto consensus on minimum levels of religious observance, a consensus which includes not only high holiday, Passover, and Hanukkah observance, but some form of Sabbath observance as well. In nearly every instance except maintenance of dietary laws, the percentage of respondents observing a particular practice exceeds the percentage reported for the respondents' childhood families.

We should not exaggerate the levels of ritual observance manifested by these LD participants. The proportion of respondents who would qualify as normatively Orthodox or even Conservative in their practice is small. (For the former, the figure would be about 5%, for the latter [measured by dietary law observance and regular attendance at Sabbath worship], perhaps around 30%. The denominational self-identification of the respondents was 6% Orthodox, 55% Conservative, 28% Reform, and 10% other.) The patterns of observance follow in general the lines of selection detailed by the American Jewish sociologist Marshall Sklare in his studies of American Jewish identity. Sklare suggests that the rituals most likely to be maintained are those which are periodic, child-centered, compatible with American cultural values, and non-segregating.[7] This is, indeed, the type of practice which commands consensual support among the respondents. Other practices which do not fall into this category were much less widely observed among the survey respondents, as among American Jews in general. Outside the consensus, considerable diversity of practice reigns among the survey respondents.

Nevertheless, the data do suggest that a "civil norm" of Jewish observance is widely endorsed by these LD participants. This norm functions on a personal level analogously to the emerging institutional norm in the Jewish polity which demands public observance of dietary laws and some form of Sabbath and holiday observance by these organizations. In both instances, the civil Jewish tenet which affirms the value of Jewish tradition seems to lie at the heart of the willingness to accept a measure of ritual observance as beneficial and appropriate even where a traditional religious motivation may not be present.[8] The civil Jewish norm hardly embraces the full range of behaviors normative for the tradition, but it appears to be a slowly expanding one.

## Attitudes, Values and Beliefs: Affirming Civil Judaism

The central question of the extent to which the individual LD participants affirm the tenets of civil Judaism was addressed primarily through an extensive set of statements with which the respondents were asked to express agreement or disagreement.[9] Taken as a whole, the responses to these statements indicate broad acceptance of the tenets of the American Jewish civil religion among those surveyed. Civil Judaism as we have described it is a part of the personal Jewish belief and value systems of a large majority. Table 3 lists a number of the key statements and the percentages of those in each of the three groups agreeing or strongly agreeing with each.

## TABLE 3—Responses to Attitudinal Statements

SA = Strongly Agree
A  = Agree
NS = Not Sure
D  = Disagree
SD = Strongly Disagree

For each statement, the responses of the groups are listed as follows:
  GA Group
  Communities Group
  Cabinet Group

| PERCENTAGE RESPONDING°<br>STATEMENT | SA | A | NS | D | SD |
|---|---|---|---|---|---|
| I feel proud when I read about the accomplishments or success of another Jew | 84 | 16 | — | — | — |
| | 82 | 18 | — | — | — |
| | 79 | 20 | 1 | — | — |
| When the State of Israel is threatened, all Jews are threatened | 70 | 30 | — | — | — |
| | 71 | 27 | 1 | 1 | 1 |
| | 72 | 23 | 2 | 2 | — |
| Jewish values are basically the same as those of all religions | 2 | 21 | 5 | 40 | 32 |
| | 6 | 29 | 4 | 43 | 18 |
| | 2 | 30 | 7 | 40 | 22 |
| It is important that there always be a Jewish people | 96 | 3 | 1 | — | — |
| | 96 | 3 | — | 1 | — |
| | 97 | 1 | 1 | 2 | — |
| Every Jew is responsible in some measure for the well-being of every other Jew | 52 | 47 | 1 | — | — |
| | 44 | 50 | 1 | 3 | 1 |
| | 61 | 37 | 1 | 1 | — |
| Without Jewish religion the Jewish people could not survive | 45 | 46 | 3 | 5 | — |
| | 50 | 39 | 2 | 8 | 1 |
| | 56 | 37 | 2 | 5 | — |

| PERCENTAGE RESPONDING[*] STATEMENT | SA | A | NS | D | SD |
|---|---|---|---|---|---|
| The observance of Jewish customs and rituals is a good way to strengthen the family | 61 | 38 | — | 1 | — |
| | 62 | 36 | 2 | — | — |
| | 63 | 37 | — | 1 | — |
| The more Jewishly I live, the more fulfilled I feel as a person | °° | °° | °° | °° | °° |
| | 28 | 48 | 10 | 13 | 1 |
| | 36 | 50 | 8 | 6 | — |
| The world is still not ready to let Jews live in peace | 25 | 55 | 6 | 13 | 1 |
| | 33 | 54 | 6 | 7 | 1 |
| | 41 | 46 | 5 | 5 | 3 |
| Assimilation is the greatest threat to Jewish survival today | °° | °° | °° | °° | °° |
| | 50 | 35 | 4 | 10 | 1 |
| | 48 | 37 | 3 | 13 | — |
| It is a miracle that the Jewish people has survived to the present day | 26 | 47 | 2 | 22 | 3 |
| | 34 | 45 | 2 | 17 | 2 |
| | 27 | 46 | 5 | 20 | 2 |
| I feel more emotional when I hear Hatikvah than when I hear the Star-Spangled Banner | 32 | 38 | 7 | 18 | 5 |
| | 37 | 33 | 7 | 18 | 5 |
| | 31 | 41 | 7 | 19 | 2 |
| American Jews place too much emphasis on Israel and not enough on strengthening Jewish life in this country | 6 | 28 | 10 | 44 | 12 |
| | 7 | 25 | 3 | 48 | 16 |
| | 8 | 26 | 5 | 51 | 9 |
| Without the State of Israel the Jewish people could not survive | 24 | 34 | 1 | 33 | 8 |
| | 28 | 28 | 5 | 33 | 6 |
| | 27 | 28 | 5 | 35 | 5 |
| A Jew who really wants to be a good Jew should move to Israel | 1 | 5 | 5 | 53 | 34 |
| | 0 | 9 | 3 | 53 | 34 |
| | 3 | 10 | 4 | 65 | 19 |
| Jews have a special responsibility to work for justice in the world | 34 | 48 | 6 | 11 | 1 |
| | 25 | 49 | 5 | 19 | 2 |
| | 33 | 52 | 5 | 9 | 2 |

| PERCENTAGE RESPONDING° <br> STATEMENT | SA | A | NS | D | SD |
|---|---|---|---|---|---|
| Jews should always strive to set an example for other people | ◦◦ | ◦◦ | ◦◦ | ◦◦ | ◦◦ |
| | 23 | 56 | 6 | 14 | 1 |
| | 35 | 52 | 5 | 8 | 1 |
| The measure of a Jew's life is his/her contribution to the people around him/her | ◦◦ | ◦◦ | ◦◦ | ◦◦ | ◦◦ |
| | 19 | 56 | 6 | 16 | 2 |
| | 20 | 64 | 7 | 8 | 2 |
| The Jewish contribution to modern civilization has been greater than that of any other people | ◦◦ | ◦◦ | ◦◦ | ◦◦ | ◦◦ |
| | 23 | 36 | 17 | 23 | 1 |
| | 33 | 39 | 13 | 14 | 2 |
| The primary loyalty of American Jews must be to the United States and their fellow Americans | 2 | 21 | 19 | 47 | 11 |
| | 5 | 29 | 15 | 42 | 10 |
| | 5 | 25 | 15 | 47 | 9 |
| I'm glad that I am an American | ◦◦ | ◦◦ | ◦◦ | ◦◦ | ◦◦ |
| | 54 | 41 | 3 | 2 | — |
| | 53 | 46 | 1 | 1 | — |
| I'm glad that I am a Jew | 92 | 7 | 1 | — | — |
| | 86 | 13 | 1 | — | — |
| | 97 | 3 | — | — | — |
| It is difficult to be a good Jew living in the United States | ◦◦ | ◦◦ | ◦◦ | ◦◦ | ◦◦ |
| | 6 | 16 | 1 | 46 | 31 |
| | 5 | 14 | 1 | 56 | 24 |
| By being better Jews, Jews will also be better Americans | 30 | 51 | 9 | 7 | 2 |
| | 21 | 50 | 16 | 11 | 2 |
| | 22 | 54 | 11 | 13 | — |
| There are times in my life when I can really feel God's presence | 15 | 32 | 17 | 27 | 9 |
| | 18 | 33 | 17 | 25 | 6 |
| | 11 | 38 | 20 | 23 | 8 |
| The Torah was divinely revealed to the Jewish people | 7 | 26 | 29 | 31 | 7 |
| | 16 | 33 | 25 | 20 | 6 |
| | 12 | 38 | 29 | 19 | 2 |

| Percentage Responding° Statement | SA | A | NS | D | SD |
|---|---|---|---|---|---|
| There is some form of eternal life after death | 5 | 24 | 44 | 11 | 8 |
| | 8 | 27 | 38 | 22 | 4 |
| | 8 | 24 | 46 | 18 | 5 |
| All suffering has a purpose, even if we cannot recognize it at the time | 5 | 19 | 23 | 41 | 13 |
| | 4 | 18 | 27 | 40 | 12 |
| | 6 | 18 | 23 | 44 | 9 |
| To be a good Jew one must believe in God | 9 | 26 | 7 | 44 | 13 |
| | 19 | 34 | 12 | 29 | 6 |
| | 19 | 40 | 2 | 32 | 7 |
| Traditional Jewish law should be accepted as the authoritative guide for Jewish belief and behavior | 6 | 27 | 9 | 42 | 16 |
| | 7 | 34 | 10 | 36 | 12 |
| | 4 | 34 | 7 | 48 | 8 |
| Even if a Jew doesn't understand the reason for a particular Jewish observance, (s)he should try to observe it | 8 | 34 | 7 | 42 | 8 |
| | 9 | 33 | 9 | 40 | 10 |
| | 9 | 34 | 10 | 43 | 5 |
| Orthodoxy, Conservatism, and Reform are equally legitimate forms of Jewish religion† | 44 | 51 | 1 | 3 | 1 |
| | 33 | 55 | 3 | 8 | 1 |
| | 33 | 52 | 4 | 11 | — |
| There is a power at work in the universe greater than ourselves | 32 | 34 | 28 | 5 | — |
| | 32 | 40 | 19 | 7 | 1 |
| | 39 | 35 | 17 | 8 | 1 |
| The Jewish people is the chosen people | 22 | 41 | 21 | 13 | 4 |
| | 22 | 41 | 18 | 13 | 6 |
| | 19 | 44 | 24 | 11 | 3 |

°Because of rounding, percentages do not always add up to 100.

°°This statement did not appear on the questionnaire used with the GA group.

†In the questionnaire used with the GA group this statement read: "Orthodoxy, Conservatism, and Reform are all legitimate forms of Jewish religion."

Virtually without exception, substantial majorities of the respondents endorse the key elements of the civil Jewish worldview and ethos. The LD participants evidently do have a powerful sense of Jewish unity—all express pride in the achievements of their fellow Jews, and all but a handful consider a threat against Israel as a threat against all Jews. A large majority also regard Jews and Judaism as in some way distinctive: Less than a third believe that Jewish values are basically the same as those of all religions. The feeling of Jewish unity and distinctiveness, we have suggested, is linked to the conviction that Jewish survival is critically important and that Jews are responsible for one another's well-being. Both assertions command near unanimous assent among the survey respondents.

So too does the proposition that Jewish survival means and depends on more than physical continuity alone. More than 90% believe that religion is critical for Jewish survival and that Jewish education is the best means of insuring that continuity. Nearly all of the respondents endorse the contention that observance of Jewish customs and rituals is a good way to strengthen the family. Jewish tradition, therefore, is, as we have proposed and as their patterns of ritual observance would indicate, important to these LD participants, both as a key to insuring Jewish survival and as a positive influence on their own and their families' lives. Well over three-quarters link the extent of their sense of personal fulfillment to the degree of Jewishness in their life-style.

For civil Judaism, we have claimed, Jewish survival is not only important, it is endangered, both from without and within. Again, the survey respondents overwhelmingly share this concern. Well over four-fifths believe that the world is not yet ready to permit Jews to live in peace. At the same time, an equivalent number regard assimilation as the greatest threat to Jewish survival today. The world the respondents see is, therefore, at once too hostile and too hospitable for them to feel secure about the Jewish future. Given this sense of perpetual threat, it is perhaps not surprising that three-quarters of the respondents believe that it is a miracle that the Jewish people has survived to the present. Whatever the notion of "miracle" may mean to the survey participants in this context, whether it reflects an aura of the supernatural attached to Jewish destiny or is merely a metaphor for the extraordinary trials and tribulations faced by the Jewish people over the centuries, its use bespeaks a sense that commitment to Jewish survial is an act of faith, an identification with a force in history which is in some way beyond human ken.

Israel is a symbolic focal point for nearly all of these elements in civil Judaism's worldview and ethos. We have seen already that these LD participants identify a threat against Israel as one against all Jews. The powerful identification with Israel is manifested in the fact that 70% claim to feel more emotion listening to Hatikvah (the Zionist anthem) than the Star-Spangled Banner. By nearly two-to-one the respondents reject the proposition that American Jews are overly concerned with Israel.

The substantial minority which does hold this view, however, is one indication that Israel does not dominate the worldview of these young leaders. Only a small majority believe that the Jewish people could not survive without Israel (compared with the much larger majority who so believe concerning Jewish religion), and barely 10% feel that being a good Jew requires that one live in Israel. As we shall see below, the LD participants surveyed are strongly supportive of Israel, but their deep concern and commitment must be seen in the larger context of civil Judaism as a whole and not as the sum total of that faith.

At the institutional level, the ethos of the civil religion is profoundly shaped by the mandate for *tzedakah:* service to one's fellows and pursuit of social justice. Here too there is general congruence between institutional rhetoric and individual commitment. More than three quarters of the respondents affirm that Jews have a special responsibility to work for justice in the world. More than four-fifths believe that Jews should strive to set an example for others, and an almost equal number view the measure of a Jew's life as the contribution he/she has made to others. This sense that Jews must be exemplary in their social responsibility can also, we have seen, provide the rationale for why Jewish survival is so important: Jews have an irreplaceable contribution to make to humanity. Indeed, more than three-fifths of the respondents affirm that the Jewish contribution to modern civilization has been greater than that of any other people. Empirically, as well as conceptually, one can construct a link between the two primary mandates of civil Judaism—survival and service—through the perception of a special Jewish mission and destiny.

The final tenet of the civil Jewish faith asserts the compatibility of participation in this destiny with full participation in American life. This conviction of compatibility appears to remain strong among the LD participants surveyed despite their fears of assimilation and their intense Jewish commitment. When pressed, only a minority (less than a third) say categorically that the primary loyalty of American Jews must be to America. But an overwhelming majority are glad to be Americans, fewer than a quarter feel that it is difficult to be a good Jew in America, and nearly three-quarters agree that by being better Jews, Jews will also be better Americans.

Thus, there are hints of ambivalence, as we described it in the previous chapter, in the responses of the survey participants. There is nothing, however, which would call into question the commitment of the vast majority to remain fully participating Americans, and to affirm that they can be such and active Jewish survivalists at the same time. Despite their concerns with regard to assimilation, fewer than 15% of the respondents believe that being Jewish will mean less to their grandchildren than it does to themselves (for whom it clearly means a lot). Somehow, these LD participants do manage to be at once extraordinarily sensitive to threats to Jewish continuity, including America's seductive embrace, yet apparently confident that those threats can be surmounted, at least with respect to their own lives and those of their families.

When we assess the relative weights of Jewishness and Americanness in the consciousness of these young leaders on the basis of this survey, we must take into account its focus on particularistic Jewish concerns. It would, nevertheless, be fair to say that the ethos of younger Jewish activists, like that of the polity as a whole, has in recent years placed increased emphasis on assertive Jewish self-expression. Despite this, there has been no searching reappraisal on the part of the vast majority of respondents of their position as Americans. Whatever ambivalence does exist is evidently not debilitating or overly troubling to these participants. They wear their dual identity well and by and large comfortably.

We have, therefore, found consensus among the respondents in this study exactly where we anticipated finding it: in their affirmation of the fundamental tenets of the civil Jewish faith. We will not find similar consensus, however, in those domains of Jewish belief which fall outside the scope of civil Judaism's worldview and ethos. With regard to theological issues and the authoritative interpretation (as opposed to the general value) of Jewish tradition, the civil religion is deliberately vague, if not silent. The responses of the LD participants surveyed demonstrate why this atheologism and pluralism are necessary: there is no consensus to articulate. Statements dealing with personal religious experience, divine revelation of the Torah, eternal life, the purposiveness of suffering, and even whether a good Jew must believe in God produced a wide range of responses, including many "not sure"s. These uncertain responses probably reflect not only the diversity of views held on such issues by American Jews, but the relatively low salience of the entire area for many respondents. The respondents were almost equally divided on the questions of whether Jewish law should be regarded as an authoritative guide for Jewish belief and behavior, and whether a Jew should try to observe even those practices whose rationales he/she does not understand. In keeping with the civil Jewish emphasis on unity, this diversity was at least a tolerant one: more than 85% of the respondents regard Orthodoxy, Conservatism, and Reform as equally legitimate forms of Jewish religion.

Among the few traditional religious assertions (beyond those taken up by civil Judaism itself) which do win substantial assent from the survey respondents two are worthy of special note. About 70% of the three groups agree that "there is a power at work in the universe greater than ourselves," and among the remainder, agnostics outnumber firm atheists by two-to-one. Similarly, better than three-fifths of the respondents agree with the assertion that "the Jewish people is the chosen people"; slightly more than 15% disagree and the rest are unsure. These substantial margins (even allowing for the high percentage of "not sure"s) may indicate that the civil religion does have a rudimentary underlying consensual theology. Of all of the propositions of classical Jewish theology, these are the ones that would seem to have the greatest relevance to civil Judaism, insofar as they anchor its assertions of a special Jewish destiny in a transcendent framework. We shall have more to say about the notion of Jewish chosenness in particular in the next chapter, and more about the relationship of transcendent religiosity to civil religious faith later in this one. At this point, however, it should suffice to note that the survey data again confirms our suggestion that civil Judaism is by no means atheistic or ideologically secular in its standpoint. Rather it is largely silent with respect to most theological assertions because it has little to say or little need to speak about them. Its claims, however, may well rest on some implicit theological/metaphysical grounding, even if this grounding is rarely and barely articulated in civil Judaism's public rhetoric.

## Civil Judaism as a Religious System

The data we have presented thus far provide clear confirmation that the young leaders whom we surveyed affirm the tenets of civil Jewish belief in large numbers. Their responses permit us to go a step further as well: we can show that the strength with which any of the elements of the civil religion's ethos and worldview are affirmed is directly related to the stength with which other elements of that meaning system are also affirmed. This relationship serves as evidence of what we have termed the coherence of civil Judaism as a religious system—the fact that its propositions form a single, organically interconnected structure through which to view the world and act within it. We have also argued that the tenets of civil Judaism are rooted in the perspective of traditional Judaism, though they are often articulated in a non-traditional idiom. Hence we would expect a positive correlation between endorsement of the civil Jewish faith and of other elements of Jewish religiosity.[10]

In order to examine these hypothesized relationships, the responses of the Communities Group to the statements in the survey discussed above were used to create several indices of Jewish attitudes.[11] Three of the indices measured strength of adherence to key components of the civil Jewish ethos and worldview: (1) positive personal identification with and concern for the Jewish people as an entity; (2) endorsement of the civil Jewish "activist" ethos of mutual responsibility, exemplary social concern, and the compatibility of Jewishness and Americanness; and

(3) positive orientation toward Jewish religion and practice. As might be anticipated from the discussion above, the mean scores of the respondents on these three indices were very high (i.e., the vast majority of respondents manifested these attitudes strongly). What is more interesting, perhaps, is that scores on the three indices of civil religious belief were also significantly correlated with one another. That is, those who more strongly affirmed any one of the dimensions of civil Judaism (identification with the Jewish people, endorsement of the activist ethos, positive orientation toward the religious tradition) tended to more strongly affirm the other dimensions as well.

This finding lends empirical weight to our contention that civil Judaism constitutes a single system of religious meaning whose components are instrinsically linked to one another. Although one could affirm some elements of its worldview and ethos without endorsing others, the evidence from this study indicates that one's commitment is likely to be to the system as a whole. Civil Judaism apparently has an inner logic and coherence for its adherents even where its propositions might to an external observer appear unrelated or even contradictory. For the elements of the civil Jewish ethos in particular, the correlations among the individual items are often striking. Affirmation of the norm of Jewish mutual responsibility and acceptance of a special Jewish responsibility to work for justice are, for example, closely related to one another.

Research in recent years has established that Jewish identity in general can best be understood and measured as a multidimensional phenomenon, but one in which the several dimensions are likely to be correlated with one another.[12] Civil Judaism relates to several such dimensions of Jewish identity in rather clear prescriptive fashion. That is, those who affirm the civil religion's tenets should also manifest that faith by maintaining active levels of communal involvement and some measure of personal Jewish observance.[13] We have noted already that the LD participants surveyed in this study do in fact maintain relatively high levels of Jewish practice and communal involvement as compared with random samples of their Jewish peers.

This finding still leaves, however, a number of questions about how strength of adherence to civil Jewish tenets relates to other dimensions of Jewish belief and behavior. We have suggested, for example, that many of the tenets of civil Judaism represent restatements in a modern idiom of classical affirmations of traditional Judaism. Is there then any correlation between strength of traditional Judaic belief and intensity of endorsement of civil Judaism? We have also claimed that underlying the civil Jewish assertion of a unique Jewish destiny and mission may lie a transcendental sensibility; that the notions of "destiny" and "mission" bespeak a worldview which resists thoroughgoing secularization, even when its proponents are reluctant to make explicit reference to transcendent reality. Thus, we may ask as well whether there is any relationship between affirmation of such transcendent reality, in experiential and doctrinal terms, and endorsement of the tenets of civil Judaism.

To explore these hypothesized relationships between civil Judaism and other components of Jewish practice and belief, several additional indices were constructed from the survey responses. These measured: (1) acceptance of the authority of traditional Jewish norms; (2) affirmation of transcendent reality; (3) Jewish ritual practices observed; and (4) Jewish communal involvement. Table 4 presents the correlation matrix for the three civil Jewish and four additional indices.[14]

### TABLE 4—Correlation Matrix of Index Scores

| INDEX | 1 | 2 | 3 | 4 | 5 | 6 | 7 |
|---|---|---|---|---|---|---|---|
| 1. Identification with the Jewish people | x | | | | | | |
| 2. Affirmation of civil Jewish ethos | .43 | x | | | | | |
| 3. Positive orientation to Jewish religion | .34 | .46 | x | | | | |
| 4. Positive orientation to transcendent reality | .15 | .29 | .39 | x | | | |
| 5. Acceptance of authority of Jewish tradition | .23 | .25 | .41 | .47 | x | | |
| 6. Ritual observance | .34 | .33 | .31 | .35 | .43 | x | |
| 7. Communal activity | .30 | .40 | .31 | .21 | .29 | .50 | x |

As is evident from the matrix, all of the indices were positively correlated with one another. Strength of adherence to the various components of the civil Jewish worldview and ethos is related at modest but consistently positive levels to both the extent of communal involvement and of personal or household ritual observance. All of these measures are in turn also related to strength of traditionalism and transcendentalism. The latter are, as might be expected, more highly correlated specifically with a positive attitude toward religion and with ritual observance than they are with communal involvement, identification with the Jewish people, and endorsement of civil Judaism's activist ethos. Still, the overall impact of the matrix is to reinforce the image of civil Jewish commitment as one component of a multidimensional, but interrelated, Jewish identity configuration among the respondents. In particular, the strong relationship between degree of communal involvement and level of ritual practice should be noted. Among these LD participants communal activism appears to be less an alternative to personal religious behavior than its complement. Thus, the institutional affirmation of the religious tradition and ritual norms characteristic of civil Judaism today finds individual expression among these communal activists as well.[15]

We can, therefore, say that civil Judaism, though articulated as a meaning system in its own right, is not empirically unrelated to other elements of Jewish faith and experience which are not part of its consensual norms and vocabulary. The precise nature of those relationships can be further defined by isolating the independent impact of any single component of commitment (as measured by one of the indices) on any of the other components (i.e., examining the relationship between the two scores while holding those on all other indices constant). This procedure can be approximated through the use of a series of regression equations, with each index in turn serving as the "dependent" variable of all of the others. Although the results must be treated with some caution, and are too complex to present in full, several additional insights do emerge from the analysis.

One is that the apparent relationship seen in the correlation matrix between a traditionalist orientation and two of the three components of the civil Jewish meaning system—identification with the Jewish people and concern for its survival, and acceptance of the civil Jewish ethos—is not as strong as indicated in that matrix. The strength of positive orientation to religion and religious practice is indeed related to the degree of acceptance of Jewish tradition as normative, but the two other elements of civil Judaism's characteristic set of affirmations appear to be manifested virtually independently of strength of traditionalist orientation. These other elements do, however, continue to show an independent relationship to maintaining a positive orientation toward Judaism and Jewish practice regardless of the extent of traditionalist attitudes. This would indicate that the civil Jewish commitment to Jewish peoplehood and to the responsibilities of Jewishness can in fact serve as an alternative to a traditionalist orientation in motivating or rationalizing a positive regard for Judaism and its practice.

The relationship of a transcendental orientation to the three civil Jewish components is somewhat more complex. Strength of affirmation of transcendent reality has no measurable independent relationship to intensity of identification with the Jewish people and concern for Jewish survival (which are almost universally very high anyway) among the respondent group. It does, however, have a positive relationship with the extent of endorsement of the civil Jewish ethos. That ethos expresses the sense of a special Jewish mission and responsibility. Thus, the fact that it is more unequivocally affirmed by those who explicitly acknowledge a belief in or experience of a transcendent power in the universe is not entirely surprising. Here again, the posited supra-rational underpinnings of civil Judaism as a meaning system come to the surface. The same relationship may be reflected in another strong positive correlation: between strength of endorsement of the civil Jewish ethos and acceptance of the proposition that the Jewish people is the chosen people. The civil Jewish ethos demands an extraordinary level of commitment in its emphasis on exemplary responsibility. That commitment, the data suggest, is perhaps itself both an expression and a reinforcement of a deeper conviction: that Jewish destiny is at once unique and in some way transcendentally validated.

The regression equations calculated for the several indices reveal other details of their interrelationship. Communal involvement is shown to be only slightly related to either a traditionalist or a transcendentalist orientation. In general, attitudes as such are only modestly related to the level of communal activity, with (as might be anticipated) endorsement of the civil Jewish ethos having the strongest relationship. On the other hand, the link between communal activity and personal observance is confirmed by the equations. Thus, among the LD participants, Jewish behavior appears to assume a holistic character. Those who are active Jews are likely to be so both publicly and privately. Personal ritual observance, unlike communal involvement, is not notably linked to affirmation of civil Judaism's public ethos as such. Such observance is, however, linked to strength of identification with the Jewish people and affirmation of one's Jewishness (though to a lesser extent than to traditionalist or transcendentalist orientations).

Taken together, the results of the statistical analysis cited above point to the complex character of civil Judaism as a religious meaning system. Clearly, civil Judaism has integrity and coherence in its own right as a way of envisioning the conditions of Jewish existence and responding to them. Equally clearly, that worldview and ethos are not unrelated to other Jewish orientations. The specific patterns of Jewish activity which the respondents to this survey manifest are linked in complex ways to both the civil Jewish faith which they by and large share, and the other components of Jewish belief and experience on which they differ from one another far more.

This is what we would expect when looking at the impact of a civil religion on overall religious belief and behavior. Civil religions rarely serve as the sole definers of reality even for those who strongly adhere to them. Civil Judaism, as we have noted, both makes room for and requires supplementation by other forms of Judaic belief which address issues beyond its scope of concern. That the way in which individuals relate to such extraconsensual propositions may affect the pattern and intensity of their commitment to civil Judaism's own several tenets, as well as their general modes of Jewish behavior, is not at all surprising.

What is perhaps most striking in all of the findings of this study is the extent to which civil Judaism does appear to shape the personal Jewish commitments of these LD participants. Not only do they broadly affirm its tenets as articles of personal belief; those tenets (and the strength with which they are affirmed) are demonstrably linked to the patterns of behavior they have adopted and the other attitudes which they hold. We cannot show, and would not claim, that their adherence to civil Judaism *causes* them to be the kind of Jews they are. But the way in which these young Jewish leaders define the world and their place in it is thoroughly informed by the American Jewish civil religion and its norms.

## Civil Judaism and Communal Policy

Even this demonstration, however, is insufficent to lay to rest another suspicion concerning the relationship of civil Judaism to social reality: that its formalization in the public rhetoric of the Jewish polity and even in the personal belief systems of the polity's leadership may be inconsequential in terms of the actual conduct of the polity's affairs. Civil Judaism, like all civil religion (indeed any political or institutional ideology) serves a vital legitimating role. That role, however, may be purely rhetorical. Policies may be generated by very different forces and values, with civil religion employed as a veneer to hide, rather than illuminate, their origins and substance. Even a more benign reading of the relationship between policy-making and its civil religious legitimation must ask whether the values and norms of civil religion—usually articulated at a high level of abstraction—can be shown to have any direct linkage to the content of social action.

This is, to be sure, a difficult question to investigate, and no less so in the American Jewish communal context. There has been much debate concerning the extent to which changing institutional rhetoric within the Jewish polity, culminating in the consolidation of the civil religion we have described, has in fact been mirrored in changing policies over the past several decades. Some evidence exists to support the thesis that substantial changes in institutional priorities and programs *have* been inspired (or at least eased) by the civil religion's affirmations of the importance of Jewish survival and of the role of the Jewish tradition in insuring that survival. The expanded support which federations have in recent years given to Jewish education is often cited, for example, as proof of this thesis. Other observers are more skeptical, pointing not only to the fact that such support has remained relatively modest in financial terms, but to a deeper problem: The tenets of civil Judaism are so broad that they can be taken to legitimate virtually any policy preference. Thus, they are relatively useless in actually guiding policy-making. In this view, civil Judaism is, if not just a veneer, then also not a powerful force in its own right in shaping communal policy. It establishes, to be sure, a context in which policy-making must take place; it sets boundaries of legitimacy. But those boundaries remain so broad that the content, the substance of policy must be filled in by other means.

We do not have the ability here to settle this debate. It would, however, be useful to know how the population of federation/UJA LD participants surveyed, overwhelmingly affirming the tenets of civil Judaism, formulate their policy preferences. Do these preferences appear to reflect the civil religion's characteristic worldview and ethos? Do they reflect a particular version of this ideology? However we might assess the general relationship between civil Judaism as an ideological system and the actual endeavors of the Jewish polity, we should expect to find the civil relgion's tenets mirrored in the perceptions and prescriptions of the young leaders who are among its strongest adherents. Were this not to be the case, then we would indeed be left with an ideological veneer, a rhetoric of legitimation without substantive significance. Such a veneer, we might anticipate, could not long serve to unify and motivate a collective whose interactions with the world were in no way shaped by its substance.

We can carry out this examination by looking at how the LD participants responded to two additional sections of the survey questionnaire. The first listed eighteen suggested "problems" facing the American Jewish community which the respondents were asked to rate as "very serious," "moderately serious," "a problem, but not a particularly serious one," or "not a problem." The second set of items consisted of fourteen suggested goals for Jewish communal action, from which the respondents were asked to identify four as of the highest and four as of the lowest priority (relative to one another). Tables 5 and 6 report the results of these two questions, with the most serious problems and highest priority goals listed first and the least serious and lowest priority listed last in the respective tables.

### TABLE 5—Seriousness of Problems Facing the American Jewish Community

VS = Very Serious
MS = Moderately Serious
P  = A Problem, but Not a Particularly Serious One
N  = Not a Problem
U  = Uncertain

| RANK[°] | PROBLEM | *Percent*[°°] *rating the problem as* | | | | |
|---|---|---|---|---|---|---|
| | | VS | MS | P | N | U |
| 1 | The conflict between Israel and its neighbors | 97 | 3 | | | |
| 2 | The treatment of Jews in the Soviet Union | 88 | 12 | | | |

| RANK° | PROBLEM | Percent°° rating the problem as | | | | |
|---|---|---|---|---|---|---|
| | | VS | MS | P | N | U |
| 3 | High rate of intermarriage | 72 | 21 | 4 | 2 | 2 |
| 4 | Alienation of youth from Jewish life | 72 | 18 | 7 | 2 | 1 |
| 5 | Anti-Semitism in the U.S. | 54 | 32 | 12 | 1 | |
| 6 | Low levels of participation in Jewish communal activities | 53 | 32 | 12 | 1 | 1 |
| 7 | Low Jewish birth rate | 43 | 27 | 22 | 6 | 2 |
| 8 | Assimilation of Jews to American lifestyles and values | 39 | 29 | 21 | 10 | 1 |
| 9 | Low levels of Jewish knowledge among lay leaders of the Jewish community | 34 | 34 | 30 | 9 | 3 |
| 10 | Inadequate Jewish schools | 35 | 23 | 17 | 15 | 9 |
| 11 | Decline in the importance of religious institutions in American Jewish life | 29 | 38 | 24 | 4 | 4 |
| 12 | Declining levels of religious observance by Jews | 24 | 44 | 26 | 5 | 1 |
| 13 | Inadequate services for the Jewish elderly | 20 | 30 | 29 | 11 | 9 |
| 14 | Insufficient Jewish content in programs sponsored by Jewish organizations | 19 | 33 | 19 | 21 | 8 |
| 15 | Inadequate rabbis | 21 | 22 | 23 | 22 | 12 |
| 16 | Lack of unity among Jewish religious denominations | 17 | 26 | 31 | 20 | 6 |
| 17 | Discrimination against women in Jewish life | 11 | 24 | 34 | 24 | 6 |
| 18 | Lack of democracy in Jewish communal life | 11 | 12 | 28 | 32 | 16 |

°Rank was determined by assigning point values to each of the responses (VS = 3, MS = 2, P = 1, N and U = 0) and totalling the points for each problem. The problem with the highest number of points is ranked #1 and so on.

°°Because of rounding, percentages do not always add up to 100.

The predominant civil Jewish concern with Jewish survival and well-being is clearly evidenced in the problem rankings. All of the items rated very serious by a majority of the respondents can be seen as immediate threats to the physical continuity and communal integrity of the Jewish people and American Jewry. That Israel's conflicts and the treatment of Jews in the Soviet Union should head the list of problems facing

### TABLE 6—Communal Priorities

H = High Priority
L = Low Priority

| RANK° | PROPOSED GOAL | *Percent ranking the goal* | |
|---|---|---|---|
| | | H | L |
| 1 | To provide financial support for Israel | 72 | 1 |
| 2 | To support Jewish education and culture | 64 | 3 |
| 3 | To provide social and welfare services for Jews in need | 51 | 2 |
| 4 | To defend Jews against anti-Semitism and discrimination | 41 | 3 |
| 5 | To provide political support for Israel | 42 | 13 |
| 6 | To support Jewish religious activities and institutions | 25 | 10 |
| 7 | To help Jewish communities in other countries | 24 | 9 |
| 8 | To increase participation in Jewish community activities | 19 | 18 |
| 9 | To promote harmonious relations between Jews and non-Jews | 14 | 23 |
| 10 | To promote unity among American Jews | 17 | 31 |
| 11 | To promote Jewish interests in American society | 6 | 41 |
| 12 | To promote the extension of civil rights and social justice in American society | 11 | 47 |
| 13 | To provide social and welfare services for anyone in need | 4 | 70 |
| 14 | To support leisure and recreational activities for Jews | 2 | 80 |

°Rank was determined by subtracting the percentage rating the goal as a "low" priority from the percentage rating it as a "high" priority and ranking the item scores thus obtained.

the *American* Jewish community may be somewhat surprising. Yet that ranking provides eloquent testimony to the powerful sense of Jewish unity which pervades the consciousness of these LD participants, and the almost unquestioned assumption that American Jews have a responsibility for the security of Jews everywhere.

Indeed, perhaps more striking than the rankings, as such, is the great seriousness attached to nearly all of the problems, and especially any which touch on the prospects for Jewish continuity. If concern for Jewish survival and a conviction of Jewish mutual responsibility have become the cornerstones of contemporary civil Judaism, then the civil religion is clearly operative as these young leaders survey the world around them. Concern for what might be termed the quality of Jewish life is by no means absent in the responses given. Low levels of Jewish knowledge, inadequate schools, declines in religious observance and in the importance of religious institutions are all perceived as serious problems by large majorities of the LD participants. Thus the broader focus of the contemporary civil religion is reflected as well. Only those few suggested "problems" which do not directly touch Jewish physical or cultural-spiritual continuity and well-being appear to spark less than serious concern.

When we turn to the respondents' priorities for communal action, we again find that the norms of the civil religion are substantially endorsed. Support for Israel (primarily philanthropic and secondarily political), for Jewish education and culture (the accepted path to continuity in the face of assimilation), and for social services to Jews in need (tzedakah at is most basic level) are the practical expression of the polity's central civil Jewish values. The next highest group of priorities—defense against anti-Semitism, helping other Jewish communities, and supporting religious activities—fall equally within the framework of civil Judaism's cardinal concerns.

Where, one might argue, the respondents depart from the civil Jewish structure is in their relatively low regard for efforts to extend social justice within society as a whole and their lack of support for Jewish efforts to serve non-Jews in need. The priorities assigned by these young leaders can be seen as reflecting the "turning inward" which has, in the eyes of many observers, diminished the polity's historic emphasis on Jewish communal responsibility for the welfare of society as a whole as part of the mandate for tzedakah.

We would add two qualifications to this analysis. One is that, as the widespread assent to the assertion that Jews have a special responsibility to work for justice indicates, the low priority accorded these items does not mean that their validity as goals is itself rejected. Rather, they do not rank as preeminent concerns for communal activity when compared with other suggested goals which may touch more centrally on the fundamental issues of Jewish survival, well-being, and mutual responsibility. Second, while we have treated civil Judaism as a single coherent meaning system, we must not overlook the fact that there is room for diversity in the interpretation of its tenets, and that emphases within the boundaries of its overall worldview and ethos may change over time and differ among adherents. The population surveyed for this study is one which has been highly sensitized to the concerns of the contemporary polity for Jewish survival. They manifest this focus consistently in their responses. Thereby, they give their civil Jewish commitment a particular tone which is characteristic especially of younger leaders today, but which does not necessarily (and we expect will not) imply a fundamental alteration in the values and norms of the system.

In terms of our overall question in this section—do the policy perceptions and prescriptions of adherents of civil Judaism reflect the tenets of that belief system?—we believe the evidence points to an affirmative answer. Civil Judasim is not merely institutional rhetoric. It is a worldview which is profoundly tied to the way in which at least these polity activists perceive the environment of Jewish life and the work in which the Jewish community (and presumably they themselves) must be engaged.

Indeed their norms for "good Jewishness" (as revealed in another section of the survey) match their prescriptions for communal policy. A "good Jew," a majority of the respondents assert, must affirm his/her Jewishness; must support Israel; and must contribute to Jewish philanthropies. Other behavioral norms too are affirmed as essential or desirable by large numbers of the LD participants, but the fundamental requisites are those of solidarity with other Jews, concern for Jewish continuity, and ethical living which the civil religion strongly affirms.[17]

Civil Judaism can be, and for most of these respondents is, very much a personal faith. Their attachment to the Jewish polity is not accidental. In the polity's work and the tenets of belief which sustain that work they evidently find a source of personal meaning, a way of locating themselves on the larger canvas of space and time and of giving their lives a measure of purpose and direction through their Jewishness.

## Conclusion

If we are right in our contention that civil Judaism has succeeded in bridging the gap between public and private religion for at least a substantial segment of American Jewry, then we must turn again to the questions "why?" and "how?" it has succeeded in doing so. In chapter 3 we suggested that the power of civil Judaism as a faith for American Jews was rooted in part in the strategy it prescribes for dealing with the ambivalence of the American Jewish condition, in the congruence between its sensibility and that of the American civil religion, and in the existence of the Jewish polity as a massive plausibility structure. Ultimately, however, there is something more which renders civil Judasim a pervasive and persuasive religious meaning system for American Jews: its capacity to paint a "true" picture of the world and to lead its adherents to a profound understanding and experience of their place in it. Civil Judaism has become a—perhaps *the*—faith for American Jews because it has come to incorporate and to generate myths and rituals which locate the American Jew in a cosmic drama of salvific import. Civil Judaism succeeds as institutional ideology because it is at heart a modern messianic faith. To the uncovering and decoding of its myth and ritual which embody its redemptive message, we turn in the next chapter.

# V

## "CHOOSE LIFE" CIVIL JEWISH MYTH AND RITUAL

### Symbols, Stories and Ceremonies

The language of religion is the language of symbols. Far more than propositions or rules, symbols give religion the power to crystallize meaning and enlist commitment. Symbols are elements of familiar reality which point beyond themselves and thereby evoke our assent to the presence of realities unseen. The wine in a cup is materially nothing but fermented grape juice. But that wine, brought forward at the proper time with the proper group, can transform both the moment and the people, making them something they were not and could not be without it. For Jews on the Sabbath eve, the wine marks the boundary between the sacred day of rest, and the week of work. For Catholics at mass, it links them to the redemptive death of their Savior. The drink is mundane, but the meanings it is able to invoke through the power of symbolism are manifold and transformative.

Symbols work on the mind and on the heart, shaping emotions, engendering associations, providing a path to understanding which could not otherwise be achieved. *How* religious symbols work to reveal the unseen and to construct a universe of meaning is part of the mystery of our humanness. *That* they work is a certainty.

Symbols are the words of religion's vocabulary; myths and rituals are the sentences through which these words express their meanings. Myths are sacred stories. They point to events (whether factual or fictional) which are paradigmatically true, which reveal reality and establish patterns for present behavior. In recounting or pointing to such stories, members of a religious group locate themselves in a context of meaning which illuminates their own experience by linking it to the experiences of their (immediate or distant) predecessors. Myths enable individuals and groups to select from the multifarious reality to which they are exposed, those elements which are "really real," which truly make sense of

129

their situation, and which, therefore, must be confronted and responded to if present life is to be meaningful. Myths reveal the simple
behind the complex, the hidden behind the manifest, the pattern behind
the chaos. In their capacity to reveal order, myths carry an emotional
force as well. Hearing the myth exhilarates; sharing the myth unifies;
and seeing the myth reenacted in one's own experience can forge a determination and commitment to respond of almost magical power.

Rituals and ceremonies are equally the shapers and expressers of religious vitality. In ritual the stuff of mundane reality, time and space and
physical substance—is restructured, deliberately and purposefully, to
make it reveal a vision of the truth contained within it. Ritual, even more
than myth, is socially and emotionally transformative. Participants and
spectators in a ritual performance are temporarily brought to a different, more intense plane of being. When they reenter the profane reality,
they do so as different persons. Rituals give the world texture and shape;
they are tools for differentiating time and space, for marking off groups
and phases of our lives. They depict and enact the paradigmatic events
and processes which render the flow of experience meaningful.

## Interpreting Civil Religious Myth and Ritual

Jewish civil religion, no less than any other religion, relies on myth
and ritual to vitalize its worldview and its ethos. The stories which the
faithful tell one another translate the abstract tenets of its belief system
into real events which happened and are happening still. The ceremonies which its adherents enact together take them out of the mundane
into a realm where their unity and purposiveness as a group become
self-evident.

Civil religious myth and ritual are not, however, always easy to identify and interpret. Civil religion is secularized. Its focus is the group itself, not a separate sacred reality. Thus, its symbols often do not have
obvious transcendent referents. Traditional religious myth and ritual
constitute, to use Mircea Eliade's term, hierophanies: they make the
power of the sacred manifest in mundane reality.[1] Even if civil religious
myths and rituals succeed in rendering aspects of the collective experience of the group paradigmatically meaningful, they rarely invoke a
trans-historical power to do so. Thus civil religions myth often does not
present itself as "myth" in the traditional sense, but simply as "history."
Similarly, civil religious ritual frequently lacks the manifest references
to sacred reality which charaterize conventional religious ritual. Thus,
the interpreter of civil Judaism must be prepared to look beyond the
surface of the stories and ceremonies he encounters in order to determine whether they serve as functinal equivalents of traditional myth and

ritual for the civil religion's adherents, indeed whether their secularized language may even mask a genuine transcendental dimension.

The difficulty in identifying the mythic components of American Jewish civil religion is compounded by the fact that these are not only secularized, but often truncated and allusive. That is to say, myths are rarely told as full-blown narratives. Rather, they are invoked in elliptical forms, referred to, alluded to, pointed to, without being explicitly recounted. Because civil religious myth is historical myth, it is often assumed that the history itself is known. A single phrase my be used to crystallize the meaning of that history, and thereby give it its mythic significance.[2] Again, it is the interpreter's task to identify the myth behind the phrase and the formulaic references. At times, this presents little challenge, but on other occasions it requires an admittedly speculative leap beyond the clear evidence of the civil religious texts themselves.

Finally, the interpreter of civil Jewish myth and ritual must recognize that there are in fact two different types of story and ceremony which give shape and substance to civil Judaism's belief system. Especially in recent years, traditional Jewish religious forms have played an increasing role within the American Jewish civil religion. Thus, the interpreter of civil Judaism must attend first to how elements of traditional Jewish myth and ritual are incorporated within the civil Jewish context. What elements are selected for incorporation, and how they are used and interpreted in the civil religion are the key questions in this regard. American civil Judaism has also spawned its own set of characteristic myths and rituals, and these too must obviously be examined, both in their own right, and in relationship to the traditional components.

### The Civil Jewish Myths

American Jewish civil religion is an activist religion emphasizing the pursuit of Jewish survival and social justice. Its worldview is dominated by the assertion of Jewish unity and distinctiveness on the one hand and the rootedness of American Jews in American society on the other. These tenets of the civil religion acquire both plausibility and power from their incorporation in three central myths. These myths make civil Judaism a uniquely appropriate structure for linking the experience and sensibility of contemporary Jews to the traditional religious vision of Judaism.

Civil Judaism's first central myth is the story of "Holocaust to Rebirth," the retelling by American Jews of the two most significant Jewish events of the twentieth century—the murder of six million Jews by the Nazis and the establishment of the State of Israel—so as to make them a paradigm for Jewish history and a continuous inspiration for Jewish action. The second great myth of American Jewish civil religion is its story of the American Jewish experience itself: "America—and American Jews—are different." America is a land in which Jews have prospered in unprecedented terms, and precisely for that reason must assume the special burden of preserving their Jewish integrity. Civil Judaism's final myth is perhaps both its most problematic, and ultimately most important: its barely disguised reaffirmation of the myth of Jews as a chosen people, a people with a special destiny and mission of world-shaping proportions. These three myths are interpenetrating in their functioning and impact. Taken together, they constitute a story about what it means to be an American Jew today which delivers a single forceful message: to be a Jew is to be part of a collective endeavor to take control of Jewish destiny, to create a future in which Jews will live in dignity and security, and in which their exemplification of traditional Jewish values will serve as a model for humanity as a whole. In short, the myths of civil Judaism are the myths of a modern messianic religion, one shorn of the naive optimism or premature universalism of earlier versions of modern Jewish messianism, but still capable of inspiring Jews who seek the meaning and method of their reentry into history.

In the next sections of this chapter we will examine each of the three central myths of the American Jewish civil religion in turn. We will then explore the structure of ritual action which civil Judaism has developed to help to dramatize and celebrate these myths. Finally, we will look again at the religious statement and message of American Jewish civil religion as a prelude to our assessment of its import for American Jewry and modern Jewish religious history in the last chapter of this book.

## From Holocaust to Rebirth

No myth of American civil Judaism is more prominent or more powerful than the myth of "Holocaust to rebirth." The historical events which form the core of this myth are the Nazi extermination of European Jewry and the founding of the State of Israel. As Jacob Neusner has written,

> These events, far from American's shores and remote from American Jews' everyday experience, constitute the generative myth by which the generality of American Jews make sense of themselves and decide what to do with that part of themselves set aside for "being Jewish". . . . [A] sizable sector of the American people sees the world in and along the lines of vision of reality beginning in death, "the Holocaust," and completed by resurrection or rebirth, "Israel."[3]

Neusner's own analysis of this myth, of its origins, its vital role in shaping American Jewish consciousness, and (from his standpoint) its ultimate and puzzling flaws as a meaning system for American Jewry, whose experience it does *not*, in fact, describe, is pointed and provocative. It is a myth, he contends, which responds to the ambiguous and ambivalent character of American Jewish existence by projecting a process of death and redemption in which the American Jew can vicariously participate. For a group living in unprecedented freedom, but knowing that it remains a vulnerable minority in a land not truly its own, this myth provides both a confirmation of its worst fears and a realization of its fondest hopes—without in any way affecting the reality of the situation in which it actually lives. For Neusner, the myth of "Holocaust to rebirth" is a veil which American Jews place between themselves and the daily reality of their lives, at once profoundly functional in sustaining Jewish group commitment and activism (primarily in defense of Jewish survival), and deeply dysfunctional in deflecting American Jews from the task of creating a mode and myth of Jewish religious existence faithful to their own chosen condition.[4]

This interpretation of the "Holocaust to rebirth" myth undoubtedly helps to illuminate why it should form the core of the contemporary Jewish polity's self-understanding. That polity has, as we have seen, found its raison d'être in the task of fostering Jewish survival. As myth, the story of the Holocaust and the creation of the State of Israel gives that work transcendent import. The power of the myth, Neusner suggests, lies in its capacity to provoke an absolutely predictable response on the part of American Jews: the Holocaust must never happen again; Israel can insure that; therefore, we must insure that Israel itself survives. Indeed, the prodigious fundraising and political efforts of the polity reflect precisely that conviction. But, as Neusner also suggests, the mythic character of the "Holocaust to rebirth" story transcends its capacity to give meaning to the specific horror of the annihilation of European Jewry and to the specific triumph of the reestablishment of a Jewish state. For American Jewish civil religion, the myth is a paradigm for all of Jewish history, even (though Neusner would not, perhaps, be prepared to concede this) for the experience of American Jewry itself.

The myth of destruction and rebirth is not, of course, a uniquely modern, nor even a Jewish, one. In a sense, all religion is about the transcendence of death. In one form or another, the passage from death, destruction, or utter degradation, to life, reconstruction, and triumph is a central feature of countless myths and rituals in a host of traditions. Religious history has probably never known, for example, a more powerful version of this "urmyth" from-death-to-life than the Christian story of crucifixion and resurrection. For Jews, the master myth of the Exodus embodies the same passage, which the Passover seder reenacts yearly. The fact that the seder remains the most widely observed of all Jewish rituals among American Jews may not be unrelated to this message, one which resonates so clearly with modern Jewish history.[5] The contemporary "Holocaust to rebirth" myth is thus not only a framework for mak-

ing sense of the two dominating historical events of recent decades, but
one which is itself rooted in a more fundamental religious affirmation:
that beyond apparent extinction lies the possibility of renewed life.

We have had occasion several times in the previous chapters to discuss the central position which the Holocaust and Israel have assumed in
the civil Jewish faith over the past forty years. Each in its own right is a
vital symbol, defining respectively two ever-present poles of Jewish experience: the perpetual threat of disappearance, and the extraordinary
vitality and creativity of the Jewish people. But the mythic meaning of
"Holocaust to rebirth" encompasses more than merely the juxtaposition
of these two poles. The passage from death to life defines a dynamic
which coexists with the polarity. The civil religion has drawn from the
"Holocaust to rebirth" myth both a confirmation of the continuity of the
present with the Jewish past, and a conviction that out of this present
can emerge a radically transformed future. It is this affirmation of a dou-
ble paradigm for contemporary Jewish existence—a statement at once
of what has always been and what is coming to be—which the "Holocaust to rebirth" myth makes possible.

This is, to be sure, a paradoxical assertion. On the one hand is the lesson of the Passover haggadah: In every generation they have arisen to
destroy us.

> We have buried many martyrs. We have stood before many oppressors
> demanding our freedom. We have learned in terrible places—Egypt,
> Spain, Bergen-Belsen, Theresienstadt; and from dreaded persecutors—
> Pharaohs, Inquisitors, Hitlers—that Jews must be concerned for one an-
> other. For the awful truth is that *no one else really cares.*[6]

The Holocaust is the awful proof that Jewish history has not changed,
that it was then in the 1930s and 1940s as it had been for the thousands
of years preceding, and even as it is today. "For the world is the same
. . . brutal, expedient, callous."[7] "The present reminds us that ancient
hatreds still seek to deny the Jewish people their future."[8] Yet, the lesson in a sense is just the opposite as well. What the horror of the Holocaust and the efforts to save its survivors in a Jewish state have taught
the Jews of our time is that history was offering them an "incredible opportunity—to change the world for our people, so long oppressed, so
long dispossessed."[9] The Holocaust remains real as ever-present possibility (as the events of 1967, in which Israel itself was threatened with
destruction, so dramatically revealed). But the Jewish revival after the
Holocaust is revelatory as well (as 1967 also demonstrated). It shows that
Jews need not be victims of history any longer, that with vigilance and
dedication they can be its masters. "During this period in man's history,
the Jews said: We care about life, and we have hope that we can build a
better world, we believe we can influence events and history—and Is-

rael was born—and Jews in America said: *We care*—we are responsible —we will *act.*"[10]

This is a theme reiterated time and again in the rhetoric of civil Judaism. "We are no longer impotent, powerless, unable to confront our problems or our enemies."[11] The proof of that proposition is what has already been accomplished—Israel, and the American Jewish role in establishing and preserving it. "There is a state where there was no state for 2000 years. There is life—Jewish life—where in the Hitler years . . . there was little more than death."[12] The future remains endangered, but in light of the mythic experience of our era, that danger looms differently:

> For if we Jews are now an endangered species . . . , we are not polar bears nor bald eagles. We are Jews, with both a millenial experience in dealing with a hostile world, and with immense new capabilities for forging our own destiny rather than being, as we were for centuries, puppets of history, manipulated by others.[13]

Israel is, of course, the preeminent symbol of that new condition, that new power, of a new era in Jewish history.

> From the ashes of annihilation has grown and is growing a nation-state, which has redeemed our people from the status of the tolerated—or untolerated—wanderer, to that of the dignity of a member of the family of nations, with his own turf, his own language, and his own national and universal aspirations.[14]

As the Holocaust illuminates all of Jewish history, so does its negation—reborn Israel: "The fact that Jerusalem is once again the center of the Jewish universe creates a new consciousness in the last quarter of this century of who we are and how far we have travelled together on this earth."[15] Israel's strength in the face of threatened death—at Entebbe, e.g.—and American Jewry's solidarity with a beleaguered Israel—when, e.g., Zionism is branded racism—thus serve as proof "that we *can* turn adversity to opportunity—that we *can* turn anxiety to hope."[16]

The myth of "Holocaust to rebirth" is, we have said, a myth of life triumphant over death, and the civil religion has used the power of its imagery to mobilize Jews for the tasks it deems to be life-giving. "Throughout Jewish history—in spite of mankind's suppression—the violence—the deprivation—the pogroms—the assaults on human sensibilities—and the barbarism—we continue to show a reverence for life."[17] "We have chosen, all through our history, in every generation, often in the face of danger and death, to meet our human obligations, to follow justice, to advance human knowledge and the human condition, and thereby to worship God."[18]

Like the great speeches of Moses in the final chapters of Deuteronomy, the myth of "Holocaust to rebirth" presents the Jew with a fundamental choice: submit to the forces of death and destruction, or join with those who are fighting for life. Both are ever-present, yet the struggle is not vain, because Judaism insists—and the history/myth of the past forty years confirms—that life must eventually win out. The activity of the polity itself becomes part of this historic struggle between the forces of life and death. Both its achievements and its challenges are often framed precisely in these terms: "We are the bridge between years of terror and persecution and new lives in freedom; between the agony of Jewishness denied and the joy of renewed Jewish identity."[19] "It is our chosen responsibility—as one people—to renew life time and again."[20]

The myth of "Holocaust to rebirth" stands at the center of American civil Judaism's mythology because it binds the work of the Jewish polity to a vision of Jewish existence which is both emotionally gripping and spiritually ennobling. But does that vision, as Neusner suggests, buy a conviction of historic significance at the price of drawing the American Jew away from the reality of his own life into a world of vicarious danger and vicarious triumph? Can the powerful sense of identification with the drama of death and life which it seeks to engender be sustained within, and give meaning to, the more prosaic life experience of American Jews, who are both more secure and comfortable than the victims, and less capable of remaking history than the heroes, of the story they tell? To answer this question we must turn to the second of the civil religion's key myths, its self-understanding of the American Jewish experience.

## America—and American Jews—are Different

From the outset of our discussion we have emphasized civil Judaism's insistence that Jewish fulfillment and full participation in American life are compatible ideals. American Jews, as one eminent professional leader has put it, want to survive as *American* Jews, not just as Jews.[21] But what precisely does it mean to be an *American* Jew? Civil Judaism's recounting of the American Jewish experience suggests that it is to be part of two great and complementary historical ventures. The American Jew is to see himself as a participant in a persistent struggle for Jewish survival in a hostile world. But he is also to recognize his privileged place in that struggle. For America is different. In America, Jews have found a society which not only permits them to be Jews, but which invites them to join in a shared enterprise, an enterprise whose values are at once American and Jewish.

The Jewish civil religious myth of America, like its myth of "Holocaust to rebirth," is rooted in real history. It reflects the achievements of American Jews—as individuals and as a group—the striking philoSemitic character of American society (at least in comparison with other environments), and, as noted above, the strongly Hebraic character of America's own self-understanding. Civil Judaism's view of America is overwhelmingly benign. Even when the polity has been attendent to threats of anti-Semitism—and it continues today to be alert to (some would say obsessed with) such threats—it has tended to view these as aberrations from the "true" America, not as expressions of America's essential character.[22]

At the core of the civil Jewish myth are the stories of America as the *goldene medine*, the land of unprecedented opportunity, and of American Jews as the people who made the most of that opportunity. The tale of Jewish achievement in America is a thoroughly familiar one in American Jewish folk mythology, but in the civil religious context it takes on a distinctive coloration by being set within the larger context of Jewish history and values. The basic affirmation is clear: "At no time or place in their history have Jews as a people, a group, been so free, affluent, accepted, influential and satisfied as they are now in North America."[23] But, with opportunity comes responsibility. "In this room," a national gathering of young UJA and federation leaders was told,

> is the most secure, the best educated, the most successful Jewish group ever to gather like this. We have every benefit of American society, and the ability to confront our problems. Compare it to the generation of our fathers and grandfathers. . . . Born in Russia, [my grandfather] came to this country in another age. While he worked for the Jewish people, he had none of the opportunity for education, wealth and influence that you and I share. Your bobes and zaydes and mine and our parents brought us a long way and together have accomplished great things. But we are a more fortunate group and this opportunity requires that we step forward.[24]

Just as the civil Jewish myth of America accords it a special status in history, so too civil Judaism views American Jews as special even within the American environment. On the one hand, "the story of the Jewish community here is the American story—boatloads of immigrants coming to these shores and fulfilling the American dream for themselves and their country. Jews are captains of industry, leaders of government, scholars, artists and scientists."[25] But Jews have written their own characteristic chapter to that story as well:

> Among immigrant ethnic groups, none can rival our personal commitment and philanthropic contributions to the welfare of the total community.
> American Jews have been in the forefront of every progressive social cause in our nation's history—the abolitionist movement, the labor movement, the civil rights movement, the anti-Vietnam movement. Long before these became universally popular, much less national policy, we were there.

Wherever the issue involved social justice it was a Jewish priority before it became an American policy. . . . We have continuously repaid our
debt for the freedom and opportunity that are the blessings of the United
States and Canada.[26]

American Jews have thus been *better* citizens precisely because of
their persistent commitment to the value of social justice. That same
commitment, as we have seen on several occasions, lies at the heart of
civil Judaism's understanding of what it means to be Jewish. The American Jew is, therefore, a participant in two complementary historic ventures.

The North American Jewish experience is unique. For here—for the
first time in world history—our spiritual and national drives coalesce.
    Dissatisfaction with the status quo, confidence that a free society can
secure equal opportunity and justice for all, is as American as it is Jewish
in character. In the history of the Diaspora no generation has been as
blessed nor has had a greater opportunity to make a creative contribution than ours.[27]

The civil religious myth of American and American Jewish exceptionalism is more than an assertion of the compatibility of good Jewishness
and Americanness. It is an understanding of the role of America and of
the Jewish people in history which places the American Jew uniquely at
the cutting edge of a world-transforming endeavor:

If America is the last best hope of mankind, and I think it is, the Jewish
people have been for several thousand years the first best hope. We hold
ourselves out, the Jewish people and the American people, as that hope.
. . . Because we in the American Jewish community hold in the one hand
the values of the Jewish people and in the other hand the values of the
American democracy, we have a special role to fill.[28]

No other nation in history has enjoyed the freedom and political guaran-
tees of American democracy. Yet, the idealism of the founding fathers
has been diminished by time. . . . It is time America rediscover the moral
clarity which in the past united the nation in the heat and passion of creative achievement.
    You and I have both our American tradition and our Jewish tradition.
As Jews we need not be afflicted by moral confusion, for there is none in
our history. Our commandments, our Torah, are clear and enduring. We
are blessed with a sure and certain sense of purpose, a set of values, a
clarity of goal. . . . We believe in the sanctity of life and the dignity of
the individual. We accept the stranger in our midst. We abhor injustice,
and are obliged to speak out against it.
    With these principles as our armaments, our mission as a people has
been to create a decent society on earth, to place men above property.[29]

Civil Judaism's mythic understanding of the unique character of the

American Jewish experience unites its two great aspirations—to promote Jewish continuity and to build a just society. The American Jew has it within his power to do both, *must* do both. Like the myth of "Holocaust to rebirth," the civil religion's myth of American Jewish exceptionalism challenges the Jew to act, and thereby to find a transcendent meaning in his Jewishness:

> I believe that we—the North American Jewish community—are poised at one of the rare historic watersheds in Jewish destiny. We have the freedom, enlightenment, prosperity and opportunity to make a momentous contribution to our culture, to our respective communities and countries and to the world. We do not have to struggle to survive.
>
> Our challenge is to thrive! To create new foundations, set new directions which will enable future generations to carry forward our historic mission into the space civilization of the twenty-first century . . .
>
> I can think of no greater legacy to leave future generations than a vital Jewish community. . . . It is our greatest opportunity to fulfill our spiritual mission as a spur to the conscience of our community, our country, and our world.[30]

This mythic vision does not entirely negate the anxieties and ambivalences which we have seen are part of the American Jewish self-consciousness. The myth of "Holocaust to rebirth," with its insistence on perpetual Jewish endangerment, and its location of the arena of Jewish renewal in the Jewish state, stands alongside that of American Jewish exceptionalism, offering an apparently very different reading of the Jewish condition. Civil Judaism has opted—clearly and forcefully—to affirm both myths. In so doing, it delivers a complex message: American Jews are uniquely secure and uniquely privileged in America, but they are also inevitably bound up in the drama of world Jewish history—a drama of threatened destruction and miraculous, though dearly earned, salvation. American Jews need the myth of American uniqueness to validate and to explain what they have done here; how, as Jerold Hoffberger, a CJF president put it, "they came to do well, and stayed to do good."[31] But they need the myth of "Holocaust to rebirth" as well, not only to remind them that America is not uniformly benevolent, but to confirm that in their enjoyment of American uniqueness they have not lost touch with a larger Jewish destiny. The myth of America tells Jews that they have found a home where they can be like others, yet remain themselves. The myth of "Holocaust to rebirth" implores them to remember that they were once and may yet again be strangers, and that for all Jews there is today a second home. For the adherents of civil Judaism, all of these assertions are true, and though in rational terms they may appear paradoxical, they are in fact faithful to the experienced reality of a paradoxical century.

This, however, is not all that can be said about these two myths and their simultaneous affirmation in the civil religion. The myths of "Holocaust to rebirth" and American Jewish uniqueness not only correct, but profoundly complement one another. Beyond the tensions they depict lies a common message: the message that contemporary Jewry must seize its destiny, that it is at center stage in a world-historical drama. Whether in reborn Israel or powerful America, the Jew is once again treading a messianic path. Out of the combination of anxiety and confidence, at-homeness and vicarious identification which the American Jew should feel when he absorbs these myths should also emerge the vital response: act to insure the Jewish future, act to validate the Jewish presence in history. Whatever they may say to American Jews in general, to those who labor in the American Jewish polity, these myths do tell a single though complex, story: a story of struggle and achievement; of being engulfed by history, only to find onself, miraculously, at its cutting edge; of seeking a rationale for continued survival, and discovering a transcendent, value-propagating mission.

## The Chosen People

The myths of "Holocaust to rebirth" and American Jewish exceptionalism have provided civil Judaism with a vocabulary with which to understand and significate the contemporary Jewish experience. To ground that experience solidly in the soil of Judaic tradition, the civil religion invokes as well a third myth, more allusively and elusively perhaps, but no less powerfully: the myth of Jews as a chosen people.

Arthur Hertzberg, the Jewish historian, has insisted that the assertion that Jews are the chosen people is the single most significant and—for modern Jews—most vexing claim of Jewish theology.[32] The struggles of American Jewish theologians and rabbinic thinkers with the myth of Jewish chosenness are elaborately documented in Arnold Eisen's book *The Chosen People in America*. Eisen describes the various strategies which these thinkers have employed to try to come to grips with the doctrine of election, at once so central to traditional Jewish religious self-understanding and so discomforting for a group seeking to integrate itself fully in a democratic, egalitarian society. From Reform's reinterpretation of chosenness as a universalist "mission," to Reconstructionism's repudiation of the concept in favor of the notion of "vocation," to Conservatism's equivocation, and Orthodoxy's affirmation without attention to the difficulties implicit in that affirmation, none of the denominational movements provided a satisfactory theology of chosenness for American Jews. What they offered instead was at best religious ideology, a functional appropriation of the symbol of chosenness to support a prescription for or legitimation of a particular American Jewish lifestyle. Even when the new generation of theologians in the post-World War II period sought to reinstitute a serious Jewish theological enterprise, and agreed, by and large, on the centrality of the concept of chosenness for such an enterprise, they could speak of it only as a "mystery" eluding convincing rational explication.[33]

Yet, if American Jewish religious thought has failed so notably to elaborate the myth of Jewish chosenness in theological terms, how do we account for its persistence as a religious symbol and its recurrent importance as religious ideology?[34] Eisen suggests that for all its ineluctability as a theological concept, chosenness retained a religious resonance of great power for American Jews. It resonated psychologically with the desire to feel some sense of reward for the fidelity Jews had shown to their religion. It was relevant sociologically to a community seeking to carve out a niche for itself in an open society. And it was historically meaningful, in light of the dramatic events of the era.[35]

Thus, what has failed as theology has succeeded as popular religion. "We, the majority of American Jews," Hertzberg has written,

> believe on rationalist grounds that there is no chosen people; we believe that the Jews have no superiority of any kind inherent within them—and yet we insist that being Jewish is something of the most profound importance, making demands on both the Jewish individual and the whole community to be something very special and centrally creative; there may be a God and it is not respectable intellectually to affirm the belief in chosenness—and yet we behave on the presumption that we are chosen and that our disappearance would be an unutterable tragedy.[36]

For this reason, the myth of chosenness, a problem (to one degree or another) for denominational theology, is a solution for civil religion. Because civil Judaism eschews theology, it could accept the concept of chosenness precisely for what it was to the folk: an intellectually suspect, but emotionally irreplaceable symbol of confirmation and continuity, an affirmation that Jews yet retained their distinctiveness, and a tool for mobilizing and legitimating commitment to the community and its professed values.

Eugene Borowitz has noted that the traditional Jewish understanding of chosenness is multidimensional, incorporating both inner-directed and outer-directed components. The inner-directed (and traditionally primary) dimensions include the acceptance of Torah as the unique revelation to the Jewish people, of the *mitzvot* (commandments of the Torah) as a normative pattern for living, of holiness as one's goal in life, and of the certitude of the redemption of the Jewish people, and, through them, of all humanity. The outer-directed components of chosenness (i.e., those which define the Jewish relationship to the outside world) are the concept of Jewish distinctiveness and the idea of Jewish service to humanity.[37] Civil Judaism embraces both of these dimensions in its understanding of the meaning of chosenness, although in reversed priority and with substantial revaluation of the traditional meaning of many of the concepts involved.

Civil Judaism's myth of chosenness is above all a myth of a unique

Jewish destiny and mission in the world. We have seen already how these themes developed in the course of the civil religion's evolution and how they undergird its commitment to Jewish continuity and the pursuit of social justice. The concept of "mission" as a modern revaluation of the idea of "chosenness" is hardly unique to civil Judaism. It was one of the centerpieces of Reform Judaism's effort to universalize and spiritualize the Jewish message. Indeed, the rhetoric of polity leaders has often echoed that of Reform preachers, speaking of a "prophetic" or a "messianic" mission. But whereas, as Eisen notes, Reform Jewish sponsorship of the concept of mission as a surrogate for chosenness often masked a contentless Jewishness and a universalizing ethos,[38] civil Judaism's sense of mission is linked to the concrete work of the polity itself.

The terms used to describe the values inherent in that work which give it its transcendent character are also hardly unique: bearing witness against injustice, laboring for brotherhood, caring. But civil Judaism insists on seeing these values as the products of a unique Jewish experience as well as the expression of a unique striving. "What guides us as a community," one professional leader has stated,

> are those Jewish values that have become part of the muscle fiber of every Jew; those values derived from multiple sources of Jewish experience; those values perpetuated in a variety of ritualistic practices of the Jewish community.
>
> It is those values to which we have instinctively given our highest priority. Those values impel us to remember we were slaves in Egypt. Those values constantly remind us of the felt recollection of redemption. Those values command us to remember our martyrs from Masada and before to the Holocaust and beyond to the fields of battle in the Negev, Golan, and Sinai. Those values command us to resist tyranny. Those values oblige us to accept our special mission.[39]

Although the values it espouses are on their face universal ethical norms, civil Judaism sees its ethos as the product and expression of Jewish distinctiveness. That distinctiveness is rooted in both Jewry's unique history and its particular religious heritage:

> We have traveled the whole world for over 3,500 years because we are Jews. We have survived the Amalekites, the Plague, Haman, the Crusades and the Holocaust. Because we are Jews, because of our Torah, because of our Ten Commandments and yes, because of our suffering, we —you and I—have been the beneficiaries of a way of life which makes us unique, not necessarily better, but unique among the peoples of the world. We have been taught to care—and we care, we really care.[40]

Civil Judaism's insistence that Jews must not assimilate, and its half-prideful, half-mournful suspicion that they will never be able to live in pece, reflect this claim that the Jewish heritage itself sets the Jewish people on a unique course. "Judaism," according to Jerold Hoffberger, president of the Council of Jewish Federations in the mid-1970s,

> is not just a religion but an all-embracing, all-demanding social ethic, requiring affirmation of God by individual and collective action. To be a good Jew, one has to know the law and abide by it. The law begins with the Ten Commandments for individual conduct and extends to a comprehensive code of social justice. It is not external pressure but this internal commitment to social justice which represents the charismatic core and cohesive course of Judaism, the force which has compelled successive generations to reach out, to reject mediocrity, to demand the best of themselves and their society. This internal drive for excellence and social justice explains why we have not, cannot, and will not assimilate—why we survive, why we thrive, and why . . . the world is often uncomfortable with us.[41]

As a comprehensive definition of Judaism, Hoffberger's statement would likely not meet with an historian's or theologian's approval. As an indication, however, of how powerfully the sense of uniqueness colors even this secularized and ethicized understanding of Judaism, it is revealing. The mythology of civil Judaism accords these essentially universal values a particularistic significance by proclaiming the Jewish people's special historical role and responsibility in their dissemination. Jews have a mission not merely to preach these values, but to construct a model Jewish community which exemplifies them for all to see—a "light unto the nations."[42] The concern of the polity for the fate and welfare of all Jews, the social service agenda of its agencies, is, therefore, as much a part of this historic mission as is its participation in the larger struggles for civil rights and social justice.

This understanding of the import and implications of Jewish distinctiveness points to a resolution of the universalist/particularist tension which has so often preoccupied modern Jewish ideology. It provides a rationale for the Jewish polity's efforts to remain both outward- and inward-looking, and it enables the activists within the polity to see their chosen course as a contemporary expression of Judaism's unique ethos.

> Directed toward its own people, the ethos of Judaism says that *some* people, in this case the Jewish people, must accept and carry the burden of the *mitzvot*, and therefore the institutional forms of this people's life must carry out the *mitzvot* in the lives of its members, and must play a role in the survival and creative development of the ethos and its people. Directed toward general society, the ethos of Judaism says that the individual Jew and the Jewish community's institutional forms must participate in, and give maximum possible help to the fulfillment of the ethical *mitzvot* among the people and within the society beyond the Jewish community itself.[43]

This Jewish commitment to "arrive at the universal through the particular" also insures, however, that Jews are and must be "marginal men." If Jewish values reflect the special character of the Jewish historical experience, the unique quality of that experience is itself rooted in the aspiration to be both particular and universal. "Our stubbornness in being ourselves on the one hand and global in our interests on the other lies close to the heart of both Jewish creativity and Jewish tragedy."[44]

The myth of Jewish chosenness enables the contemporary polity to envision its own mandate in terms of the religious categories embedded in the classical Judaic tradition (at least as understood in the civil religion). "If we take hold of, or reassert at this time, our prophetic tradition," asserted Irving Blum, a CJF president,

> it is out of no reflex of insecurity. It is a vital response rather stirring within us almost genetically: once again we realize that we must do battle with the historic themes of Exodus and Return—rude leave-taking of our fixed patterns of thought, behavior and social action to go wandering, groping, towards a vision of promise and of man's excellence. . . .
>
> [We] can give a new vigor and thrust to that prophecy which insists on the practice of fulfillment and the healing of society. Not only for ourselves and our people, but for all of peace loving and freedom loving mankind. We Jews have been and must continue to be the conscience of history.[45]

"Our Jewish communal structure," asserted Charles Zibbell, "cannot be merely a 'service-station' geared to meet a series of personal needs. It is also the expression of a value system and interpretation of the covenant."[46]

In claiming lineage from the prophetic tradition or from the covenant which seals Israel's special relationship with God and binds it to observe the Torah's *mitzvot*, civil Judaism is not speaking frivolously. The civil religion has in fact generated its own sense of *mitzvah* and of the sacred. If this sensibility is not, to be sure, equivalent to that which the classical Judaic tradition associates with these terms, it constitutes at least an opening toward transcendence, a bridge between the apparent mundaneness of the polity's daily work and the portentous character of its self-assigned mission. Responding to a critic who had characterized federations as mired in the secular realm, Sidney Vincent expressed the case in these terms:

> God is approached Jewishly not through a search in the woods but basically through 'mitzvot,' through good deeds, through practical acts. I would say that the office of a social service agency that is finding housing for a new immigrant is a very good way indeed to approach God. . . .
>
> What we do by day and by night in working on detailed Jewish tasks takes on magical properties when viewed under the aspect of Jewish history.[47]

"When a Federation leader makes a motion after months of hard work
. . . ," argued another professional leader,

> that will enable the community to create a hundred units of subsidized
> housing for the elderly, or a new Jewish day school, the making of that
> motion is literally a sacred activity from every Jewish perspective.[48]

Civil Judaism's assertion that the work of the Jewish polity is holy
work, a fulfillment of the covenant, is not made lightly, but neither does
it become the basis for a full-fledged theology of chosenness. The inner-
directed dimensions of the concept are embraced, but not elaborated.
Indeed, the civil religion often employs a deliberately "softened" vocabulary in its allusions to these dimensions of the myth of chosenness:
Torah and *halakhah* appear as the "tradition" and "heritage"; *mitzvot*
are "Jewish values"; the quest for holiness becomes the striving for
"quality" and "excellence" in Jewish life; the active choosing God is
eclipsed by the activist, responsible community; and revelation and redemption are virtually ignored.

Civil Judaism, like many modern Jews, often finds the traditional language of chosenness, and the implications of that language,
discomforting. For this reason, it is possible to lose sight of how critical
the myth of chosenness really is, to fail to recognize that it is the glue
which holds together the pragmatic ethos and the transcendent vision of
civil Judaism. For the civil religion, the distinctiveness of the Jews—of
their experience and of their religious tradition—is not an historical accident, but a calling which each generation must reaffirm. "We seek not
normalcy, not a desire to be simply like others, but something better."[49]

Beyond this aspiration lies an inchoate conviction that the historic fact
and the world-transforming significance of Jewish distinctiveness ultimately reflect the workings of forces beyond human ken. Here again,
the myth of Jewish chosenness serves civil Judaism as a bridge to the
confrontation with transcendence, however tentative that confrontation
may be:

> [F]inally, as is always the case with Jewish life, there is mystery. Our sur-
> vival . . . violates the conventional wisdom and the usual rules of history.
> We were an exception in how we emerged, we have been an exception
> in how we resisted assimilation, and we are an exception in how we are
> meeting our responsibilities. . . . May we continue to be an exceptional
> people—in both senses of the word—exceptional in being different, ex-
> ceptional in being extraordinary.[50]

For the American Jews to whom civil Judaism addresses itself, the
myth of Jewish chosenness is perhaps not one to speak about too openly
or too clearly, but it is one that is told and retold nevertheless in a myr-
iad of barely concealed ways. It is one confirmed by the extraordinary

history of this century and by their own remarkable presence on the American scene. To the myths of "Holocaust to rebirth" and the uniqueness of the American Jewish experience it adds an intimation of inevitability—this is the way it was meant to be. The myth of chosenness opens for civil Judaism a path into a religious sensibility and vocabulary which elevates its ethos onto a new plane: a vocabulary of covenant, of *mitzvah*, of sacred deeds. Perhaps most important, it anchors the messianic mission to shape history which the contemporary polity has accepted for itself, in the depth of a tradition which has always seen Jewish existence as central to God's plan for human redemption.

### The Religion of Communitas: Civil Jewish Ritual

Civil Judaism is an activist religion. Its thrust is ethical, even messianic. But to succeed as civil religion, it must be able to perform the critical functions of unifying its adherents, mobilizing their energies and legitimating their activities which we identified in chapter 1. The myths of civil Judaism play a key role in performing these functions, but the power of civil Judaism as a religious ideology rests equally on its capacity to generate an experience of unity and a sense of purposiveness through rituals which have become parts of its symbolic structure.

The development of clearly identifiable civil Jewish ritual is in itself a sign of the transformation which has taken place in the essential character of the Jewish polity and the meaning of its activities. What was once merely a philanthropic system has become a vehicle through which many contemporary Jews both discover and express their group solidarity and their participation in that group's unfolding destiny. The Jewish civil religion has thereby begun to reverse the process of deritualization which is so characteristic of modern Western religion. Mary Douglas, in her book *Natural Symbols,* has suggested that when the individual's sense of group dependence begins to break down, religious expression moves away from the ritual realm toward greater ethical concern. Conversely, as stronger ties to the group develop and the sense of personal autonomy diminishes there is greater propensity for and receptiveness to ritual activity.[51] The historical events—the Holocaust, the founding of the State of Israel, the Six-Day War—which galvanized Jewish commitment to the work of the contemporary Jewish polity helped to restore a sense of solidarity and even group dependence which had dissipated among American Jews. Thereby, they also opened the polity to a renewed appreciation of the power of ritual, not only as a functional tool (which it surely has been), but as a necessary expression of a new sensibility.

As with all civil religion, the ritual of American civil Judaism can be divided into two categories. The first is ritual which the civil religion appropriates from traditional religion, in this case, traditional Judaism. In chapter 3 we noted that American Jewish polity's growing acceptance and utilization of traditional ritual forms over the past several decades. Jewish dietary laws are regularly observed in communal facilities and at public functions. Grace after meals is recited as a matter of course at such events. Celebration and observance of the Sabbath has become an important feature of polity events which are held over weekends; indeed (as we shall discuss below) polity organizations have often become the sponsors of events, such as retreat weekends, designed specifically to promote such celebration and observance. Even ritualized study has become part of the polity's behavioral repertoire in the form of *divrei torah* (brief expositions of biblical portion or other Jewish theme) which are frequently used to open meetings and events.

This civil religious appropriation of traditional Jewish ritual clearly reflects the growing appreciation of and commitment to Jewish tradition in general which we noted as one of the tenets of civil Judaism. It also has been triggered in part by the expanding participation in the polity of individuals who are religiously observant in their personal lives, and the desire to insure that such individuals are made to feel welcome in the organizational system. But more is at stake here as well. The incorporation of Jewish ritual into polity activities anchors these more firmly within the framework of the tradition, and enables the civil religion to evoke some of the emotional resonances of such ritual on its own behalf. Traditional ritual helps to transform meetings into sacred occasions. Thus, when a polity leader claims that his motion or committee service is a religious act (as we saw some do), that claim is made within a context of plausibility created in part by the religious legitimation which traditional ritual lends to polity activity.

Even this, however, is not the whole story. For civil Judaism is characterized by a second type of ritual which is even more revealing of its fundamental religious meaning and message. These are the rituals of the polity itself, rituals which often surround and penetrate its most central activity: fundraising. These rituals are intimately bound up with civil Judaism's key myths, especially the myth of "Holocaust to rebirth." The ceremonial aspects of fundraising have long been noted: the dinners with their honorees, the plaques and rollcalls, the trips to Israel to meet prominent leaders. In the context of civil Judaism, these are not merely pseudo-religious performances; they are the most visible elements of a ritual system which is both institutionally functional and personally transformative for the activists of the Jewish polity.

The impact of the rituals of the civil religion lies in their power to reflect and foster a particular experience of Jewishness which is consonant with civil Judaism's fundamental worldview and ethos. This experience can be characterized in the terminology of the anthropologist Victor Turner as one of "anti-structure" and "communitas." Turner characterizes social life as a dialectical process in which social structure—the differentiated pattern of roles, statuses, and accompanying norms of behavior within which social interaction customarily takes place—is periodically disrupted by periods of anti-structure, when this pattern is suspended or dissolved. The suspension may take place factually—i.e., norms may actually be temporarily dissolved—or it may take place symbolically—i.e., through ritual enactments in which the disruption of social structure is depicted, albeit never actually consummated.[52]

In Turner's view this suspension or dissolution is important because it is only by exposing the ultimate contingency of all differentiated social structures that humans can experience social life in its ontologically prior form, as a direct, intense, relatively undifferentiated mode of human interaction which he terms "communitas." Communitas is an especially intense form of group solidarity which carries with it a conviction of shared destiny. Such an experience can arise spontaneously—particularly when the group shares a common exposure to threat or danger, when it faces a great historical challenge, or when it finds itself standing outside normal social structural categories—at the margins of society, as liminals caught betwixt and between stable categories, or as a group relegated to the very bottom of the social hierarchy as slaves or virtual subhumans. But the achievement of communitas can also become an explicit goal of religious or political activity, either directly or through the deliberate cultivation of feelings of marginality, liminality, or inferiority. The experience of communitas is both an end in its own right and a source of values which can then be brought back into the social structural sphere as well. In this fashion, the intense feelings of unity and interdependence which are achieved in moments of communitas become ethical norms and social ideals for daily behavior.[53]

Anti-structure and communitas are social experiences which, according to Turner, are almost universally interpreted and transmitted in a religious context.[54] Religious myths and rituals provide the matrix within which communitas is preserved and pursued. For civil Judaism, myths and rituals of anti-structure and communitas provide the essential vehicles for communicating its characteristic ethos and worldview—perceptions and prescriptions which themselves emphasize precisely those experiences of solidarity, endangerment, and historic challenge which Turner identifies. For American Jews, the historical events of the Holocaust and the establishment of the State of Israel have unquestionably been the most powerful sources of anti-structural experience in this century. The myths and rituals of civil Judaism are devoted to keeping these experiences and the commitment to Jewish solidarity and activism which they produce alive. Even the civil religious understanding of the American Jewish experience, with its cultivation of that measure of ambivalence necessary to sustain an ethos of both integration and group continuity, supports this religious thrust. From the perspective of civil

Judaism, American Jews are inevitable liminals and marginals, "in all but the legal sense citizens of two worlds" (the United States and Israel).[55] American Jews have two homelands and two promised lands; they are of the new Israel and the old Israel at once. The sense of being what Neusner terms "strangers at home" is vital to maintaining the delicate balance of in-group solidarity and universal ethical activism which the civil Jewish ethos demands.

Civil Judaism's embrace of traditional rituals—usually in forms which are designed to minimize the potential for alienating either traditionalists or modernists—helps to foster the sense of identification over time and space which makes its communitas a more encompassing one. But it is the rituals which are largely of its own devising—missions to Israel, retreats, major meetings and conferences—which form the heart of its transformative arsenal.

Probably the single most effective ritual of the civil religion is the "mission" (the very name carries with it, of course, multiple religious and ethical connotations). This is a carefully orchestrated group trip to Israel (and at times to other countries) which is designed to increase the participants' knowledge, concern, and commitment, and hence the size of his/her contribution to the federation/UJA campaign as well. Select groups of leaders began making such visits—"study missions" as they were originally referred to—in the immediate post-World War II period. But the size, number, and civil religious significance of these missions began to grow dramatically in the 1960s when UJA's Young Leadership became intensely involved in the missions program. These young leaders perfected the type of mission which most directly and unambiguously captures the message which the missions program as a whole is designed to deliver. The mission was called "From Holocaust to Rebirth," and it took young Jews on the journey which the death camp survivors made from the hell of Auschwitz to the promise of new life in Israel. The emotional impact of such a mission proved, not surprisingly, to be enormous. Here, normal successful American Jews were being made to feel as helpless as the victims of Nazi murder and as powerful (albeit besieged) as the Israeli army officers from whom they received private briefings. Having personally experienced the mythic journey of the Jewish people in our time, how could they fail to identify, how could they fail to respond?

Today, missions to Israel have become a staple of federation-UJA fundraising and leadership development. Dozens of missions from individual communities or organized nationally take place each year involving thousands of participants. Some involve whirlwind trips at a dizzying pace; some include journeys to see other oppressed or impoverished Jewish communities which are sustained by funds raised by the federations and UJA. Some missions have become enormous pilgrimages, with thousands of Americans arriving in a span of a few hours, spreading out over the length and breadth of the land in busloads, and gathering for massive demonstrations of solidarity with Israel, sometimes accompanied by the signing of pledges and proclamations. The names of these super-missions are revealing as well: "This Year in Jerusalem," "Koach" (Strength), "Hashiveinu" (Return Us)—all with mythic overtones. Virtually all missions incorporate a few key elements: a visit to Yad Vashem (the Holocaust museum); a trip to a border settlement, where the ongoing threat to Israel's security is palpable; a briefing by a high government or army official to provide a sense of intimate insidership; a climb up Masada, symbol of Jewish heroism and the modern Israeli determination never to be driven from the land again; a visit to an immigrant absorption center, an impoverished neighborhood, or a development town—both to see Israel's problems and how American contributions are helping. Finally, there is the solicitation—the personal request for an enhanced commitment—which all participants undergo, either singly or in a group.

Missions work. They transform mildly supportive individuals into dedicated contributors and activists, and committed workers into driven leaders. Like all good rituals they are artfully manipulative, playing with the emotions, overwhelming mind and body with a flow of sensations. But they work primarily because they are enormously effective mediators of the fundamental religious myth and experience of civil Judaism. Critics contend that missions present a distorted picture of Israel, and in one sense that it is probably correct. Yet, they are brilliantly successful in presenting the Israel of civil Jewish mythology, in all its confused profusion of meanings: the Israel of strength, and Israel threatened; the bold, new, technologically sophisticated Israel, and the Israel of ancient Jewish tradition; the Israel which is exotic, and the Israel which is "home."

The American Jews who go on a mission are experiencing a ritual of anti-structure and communitas. Removed from their familiar surroundings, they are thrown together on a bus in enforced solidarity. They are enveloped in the story of a nation built on the ashes of six million dead, rising like a phoenix, struggling at once just to stay alive and to be a beacon of hope for the world. And they are told what they must do once they return to their "real world" to maintain the unity they have come to feel and to continue to share in the destiny they have glimpsed unfolding. It is a ritual of unique power, a rite of passage which leaves few untransformed.[56]

No other ritual of the fundraising campaign is as effective or as dramatic in its civil religious message as the mission. But the entire process of the campaign—with its banquets and speakers, card calling and phonathons—has become, as noted above, a ritual in its own right. The elements of that ritual have often been criticized and satirized for their shallowness and ostentatiousness on the one hand and their over-heated rhetoric and portentousness on the other.[57] Despite this, the ritual of campaign has been a singularly effective instrument for mobilizing Jews and producing a sense of communal solidarity. For many participants the ritual dimensions of the activity have helped it become something even more: a deeply felt means of Jewish identification and self-expression. As Eugene Borowitz has put it: "The experience of campaign leadership has affected American Jews so deeply because, in the midst of their otherwise highly secular existence, it has brought them a 'rumor of angels.' "[58] At its best, the fundraising campaign, like the mission to Israel, can be a profoundly meaningful step beyond the boundaries of daily concerns into a realm of mythic import. "The journey we have been taking in our campaigns, physically and spiritually, has been one from remembrance to renewal."[59] The ritual of campaign helps to mark off and highlight that spiritual and symbolic journey. Divorced from this civil religious meaning, the ceremonies themselves indeed often appear to be gratuitous showmanship, but as civil Jewish ritual they are indispensable and effective.

Civil religious ritual has centered around the fundraising campaign, but its essential structure and themes have been transported to other settings as well. In recent years, for example, the organizations of the polity have made increasing use of the "retreat" as a format for leadership development and other institutional business which requires an intensive and concentrated period of group work. Like the mission, the retreat is intended to be an organizationally functional activity. Its effect, however, ofter transcends this intent. The retreat too becomes for many a "religious experience." Regardless of its specific content, the retreat acquires much of its power from its ritualized structure, not very different from that of the mission: removal of the participants from their everyday reality; communalized activities, typically with an emphasis on broad participation; the building of a sense of fellowship; achievement of insight and/or renewed commitment; reentry into the world with a desire to change it.

This implicit structural message is made explicit expecially in the many retreats sponsored by federations and the UJA which are designed to strengthen new leadership. Here, the ritual forms of the civil religion are often blended with those of traditional Judaism to create a highly effective socializing and mobilizing experience. Such retreats are generally held over a weekend, sometimes involving individuals and couples and sometimes whole families. The Sabbath serves as the initial focal point, with religious services of some sort, a festive meal, singing and dancing. For some participants the Shabbat experience itself involves an immersion in a Jewish world which they do not normally experience. A retreat Sabbath will likely not be observed in a fully traditional fashion: services may be abridged or "creative," various prohibitions may not be observed. But the atmosphere of Shabbat is ideal to create the intermingled feelings of community, nostalgia, and "specialness" which produce a sense of identification with the Jewish purposes of the polity enterprise. The emotional commitment is reinforcd through the content sessions of the retreat—lectures from a "scholar-in-residence" on Jewish themes, updates and discussions of critical issues affecting the community, experiential explorations of Jewish identity and values. Retreats are designed to achieve a mix of serious Jewish activity, Jewish fun (singing and dancing), and general recreation (the participants do, after all, enjoy swimming, softball, and movies). The overall effect of a typical retreat weekend is often summarized in the word "renewal." The participants emerge with "their Jewish batteries recharged," feeling more like a Jewish community, more prepared to take on the responsibilities of communal activism.

As a ritual performance, the retreat embodies a powerful civil Jewish message: To be a better and more fulfilled Jew one must—at least periodically—escape from the daily routine and carve out a time and space where Jewish fellowship, study, and renewal of purpose can take place. Then one must reenter the world and try to insinuate these values into that reality. The retreat provides a setting where Jewish communitas can be realized, where the norms of daily life (which often mitigate against uninhibited expression of Jewishness) can be suspended and replaced by Jewish ones. Designed properly, such a retreat can be, and has often become, an important, life-transforming experience for participants. Two Sabbaths observed by all Israel would, according to a Jewish saying, bring redemption. One Sabbath spent at a retreat can provide a glimpse of a realm of Jewish living in which both Jewish distinctiveness and solidarity are self-evidently manifest. In the afterglow of such an experience, the worldview and ethos of civil Judaism seem themselves more "right" and more compelling.

The discovery and development of the weekend retreat as an effective ritual of the civil religion has been paralleled by a growing awareness among polity leaders that other occasions too, where large numbers of polity activists come together, have taken on a ritual character. Undoubtedly the best example of this is the transformation of the General Assembly of the Council of Jewish Federations into a major civil religious ceremony in its own right. Again, we speak here not of some of the more obvious, but not necessarily religious, rituals of speechmaking and awards, but of the impact which the General Assembly has come to have as a Jewish experience. That impact is compounded out of a number of elements, including, but hardly limited to, the ceremony which surrounds its formal proceedings.

One critical element is simply the number and variety of the participants. The General Assembly has become one of the largest regular Jewish gatherings outside the State of Israel, bringing together approximately three thousand Jews from throughout North America and the world. At times it appears that "everyone who is anyone" in the Jewish world is present, and, indeed, virtually every Jewish organization of any significance is represented among the participants. Coupled with the comprehensive agenda of formal sessions dealing with nearly every issue in Jewish life, and the endless rounds of meetings, consultations, and receptions, the crowd of participants produces the impression that one is at the center of a vast and important Jewish world. Jewish community is palpable—and exciting.

A second element which has helped to transform the General Assembly into an important ritual occasion is the intensified Jewish atmosphere which has pervaded it in recent years.[60] The appropriation of traditional and contemporary Jewish ritual forms by the civil religion is clearly evidenced at the General Assembly. Shabbat again serves as a focal point, with services, dinners with singing and dancing, study sessions, a *havdalah* ceremony marking its conclusion, and other special programs. But the overall tone as well has become increasingly infused with elements of traditional Judaism: only kosher food is served at official functions; meals are preceded by the traditional *motzi* (blessing over food) and end with a version of the *birkat hamazon* (grace after meals); services are held daily.

It is important to emphasize that as in most other cases where elements of traditional Jewish practice have been incorporated within the framework of the civil religion, the absorption has been by and large unreflective, certainly at a theological level. Civil Judaism finds in traditional Jewish forms suitable media for expressing its identification with the tradition and respect for its values. It incorporates traditional norms to the extent that these are socially and religiously functional within the context of its own expressed purposes. Shabbat observance at the General Assembly is, for example, an effective way of experiencing and demonstrating the Jewish character of the enterprise in which the participants are engaged. It enhances the sense of fellowship and specialness, and indicates a sensitivity to and appreciation of the rhythms of Jewish living. But the civil religion makes no effort to enforce Shabbat as a norm, and the Shabbat atmosphere at a General Assembly is far from that which one would find in a traditional Jewish environment.

The final element which gives the General Assembly a religious dimension is the character of the agenda itself. Here, as we stated above, the major issues of Jewish life are addressed. Here the speeches are given, the resolutions passed, which demonstrate what the civil religion is about. Here the priests and prophets of civil Judaism carry out their offices before the assembled congregation of Israel. Thus, one cannot help leaving a General Assembly with a sense that one has been part of an event of profound importance and meaning, a "holy convocation" with the potential to transform the Jewish world. One comes to and departs from a General Assembly almost like a pilgrim on a journey to Jerusalem, with a sense of exaltation at having confronted the entire meaning of the Jewish experience in dramatically condensed form.[61]

This experience of the General Assembly as ritual performance and as a microcosm of the meaning of Jewishness has been noted repeatedly by speakers at the assembly itself. It is an occasion for "a *Heshbon Hanefesh*—a soul-searching of truly giant proportions."[62] It is an event which "fortifie[s] our confidence that our mission in behalf of Jewish continuity draws upon inner resources of Jewish history and experience which have been indelibly affected by the travails of our generation."[63] Above all, the General Assembly has become a place for achieving and renewing the sense of communitas: "We felt more and more that we were 'mishpochah'—one family—we talked together, we prayed together, we wept together, we danced together—all as we rededicated ourselves to serve the purposes for which our community organizations had been established."[64]

The General Assembly is thus both an event and a symbol, a means of effecting the purposes of the polity and of rediscovering the religous sensibility which lies behind those purposes. Reflecting on the 1977 General Assembly, Sidney Vincent put its meaning in these terms:

> I think our ultimate strength is precisely in these warm and intimate relationships achieved while we face sober and practical and grim challenges. That combination of warmth and toughness has made our communities into an amalgam of the personal and the organizational—a unique instrument forged on this American soil combining the Jewish heritage of personal responsibility for each other with the effectiveness and efficiency of American know-how. . . . [W]hen we operate at our best in our community work, we do more than fundraising and budgeting and planning. We are also creating our own version of *havurah* (communion), not in structure, but in spirit.
>
> I leave Dallas feeling that I have spent five days with my extended family, to whom I am bound by ties of shared anxieties and shared concern and shared activity and shared love, not only for the Jewish people as a whole, but for very precious and very individual Jewish people.[65]

Without this sense of communitas, the Jewish polity could not make the demands that it does of American Jews. And without the rituals of a General Assembly, a retreat, or a fundraising campaign, communitas itself could not be so powerfully achieved.

Civil Judaism has rarely set out to create religious rituals. Neither has it had any program for consciously revaluating traditional rituals. Where it has self-consciously sought to develop sancta, these have focused almost exclusively on the two major symbols of its dominant myth: the Holocaust and the State of Israel. Federations have played a major role in many communities in establishing Holocaust memorials and promoting Holocaust Day observances.[66] Polity organizations have also been prime movers in stimulating celebration of Israel Independence Day through parades, festivals, and public ceremonies. In neither of these areas, however, has a standardized ritual form been created; nor are these events marked exclusively by polity institutions.[67] Indeed, in keeping with the encompassing nature of civil religion, efforts are often made to involve the broadest possible range of communal organizations, including the synagogues, in these celebrations and observances.

It is as unlikely that civil Judaism will develop a full-fledged ritual system as it is that it will develop an explicit theology. The emphasis of civil religion is on the public sphere; it has little interest in or capacity for illuminating and sacralizing the private moments of life. It is content, by and large, to let traditional Judaism speak to these with whatever power and through whatever ritual and theology it can muster. Nevertheless, in seeking to invest the public and historical life of the Jewish people with meaning, civil Judaism has created a set of rituals which link its mythic vision of Jewish solidarity and distinctiveness to the felt experiences of anti-structural suspension of the everyday and of encompassing communitas. They thereby help to shape and sustain the civil religion's definition of what it means to be an American Jew: a member of a group irrevocably bound together by a common and exceptional fate and seeking to create of that a shared destiny

## The Religion of Destiny

American civil Judaism is a religion in the process of self-discovery. For its adherents, its import and relevance has been so self-evident that there has been little reason to seek underlying themes or an encompassing religious intentionality in its tenets. We have tried to suggest in the preceding three chapters, however, that there is a consistent structure and dynamic embedded in the worldview and ethos, the myths and rituals of the civil religion.

The structure is built out of classic polarities—between Jew and non-Jew, survival and disappearance, community and individual, exceptionalism and normality, renewal and destruction, life and death. The dynamic is one of passage—from passivity to activity, from victim to maker of history, from death-witness to life-giver. Civil Judaism is a religion of tensions recognized, confronted, held in the balance, and thereby transcended.

The polarities through which the civil religion defines the Jewish condition in the modern world are by no means unique or original to it. They are the stuff of traditional Judaism's worldview as well. They are, in a sense, eternal polarities, and accepted as such. The Jew, civil Judaism affirms, will always find himself poised between survival and disappearance, the command to be exceptional (holy) and the pull of normality (the profane), between life and death. This is the core of civil Judaism's legitimate claim to the mantle of Jewish continuity. The civil religion preserves not merely Jewish social values, but the fundamental antinomies, the fundamental demand for choice, of the Jewish tradition.

Yet, civil Judaism also recognizes a profound break with the classical past of the Jewish people. Its dynamic seeks a new way of appropriating these polarities, of confronting and transcending them. Civil Judaism proclaims a new (or renewed) era of Jewish activism. It chooses to face the world with the proclamation that Jews will no longer be content to cultivate their inner life; they seek the power to control their historical destiny as well. No longer will they wait for the world to recognize the value of Torah; rather they will bring these values to the world, confident of their efficacy in the arena of social change.

For American Jews this combination of a worldview which accepts the Jewish condition as inevitably ridden with tensions and an ethos which prescribes the active, creative appropriation of that condition is especially compelling. The civil religion tells them that their own ambivalence is part of their essential Jewishness, and that an activism which does not shrink from either pole—which affirms both their Jewishness and their Americanness fully and unhesitatingly—is precisely the response which can make of that ambilvalence a creative rather than an immobilizing force. There is, perhaps, more than a little sleight of hand in this assertion. But, as Cliford Geertz reminds us, this meshing of ethos and worldview so that each seems to render the other supportable and inevitable is of the very essence of religion.[68] Civil Judaism achieves this by demanding that Jews preserve their awareness of the awesome dualities they face. But it promises them as well that they now can face these tensions not as helpless victims but as shapers of their own destiny.

To give Jews the strength they need for the confrontation and the choice, the civil religion calls on the dynamic of anti-structural renewal which Turner finds at the heart of so much religious ritual. By experiencing their own marginality, by remembering that not long ago and perhaps again their lives counted for nothing, by allowing themselves to be transported out of their everyday reality, civil Judaism's adherents are reformed into communitas. Their shared destiny becomes manifest, and so too the source of their social commitment. Civil Judaism confronts American Jews with the abnormality of their condition, and challenges them to accept this as their "normality." The experienced polarities of Jewish existence are themselves generative of solidarity and ethical activism.

This, then, is the answer which American Jewish civil religion proposes for the modern Jewish quest. American Jews can keep faith with the past, but only by replacing its passivity with activism. They can preserve Judaism and its values, but only by taking these into the arena of history. They can be part of the unfolding of the destiny of the Jewish people, but only by placing that destiny in their own hands. They can be a *kehillah kedoshah*—a holy community—but only by blending their Jewish impulses with their American know-how.

Civil Judaism, like other forms of modern Jewish ideology, offers a vision of continuity through change. Its unique power rests in the dramatic promise it offers as well: that the Jewish people can once again be at the cutting edge of history, that the work of sustaining a Jewish polity is work of transcendent significance. The history of the Jewish people and of American Jews in the twentieth century has seemed to confirm this promise. And thereby, the religious worldview and ethos of civil Judaism have come to define the meaning of Jewishness itself for much of American Jewry.

# VI

# TOWARD A DIALOGUE OF JUDAISMS

### Civil Judaism: The Return to History and Polity

Two thousand years ago, during the period of the Second Commonwealth, two major camps—the Pharisees and the Sadducees—contested for primacy in defining the character of Judaism as a religious system. From the sources available to us, it is difficult to reconstruct with certainty the details of each's philosophy of Judaism and of the struggle they waged with one another.[1] Nevertheless, we can infer that one element of that struggle was over the question of where the primary locus of meaning in Jewish life was to lie.

The Sadducees, following the precedent of the biblical period, placed primary emphasis, it would appear, on the public institutions of the Jewish people and religion—the Temple, the priesthood, the political structures of the state. Judaism's meaning and message were addressed to and embodied in the conduct and fate of these institutions. The Pharisees, while acknowledging the importance of this public realm, focused their teaching on another. They emphasized the personalization of Judaism, the construction of a system of norms of holiness—and a promise of salvation—addressed not only to the collective, but to the individual as well. Their Judaism centered not around the Temple, but around the table, where all could eat like priests, and the school, where their dual Torah—the written and the oral—was taught.[2]

The Pharisees and Sadducees had much in common. They shared the biblical text and the history, vocabulary, and symbols which it enshrines. They recognized themselves as part of a single people and community. But, if our sources are to be believed, they also differed on some of the fundamental questions which religion, as a life-shaping worldview and ethos, must address. The contest between the Pharisees and the Sadducees was in large measure decided by a third party: Rome, which in destroying the Temple and defeating Jewish thrusts for national independence, effectively undermined the institutional base for Sadducean Judaism. Only the Pharisees were equipped to survive this historic catastrophe. Out of their response to the crisis of the Temple's destruction emerged the Judaism which was to be normative for the succeeding seventeen centuries. It was a Judaism of study and self-discipline, of faithfulness to the Torah and its laws—and of the deferral of hope for a national revival until God himself was ready to bring the messianic consummation in the end of days.

For nearly two millennia, therefore, the essential structure of Judaism reflected the Pharisaic-rabbinic triumph. The sense of Jewish nationhood was preserved, but the religion of the Jew was not that of actors on the stage of history, but of a pious community standing as much as possible apart from the clamor of great events. The Jew met God in the rhythms of daily life and the observance of his law. He prayed daily for the redemption of Israel, the coming of the Messiah, but he did not act in history to hasten that end.

Nevertheless, the example of the Second Commonwealth period (and of the biblical period before it) stood as a demonstration that Judaism need not only be defined in these terms. The Judaism which we have imagined as "Sadducean" remained as a strand in the Jewish religious consciousness, one which might well reemerge when the conditions which had doomed it no longer obtained. With the new era ushered in by the Emancipation and the Enlightenment, those conditions in fact began to change. Jews no longer saw themselves as bound to an eternal present. They had returned to history, to the arena of public events, and the challenge to Judaism was to validate this reentry in Jewish terms, or to lose its hold on those Jews who had opted for time over eternity.

What has emerged among an important segment of modern Jewry in response to this challenge is in fact a new religious sensibility, one which Daniel Elazar has termed "neo-Sadducean Judaism." The "new Sadducees," according to Elazar, are "Jews who seek to be Jewish through identification with the Jewish people as a corporate entity, its history, culture and tradition, but without necessarily accepting the authoritative character of *halacha* or the centrality of *halacha* in defining their Jewishness."[3] Neo-Sadducean Judaism places at the center of its world not Torah, but the Jewish people, and makes the maintenance and expression of Jewish peoplehood its primary religious obligation.

What Elazar calls neo-Sadducean Judaism represents a tendency and an approach, not a fully institutionalized religious system. There is no explicitly "neo-Sadducean" religious movement, camp or party in the contemporary Jewish world. All of modern Judaism, as we argued in chapter 1, has been profoundly affected by the Jewish return into history and the reemergence of Jewish peoplehood and polity as focal points for identification and Jewish self-expression. Further, if fidelity to *halakhah* serves as a defining hallmark of the Pharisaic-rabbinic tradition, then all of Reform Judaism (and many Conservative Jews) may be said to have left that camp, without thereby becoming, and certainly without viewing themselves as, "neo-Sadducean."

Nevertheless, Elazar's conceptualization draws attention to the fact that what we have termed American civil Judaism expresses a characteristic religious sensibility (as does the Israeli civil religion described by Liebman and Don-Yehiya) different from that of the classical Pharisaic-rabbinic tradition. American Jewish civil religion departs from the Pharisaic-rabbinic mode not only in its refusal to embrace *halakhah* as a binding norm, but by explicitly shifting the primary locus of Jewish meaning back into the public realm. Civil Judaism is not essentially a Judaism of the home, the synagogue, and the school (though, as we have seen, it has come to value these increasingly in recent years). It is a Judaism of the historical-political arena, of an elaborated polity and of public activism. And, though it has no Temple, it does once again have a Jewish commonwealth to serve as its focal symbol.

There is more to civil Judaism than this "neo-Sadducean" affirmation. Indeed, as noted above, it is doubtful that most of those who embrace the civil religion would think to identify themselves with such a label. (The vast majority continue to identify with one or another of the denominational movements.) Yet, regardless of whether one accepts his specific designation as historically valid, Elazar's central claim merits elaboration: The evolution of Jewish civil religions in the modern era must be explored not as a Judaic aberration or as a purely political phenomenon, but as part of the reopening of an alternative pathway into Jewish religious life for the modern Jew.

The central question we must ask is where this pathway is likely to lead. Elazar suggests that with four-fifths of world Jewry living outside the traditional Pharisaic-rabbinic framework (in America the proportion would be at least as high), the further development of neo-Sadducean Judaism is inevitable. The question, he asserts, is what the content of that Judaism will be.[4] If the "dialogue of Judaisms" broken off centuries ago is to resume in a new form in our day, the elaboration of "neo-Sadducean" Judaism will be a necessity. In America today, civil Judaism is the primary locus of such a "neo-Sadducean" faith. Its tenets and its symbols can serve as the kernals of a more fully developed and articulated religious meaning system which could take its place in a modern Judaic dialogue. If this is to occur, however, civil Judaism must be recognized as the bearer of a serious religious message. Its presuppositions and implications must be spelled out, examined, and argued, much as those of Reform, Conservatism, Orthodoxy, and Reconstructionism are today.

Some students of American Jewish life have expressed doubt that what we have called "civil Judaism" could be developed in this fashion. They regard the belief system we have described as essentially a "lowest common denominator" faith, i.e., an inoffensive set of assertions commanding consensual support among Jews of various denominational persuasions, but lacking a theological perspective in its own right which could be systematically and self-consciously elaborated. As we have acknowledged, there is some validity to this point of view. Nevertheless, it underestimates the distinctiveness of the religious sensibility underlying civil Judaism and the historic significance of its emergence to prominence in the consciousness of the modern Jew. The "neo-Sadducean"/"civil Jewish" sensibility has, in addition, deep roots within the Judaic tradition itself. The elaboration of this faith stance may not necessarily come out of the civil religious institutional context. But civil Judaism provides the popular base from which a more theologically articulate modern "neo-Sadducean" Judaism could emerge.

For the institutions of the Jewish polity, undertaking such a process of theological elaboration would indeed be difficult, if not impossible. The theological and philosophical reticence of civil Judaism on fundamental issues of belief and obligation reflects not only its functional role, but the activist, non-reflective ethos of the polity. We should not expect federation or UJA leaders, even the more thoughtful among them, to embrace the theological endeavor. Yet, there are other institutions —primarily the synagogue and the rabbinate—which might take up the task of elaborating the "neo-Sadducean" religious stance. Precisely these institutions, however, have historically been the sponsors and interpreters of the Pharisaic-rabbinic tradition. Thus, whether a dialogue of Judaisms eventually develops depends as well on how they respond to the implicit challenge and opportunity which the emergence of a "neo-Sadducean" religious sensibility offers. The relationship between civil and "church" religion has, as we noted in chapter 1, often been ambiguous and even ambivalent. Can the American synagogue absorb and refine the ideological thrust which civil Judaism represents? Will it seek to? Should it? Or, will the synagogue set the stage for a dialogue in a different fashion: by defining itself and its message over against civil Judaism, by—in effect—choosing to renew the Pharisaic challenge to Sadducean religiosity?

The question of the religious fate and potential of civil Judaism forms, we believe, the appropriate conclusion for this book. The future of the civil religion as an integrating and mobilizing ideology for American Jewry seems relatively secure. It continues to speak effectively to and for the Jewish polity and the bulk of its activists as they seek to define the bases and nature of their Jewish commitment. No other ideological formulation has emerged to challenge seriously its hold on these activists, or the substantial number of American Jews who find its tenets and symbols expressive of their own Jewish worldview and values. If it is not a universal faith, if it does not unify *all* American Jews as a moral community, it certainly is, and is likely to remain, the core of as much commonality of belief and behavior as American Jews are capable of attaining. Civil Judaism remains dynamic and evolving. It has not lost its capacity to stimulate prophetic reassessment of the adequacy of the polity's performance in the fulfillment of its mission,[5] as well as to provide the symbols and ceremonies for collective reaffirmation and celebration of that mission.

Still, this assessment of the civil religion as fundamentally healthy and effective does not go far enough. We are not, to be sure, in a position to assess whether civil Judaism is true or false in any absolute sense. Neither, however, can we be satisfied merely to demonstrate its functional significance for American Jewry. Between the questions of contemporary vitality and ultimate truth lies the question on which we wish to focus: the role civil Judaism may play in the modern development of Judaism as a religion. We have identified two central issues which must be addressed in this context: (1) the response of the traditional religious institutions of the Jewish community to the emergence and consolidation of this "neo-Sadducean" Jewish ideology; and (2) the potential for elaboration of civil Judaism itself into a more encompassing philosophy of Jewish existence. Whether civil Judaism will become a footnote in Jewish religious history or an important chapter in its modern development will likely be determined by how these two issues—one institutional and the other intellectual—are resolved (or not resolved) over the next few decades.

## Civil Judaism and the Synagogue

The modernization of Judaism beginning at the end of the eighteenth century effected major transformations in the roles of two of the primary institutions of Pharisaic Judaism: the synagogue and the rabbinate. Initially, modernization brought enhanced prominence and significance, largely by undermining the communal structure and lay leadership of the kehillah. The synagogue and the rabbinate assumed a position of primacy in Jewish religious life which was, until recent decades, unshaken, if not unchallenged. As late as the 1950s, observers of American Jewish life were celebrating a new wave of institutional growth marked by the building boom of suburban synagogues. As Judaism took its place as one of America's three great religious traditions in Will Herberg's "triple melting pot,"[6] there was a good reason to believe that the synagogue and rabbinate were poised on the brink of a new era of institutional expansion and domination.

Yet, the period after World War II and especially since 1967 has been notable for the ascendance not of the synagogue, but of the federation and the institutional network which we have called the American Jewish polity. This is not to say that synagogues and the rabbinate have been displaced entirely from their positions of importance in the matrix of American Jewish institutions and leadership. The synagogue remains the place where most Jews gather to give ritual and symbolic expression to their Jewishness, to educate their children, and to find a Jewish context in which to share the joys and cope with the sorrows of human existence. But the synagogue is no longer the exclusive venue for any of these activities, and the rabbi is no longer the unquestioned leader of the Jewish community. That community has become increasingly bimodal, built around two institutional complexes which view one another sympathetically in theory, but often warily in practice. And of the two, the federation and its associated agencies today represent, in the eyes of many, the more dynamic force in Jewish communal life.

There is no little irony in these developments. Our own analysis argues that the institutional ascendance of the federation has been marked and aided by the decisive defeat of Jewish secularism as an ideological basis for contemporary Jewish life. The synagogue, which held its own and eventually triumphed against secularist and/or assimilationist challengers for institutional primacy—*landsmanshaften*, trade unions, Y's and settlement houses—has proven unable to retain clear primacy precisely at a time when most active American Jews have endorsed the preservation of the religious tradition as a major communal goal.

Behind the tenuous relations of federation and synagogue lies, therefore, not merely an institutional encounter, but a religious ideological one, that of one form of Judaism—the "neo-Sadducean" civil religion—with another. The contemporary federation poses quite a different challenge to the synagogue than that posed by the secularist institutional rivals (including the federations) of another era. The fact that the fundamental tenets of civil Judaism are neither radical nor unfamiliar to the synagogue world heightens its appeal, even, and perhaps especially, for those Jews who are comfortable in the synagogue and committed to its endurance. The challenge of civil Judaism to the synagogue lies not in its irreligiosity (for it is not irreligious), but rather, as we have suggested, in the *type* of religion it is. Civil Judaism legitimates a way of being Jewish and a program of Jewish activity within which the role of the synagogue and the rabbinate—the life of study, prayer, and ritual observance—are no longer primary. What the synagogue does and stands for is important, but not central. Alongside its work and teaching there are other *mitzvot* equally sacred, other rituals equally powerful, other lessons equally vital for the Jew. The federation campaign lends its own rhythm to the Jewish year. Federation-sponsored events provide occasions for religious exaltation and inspiration which rival or surpass what is available in the synagogue. Service on federation or agency boards, attending to the urgent needs of the Jewish people, takes on the character of a sacred calling. "We Are One" becomes a more immediate and compelling watchword of the faith than *"Hashem echad"* ("the Lord is One").

## Strategies of Response: Integration

How the synagogue can and should respond to this civil Jewish challenge is not self-evident. At least five possible strategies of response can be identified, each with different implications not only for the institutional relations of synagogue and federation, but for the developmental prospects of "neo-Sadducean" Judaism as well.

The first of these strategies might be termed *integration*. Civil Judaism is, after all, not the enemy of the synagogue. It reserves for the synagogue an important role as a transmitter of Jewish identity and as a place for Jewish association and religious self-expression. What is more, civil Jewish ideology is widely endorsed by large numbers of synagogue affiliated Jews, including rabbis. Based on this mutual appreciation, one can envision the synagogue becoming in effect a cosponsor of the civil religion, incorporating its symbols and values into its own teaching and worship, and making them central to its own mission and message. So-called "neo-Sadducean" themes would be explicitly rewoven into the fabric of conventional Judaism, perhaps even pushing more traditional themes to the side.

The integrationist approach is already reflected in much of American synagogue life. Precisely because all forms of Judaism have been affected by the historical upheaval which has brought the religious sensibility of civil Judaism to the fore in the modern world, this type of response is less a matter of accommodation to an outside force than of reinterpretation of the synagogue's own ideological heritage. The values which civil Judaism proclaims can be easily and authentically voiced by the synagogue as well—so much so that their implication in an alternative meaning system may be entirely submerged or forgotten.

The practical ramifications of this strategy can be seen in a number of common phenomena: rabbis whose sermons deal largely with current issues of community concern; synagogue educational and youth programs which emphasize Israel and a heroic presentation of Jewish history; the incorporation of Holocaust remembrance and celebration of Israel's independence into the liturgical calendar. Many synagogues have gone even further: they sponsor federation/UJA campaign events, or participate in the national UJA Shabbat. Their rabbis may be active on the local federation board, or the national UJA Rabbinic Cabinet (activities which may also add to their prestige).

Whether unconsciously or as a deliberate strategy, this integrationist approach attempts to make a virtue of necessity. They synagogue incorporates and celebrates the symbols and values which have proven so powerful when utilized by federations, and weds them to its own programmatic strengths. In so doing, it promises to restore the synagogue to a position of prominence, if not primacy, as the repository and transmitter of those ideals which matter most deeply to American Jews.

The integration of civil Judaism into the synagogue does not require that the synagogue give up its traditional rite of passage and associational functions. Indeed, these are precisely the domains of synagogue activity most significant to civil Judaism, with its emphasis on communality and continuity. Because these activities—bar/bat mitzvahs, high holy day services—are so often devoid of genuine spiritual significance for the participants, highlighting civil Jewish ideological dimensions in their performance might even enhance their overall Jewish import.[7]

Nevertheless, the integrationist strategy raises serious questions on two levels: First, it is not clear whether the synagogue can indeed prosper as a civil religious institution. The accommodations already made have not substantially altered either its image or the expectations placed upon it in the Jewish community. It is doubtful whether the synagogue could ever displace the federation as the focal point for expressing support for Israel or concern for the welfare of other Jews. As the primary transmitter of Jewish tradition, the synagogue may indeed remain preeminent, but this only leads back to the question of how the content of that tradition shall be defined—i.e., what value system will dominate the synagogue's teaching and preaching.

It is at this second level that the potential danger in a strategy of integration becomes visible. At least in its present form (pending the question of how it might achieve theological elaboration), civil Judaism leaves vast realms of human concern unexplored. It is difficult to imagine that any synagogue could build its program entirely around the set of civil Jewish assertions, since they are deliberately vague with respect to critical issues of belief and behavior that have traditionally preoccupied the synagogue, the rabbinate, and the Judaism they have sponsored. A synagogue that would itself be little more than another vehicle for proclaiming the civil Jewish consensus would facilitate not a dialogue of Judaisms, but a shallow monologue. "Neo-Sadducean" Judaism without its Pharisaic-rabbinic counterpart might prove as spiritually unsatisfying to contemporary Jews as rabbinic Judaism without a "neo-Sadducean" sensibility did to many of their forebearers a century and a half ago.

## Supplementation

This caveat suggests a second strategy of response for the synagogue to civil Judaism: *supplementation.* Many synagogues and rabbis are prepared and even eager to accept civil Judaism as an important ideological framework for mobilizing Jewish communal energies on behalf of vital collective concerns. But they are also aware of civil Judaism's superficiality and narrowness as a system of Jewish belief and behavior. In this context the role of the synagogue can be conceptualized as one of providing what the institutional loci of civil Judaism either cannot or will not: intimacy of Jewish contact; a multihued Jewish aesthetic and cultural experience; sustained reflection upon and study of the texts which are the well-springs of Jewish ethical and spiritual values. In adopting these as its institutional goals, the synagogue would complement the

strengths of civil Judaism with its unique ethos and style. It would provide an antidote to a Judaism of unrelieved activism, without denying
the significance of the public domain.

There are many civil Jewish activists who seek precisely this resource
in the synagogue and rabbinate. They look to the synagogue to affirm
the values of Jewish communality and mutual support, but they also
want a deeper and more personalized Jewish experience. A synagogue
that celebrates Israel's Independence Day *and* offers the opportunity to
become part of a *havurah* (small fellowship group), a rabbi who can address him or herself to incidents of anti-Semitism *and* the subtleties of
the weekly Torah portion—these may be in the strongest position to appeal to civil Jewish enthusiasts who do not want or need another federation or Jewish community center under a different name.

Indeed, the challenge of civil Judaism to the synagogue may represent
less a desire to subordinate the latter's message than a call for the synagogue to do more effectively what it claims as its mission: defining and
transmitting Judaism's religious heritage. Like most civil religions, civil
Judaism does not seek a monopoly in the religious sphere.[8] There is,
from this standpoint, ample room for two distinctive but complementary "religious" institutions at the core of modern Jewish life. Each will
appreciate and support the other. Each will offer a unique setting
in which to absorb a holistic—public-and-private, collective-and-
individual—teaching that embraces both civil and "synagogue" Judaism.

## Independence

The strategies of integration and supplementation rest on the
assumption that civil Judaism is and will remain a force shaping the Jewish commitment of large segments of American Jewry. Each strategy
proposes to meet the civil Jewish believer where he or she is, although
they differ in their estimation of whether it is reaffirmation or supplementation and extension of the civil Jewish faith which they seek
from the synagogue and rabbinate.

This assumption is by no means unquestioned today. Rabbi Harold
Kushner, a prominent Conservative intellectual figure, has, for example, written of a profound shift in the sensibility of the Jewish community which challenges civil Judaism at its core:

> For two generations now, we have lived with a view of ourselves as a
> community which was rooted in peoplehood and found its underlying
> "mythology" in the Holocaust and the State of Israel, historical rather
> than theological or halakhic fundaments. I would venture to predict that
> that kind of Jewish self-perception has had its day, and is in the process
> of change. It worked well for two generations. . . . But the American
> spiritual temper is changing, and so is American Judaism.

What Kushner finds are Jews who "are asking questions about faith, about God, about moral values," who are preoccupied by inwardness and spiritual concerns.[9] His testimony is not unique. Several other perceptive observers of American Jewish life—notably Harold Schulweis[10] and Charles Liebman[11]—have pointed to a similar trend. We might cite as well the revitalization of American Orthodoxy and the related, though larger, phenomenon of the *ba'al teshuva* ("returner") movement —Jews who are moving or moving back toward traditional Jewish life-styles.[12] In a sense, one could speak of a neo-Pharisaic turning in American Jewish life, a restatement of the concerns and even a recreation of the institutions (the *havurah* being the most notable example)[13] which seem to have animated the Pharisees centuries ago in their rejection of Sadducean Judaism.

Thus, alongside the neo-Sadducean renewal represented by civil Judaism, the synagogue must contend with a new energy emerging from individuals operating within a very different ideological framework. This phenomenon makes conceivable a synagogue response to civil Judaism which is essentially a declaration of independence. Rather than emphasizing its compatibility with Jewish civil religion, the synagogue should, from this perspective, boldly deliver its own message, speaking once again of God, of Torah, of faith, of spirituality.

A refocusing of synagogue and rabbinic energies on "biography" rather than history, on the Jewish person and his/her spiritual needs rather than on the Jewish people and its collective fate, need not be tied to a total rejection of civil Judaism's concerns. There is, nevertheless, a growing feeling in some segments of the Jewish community that loyalty to Israel, communal responsibility, and opposition to anti-Semitism have been "oversold" as the prime motivators and ingredients of Jewish commitment. Many Jews are seeking in Judaism not a public cause, but a guidepost and rationale for their daily lives. Can Judaism provide a spiritual focus, a moral compass, a transcendental purpose in immediate and personal terms? Can it enrich their family lives, restore a sense of personal worth, help them cope with success and failure? These questions —though central to all religious meaning systems at some level, including civil religion—suggest an agenda for Jewish institutions and leadership very different from that which by and large preoccupies the Jewish polity today. By pursuing such an alternative agenda, by addressing itself to the individual and the family seeking spiritual succor and guidance, the synagogue can perhaps reestablish its primacy as the focal point for Jewish identification and self-definition. It is even conceivable that the federation and its neo-Sadducean Judaism will eventually fade into the background as Jews once again turn from history and politics to daily life and its rhythms as the arena of their self-fulfillment.

This vision of a reassertive neo-Pharisaism should be viewed with some caution. The empirical evidence for the transformation in American Jewish consciousness which Kushner and others describe is limited.

This does not mean that the change is illusory, only that its dimensions and depth are unknown. While some American Jews may indeed be manifesting a heightened concern with observance, spirituality, and theology, others, as we have suggested in previous chapters, are pursuing and broadening the civil Jewish agenda of public activity with equal enthusiasm. There is and undoubtedly will be a constituency for a synagogue and rabbinate which define themselves primarily in neo-Pharisaic terms. But it is not clear whether the supposed movement in this direction represents a major reorientation in the direction of American Jewish life, or a limited reaction among a relatively small segment of the Jewish populace.

More importantly, there is the question of whether a declaration of synagogue independence from the civil Jewish faith, should it be possible, would be healthy for Jewish life. Charles Liebman, who accepts the notion that there has been a turn away from the public arena by some American Jews and an embrace of an ethos of personal spirituality, suggests that this development might lead to an unwarranted and ill-advised abandonment of the authentic political-communal component of the Jewish tradition with which civil Judaism is identified.[14]

A clear demarcation between neo-Sadducean and neo-Pharisaic camps, while perhaps responsive to differing sensibilities in the Jewish populace, would isolate each from the corrective influence of the other. Indeed, the prospect of independence in any substantial sense is virtually inconceivable. One can hardly imagine rabbis ceasing to speak about the Holocaust and Israel, even if these are no longer the topics which most energize their constituency. A neo-Pharisaic renewal in contemporary Jewish life may provide the synagogue sphere with a heightened incentive and confidence not to become a mere adjunct to civil Judaism. But it is unlikely to lead to a response of "live and let live." Rather, it may provide the ground for opening a genuine dialogue through which both religious impulses—the neo-Pharisaic and the neo-Sadducean—may be deepened and strengthened.

## Confrontation

The aspiration for such a dialogue is predicated on the assumption that there is indeed a genuine religious teaching to be found in the civil Jewish camp. This is not the universal view of those in the synagogue–rabbinic community. Some are far harsher in their judgment of civil Judaism than even those who claim to find its message falling increasingly on deaf ears. For these critics, what we have called civil Judaism is nothing more than a species of secularist ideology in Jewish clothing. It defines not a religious way of life, but an organizational culture in which God is effectively absent and true piety is unknown. Rather than absorbing its message or even seeking to go their own way, religious leaders must respond to the civil Jewish challenge by confronting and resisting its substitution of a shallow "Jewish-style" worldview and ethos for the genuine article.

It is relatively rare today to find such a straightforward assault elaborated in print.[15] Yet the position should not be dismissed out of hand. Civil Judaism does refuse to commit itself on issues of behavior and belief which are central to the classical Jewish tradition. From a principled perspective, one could argue that its partial accommodation to Judaic norms—e.g., kashrut at public functions, but implicit approval of any dietary practice in private—is worse than a clear rejection of them, precisely because it promotes the image of religious seriousness where none actually exists. Similarly, the critic can legitimately contend that for all its talk of "insuring Jewish continuity," civil Judaism has not in fact inspired significant devotion among its adherents to study or worship to accompany their commitment to "good deeds." Indeed, even the elaborate institutional apparatus of *tzedakah* which civil Judaism hallows can be depicted as little more than a monument to Mammon, trading donated dollars for status and power, a fundraising business, not an expression of a deeply religious charitable impulse.

If this critique is ultimately unfair and one-sided (and we believe it is), it is not totally groundless. For those whose vision of the Jewish community as a *kehillah kedoshah* embraces more than what civil Judaism is prepared to urge on its adherents, the ideology of the polity may indeed present itself as a threat rather than a potential ally. If civil Judaism were to succeed in substituting its vision of what is incumbent upon the Jew —indeed of what Jewish religiosity is all about—for one in which faith, study, and personal observance (whether in strictly traditional form or not) are central categories, it would represent a fundamental shift in the nature of Judaism. That, in a sense, is what a thoroughgoing neo-Sadducean revolution might portend—though not, we suggest the evidence shows, what civil Judaism intends. For one committed to the traditional faith, one who sees in civil Judaism the still evident signs of its far-reaching accommodations to secular culture and the ideal of integration, confrontation and resistance may be the only acceptable response.

Nevertheless, it is not, we believe, likely to be a productive one. It underestimates the extent to which civil Judaism has moved to embrace a more traditional religious sensibility, and its openness to further elaboration and development along these lines. Like a posture of independence, a strategy of confrontation with civil Judaism—even where the themes which the civil religion emphasizes are taken up through a more traditional vocabulary—is less likely to produce a strengthened religious sector than a divided one. Institutionally, federations and synagogues are unprepared and unwilling for a *Kulturkamph*. To espouse what would amount to such a struggle, however well-intentioned the motives, would likely result in a polarization within the synagogue camp which would weaken its capacity to impact upon the civil Jewish sphere. For most rabbinic leaders, civil Judaism is an inadequate ideological basis for a full Jewish religious life, but not a false one. Hence, what they seek is not the dismantling of civil Judaism, but its enrichment and transformation into a more encompassing, more Judaically authentic system of belief.

## Transformation

The need for deepening and strengthening the religious message of civil Judaism is one felt keenly by many who are on the whole sympathetic to that message. In this view, integration, supplementation, independence, or confrontation are all inadequate responses from a religious standpoint. What is required is a strategy of infiltration and *transformation*. Essentially, it is necessary for what Martin Marty calls "public theology" to reemerge as a force seeking to rectify the shortcomings and fill the gap in self-understanding which civil Judaism manifests.

We have already noted the grounds for such a critique: Civil Judaism substitutes vague terminology—"maintaining the quality of Jewish life," "serving Jewish needs," "pursuing excellence"—for an authentic Jewish vocabulary of Torah and *mitzvot*. Even where it uses such terms, it tends to rob them of their depth and full import, their rootedness in a worldview which embraces divine creation, revelation, and redemption. Civil Judaism's redefinition of the Jewish "mission" emphasizes the practical, almost to the exlusion of the spiritual. And, in urging the fulfillment of Jewish responsibilities through the instruments of the Jewish polity, it inadvertently fosters the depersonalization of the *mitzvot* of *tzedakah* and *gemilut hasadim* (acts of kindness) which it values so highly. Above all, in virtually ignoring the task of disciplined reflection on issues of Jewish belief and behavior—i.e., in its atheologism—civil Judaism may unwittingly undermine the basis of the commitment to Jewish life which it seeks so demonstratively to promote.

If civil Judaism is at once important for what it says and flawed in its manner of speaking, then the response which the synagogue and rabbinate offer to it can be neither cheers nor catcalls. The task from this perspective is one of provoking the institutions and leadership of the Jewish polity to deepen their professed commitment to Jewish values by studying them more intensely, thinking about them more seriously, and applying them more self-critically. Civil Judaism can be opened to its own most challenging implications by raising questions about the "why" of Jewish survival and the "how" of Jewish services.

This is a role which should be attractive and accessible to leadership in the synagogue and rabbinic community (and perhaps even more to the growing cadre of university-based Jewish thinkers). There are models which emanate from the classical tradition and from the "neo-Pharisaic" religious sensibility of the current period—models such as the *tzedakah* collective, whose members examine the meaning of what they do and the purposes for which their contributions are spent, or *hev-rot* (voluntary associations) which personalize the commandments to visit the sick, care for the aged, teach the young, and bury the dead—which could extend the civil Jewish ethos more centrally into the life of the individual. There are teachers—Irving (Yitz) Greenberg, David Hartman, and Harold Schulweis among others—who have sought with considerable success to stimulate the polity leaders with whom they have worked to explore the religious bases and horizons of their own commitments. What the strategy of transformation envisions is a civil Judaism which would outgrow the limitations of its own secular origins, and move more overtly and securely into the mainstream of Jewish religious tradition.

Is this strategy, then, the most appropriate response of the rabbinate and synagogue world to civil Judaism and the ascendance of the federation? That may depend on whether the impulse to transformation is one-sided or two-sided. The religious teachers who have been most effective in reaching out to the polity and its leadership are those who have let themselves be affected in turn by the power of civil Judaism to shape a significant collective Jewish commitment in our time. Transformation of civil Judaism cannot mean the loss of its unique unifying, mobilizing, and legitimating force. Thus, we return to the notion that what is required is a dialogue of Judaisms, an exchange between those who recognize themselves as bearing overlapping, perhaps ultimately complementary, but not yet fully synthesized visions of what it means to be a Jew in the modern world. Eventually, we might hope, the synthesis will be achieved, and civil Judaism will contribute its energy to a holistic definition of Jewish belief and behavior. For this to occur, however, both the synagogue and the federation-framed polity must embrace a dialogue on this level, and not merely one aimed at an institutional modus vivendi. And for that to take place, both the synagogue and the polity itself must begin to attend seriously to the religious message of civil Judaism.

## Toward a Civil Jewish Theology?

The question remains, however, whether such a movement toward religious and theological self-consciousness is indeed possible for civil Judaism. The barriers are both practical and intellectual. On the practical level, the key issue is whether civil Judaism can function effectively as an integrative meaning system were it to become more articulate with respect to its own premises and implications. Before hastening to judgment on this question, it is well to remember that civil Judaism as it exists today is already far more "religious," far more "commanding," far more "Jewish" than anyone projecting its development thirty years ago might have anticipated. Civil Judaism must, indeed, articulate a consensus, but the depth and breadth of that consensus can itself grow over time, as the last several decades have revealed. There is no a priori reason why a civil religion which speaks more explicitly of God, of revelation and redemption, of the election of Israel and its meaning, of the sacred significance of the work it prescribes, could not also command a consensus of faith in the not too distant future.[16]

The real problem, then, is the intellectual one: finding a vocabulary, a theology, a philosophy of Jewish life which takes the civil religious sensibility and exposes its spiritual roots and import. It would not be enough merely to absorb the civil Jewish message into the fabric of traditional rabbinic or modern denominational ideologies. Such a course is superficially plausible. As we have emphasized on several occasions, there is almost nothing in civil Judaism which is foreign to the classical tradition or the modern versions of Judaism which claim to be its successors. Yet the significance of civil Judaism lies in its embodiment of what we have been calling the "neo-Sadducean" religious sensibility: the conviction that the meaning of Jewishness is located centrally in the experience of Jewish peoplehood, in the engagement with history, and in the response of the Jewish people to the great events which challenge them as a polity and call forth a reaffirmation of their historic mission. Although this sensibility is hardly foreign to either pre-modern Jewish tradition or the major modern Jewish religious ideologies, it is not their starting point nor their focus.

What is needed is, then, a greatly expanded endeavor in Jewish public theology. Public theology is the appropriate complement to civil religion. It attempts to build a more sweeping religious edifice on the foundation of the usually parsimonious assertions which the civil religion itself puts forward. Because it is inherently more idiosyncratic and speculative, public theology rarely enjoys the wide and unquestioned legitimacy of the civil religion itself, but it is the impetus of such theologizing which often propels the civil religion forward into new self-understanding and self-criticism.

In order to help foster a dialogue of Judaisms a Jewish public theology must be at once faithful to the fundamental religious worldview and ethos of civil Judaism, and articulate concerning a range of issues which the characteristic rhetoric of the civil religion leaves largely unexplored. A theology cannot be merely exhortative; nor can it be purely celebratory. It cannot simply *assert* its view of reality; it must, in some fashion justify that view by grounding it in a reasoned set of premises and conclusions. This does not mean that a civil Jewish theology must be systematic and propositional. Most Jewish theology has not been such. It does mean, however, that Jewish public theology should be concerned with questions which civil Judaism itself, as a system of religious *practice*, can avoid.

If it is to speak intelligibly to the adherents of the civil religion, public theology will necessarily reflect some of the fundamental tensions which we have found implicit in civil Judaism. Civil Judaism, we have suggested, is messianic in tone, yet prides itself on maintaining a posture of pragmatic realism. It regards the Jewish people and its destiny as exceptional, yet it aspires to see Jews fully integrated and accepted in the modern world. It preaches solidarity with the Jewish people and a nearly sacrificial sense of mutual responsibility, yet it concedes autonomy to the individual and refuses to sanction norms of religious behavior. A public theology for civil Judaism must confront these tensions and, if not resolve them, at least render them supportable as dimensions of a viable religious stance in the contemporary world. Perhaps more than anything else, a civil Jewish theology must bridge the gap between the "religious" and the "secular" domains, for if civil Judaism is to enter a religious dialogue it must be able to demonstrate that its highly secularized ethos is in fact a faithful expression of Judaism's religious heritage.

A civil Jewish theology must, therefore, give substance to the rhetoric, the mythic allusions and the symbols which are central to the civil religion, but which rarely are accorded sustained reflective consideration. What is the "destiny" of the Jewish people? Whence does it arise? How can the Jew be sure that the Holocaust and the State of Israel indeed carry religious meaning, and are not merely links in a chain of historical accident? Why must a Jew maintain his bonds to the Jewish people when the ethical values he espouses are universal in character? For civil Judaism, the answers to such questions are implicit in the ethos of active response to which the Jewish polity is devoted. But the answers need to be made explicit as well, to be affirmed as intellectually persuasive (though never provable), in addition to being emotionally compelling. Civil Jewish faith must be linked, carefully and thoughtfully, to the textual foundations of Judaism and to the rich conceptual repository of Judaic tradition.

Civil Judaism's individual themes have, of course, been addressed often by modern Jewish thinkers over the years. What has typically been lacking, however, is an elaboration of these themes as elements of a coherent meaning system. Neither civil Judaism nor "neo-Sadducean" Judaism have had or are likely to have theological expositors as such, largely because neither exists as an identifiable religious or intellectual movement. But there have been and are today important Jewish intellectual figures whose thought reflects a particular sensitivity to the concerns and themes which dominate the Jewish civil religion. It is in their work that we will find the Jewish "public theology" of our era. Their theologizing does not necessarily address civil Judaism or its adherents explicitly. It could not be labeled "neo-Sadducean" in any rigorous sense (although, interestingly, neither is it generally traditionally rabbinic or denominationally rooted). Yet it speaks both out of the civil religion and to it in strikingly appropriate ways.

While many could perhaps be named, we would point to five such individuals—Mordecai Kaplan, Martin Buber, Emil Fackenheim, Eugene Borowitz, and Irving Greenberg—as potential contributors to a civil Jewish theology. The grouping of these men (especially such radically different thinkers as Kaplan and Buber) may appear at first glance arbitrary and idiosyncratic. They form no "school" of Jewish thought, no theological movement. But all have taken their intellectual cue from the fundamental civil religious/"neo-Sadducean" sensibility: that the meaning of Jewishness today lies in the return of the Jewish people to history and in the possibility of making that return a life-transforming event for the individual, the Jewish people, and perhaps even the world. All have attempted to outline a path of response to the tensions and contradictions which have bedeviled the Jews in that process of return, a path which bridges the gap between the "secular" and the "religious." And all have pointed to a renewal of the Jewish conviction of living a covenanted existence as the key both to uncovering the religious, redemptive meaning of being a Jew and to cementing the link between modern Jews and the Judaic tradition which modernity has called into question.

We cannot in the course of a few pages hope to do justice to the full scope and depth of the thought of any of these men. Buber and Kaplan are giants of the modern era whose creative work over blessedly long life-spans will occupy scholars for years to come. Fackenheim, Borowitz, and Greenberg are contemporaries, men whose own thought continues to evolve and to whom we are too close to pass definitive judgment. Yet, if we are to sketch even the outlines of the direction which a civil Jewish public theology may—perhaps must—take, we must attempt to draw together the themes in these men's work which point the way forward toward such a theology.

## Mordecai Kaplan: The Religion of Ethical Nationhood

In the case of Mordecai Kaplan that task is made somewhat easier by the consistency of his thought and emphases over the course of his career. From his first major work, *Judaism as a Civilization*,[17] to his last valedictory (as it were), *The Religion of Ethical Nationhood*,[18] Kaplan insisted that the reconstitution of Jews as a trans-national people and the reconstruction of its religious civilization in a modern key were the requisites for restoring Judaism's integrity and vitality as a path to salvation for the contemporary Jew. Kaplan's program speaks directly to many of civil Judaism's central concerns: It places Jewish peoplehood at the core of the Jewish religious experience. It affirms the importance of Zion without negating the Diaspora. It holds out the possibility of living authentically as both a Jew and an American in two civilizations at once. It locates the unique Jewish vocation in the modern world in the embodiment of "ethical nationhood," organized collective existence in the service of international cooperation and world peace. Kaplan's thought is in fact a virtual blueprint for a Jewish public theology; it is the most single-mindedly communal, pragmatist, and modernist ideology which American Jewry has ever produced.

That Kaplan's Reconstructionist philosophy should bear such direct thematic links to the civil Judaism we have described is not surprising. If civil Judaism is, as we have suggested, deeply rooted in and closely related to American Jewry's folk religion, Kaplan's Reconstructionism is (as Charles Liebman has noted) the quintessential "elite" formulation of that folk religion.[19] Kaplan understood American Jews—or at least second generation American Jews of Eastern European origin—better than any other American Jewish thinker. He understood that their attachment to Jewish life was strongly ethnic in character, but that they sought to validate this ethnic feeling in religious terms. He understood their need to feel fully American and fully modern, without feeling that they were thereby being disloyal to the faith of their fathers. He understood that ethical values represented the summit of their religiosity, but that they believed their commitment to those values to be intrinsically linked in some way with their Jewishness. He understood the important role which the struggle for a Jewish state played in enhancing their self-respect as Jews, and the fact that Zionism therefore served as a spur to the development of a profound commitment to the survival of a strong Diaspora communnity. Because Kaplan understood American Jewry so well, much of his thought has been thoroughly integrated into the fabric of American Jewish life at every level. Many Jews who never think of themselves as Reconstructionists, indeed even some who are antagonistic to elements of Kaplan's theology, nevertheless approach Jewish life and its problems with perceptions and assumptions profoundly colored by his perspective.

Kaplan's ideas, elaborated in a series of works,[20] are an attempt to blend modern social science and ancient prophetic vision. Religion, he argued, must be understood in naturalistic and humanistic terms as the expression of a group's striving toward a way of life which promotes the fulfillment of man's ethical and spiritual potentialities. Its mission is to inform character with the values and moral commitment needed to sustain human survival and to help the individual experience salvation through his attachment to his group and its civilization. Religion is properly, Kaplan contended, the expression of what the Bible calls "wisdom": a mature sense of values which permits man to satisfy his needs and to maintain harmony with the natural and human orders.

Judaism is, in perhaps the most famous of all Kaplan's assertions, the evolving religious civilization of the Jewish people. It embraces three intertwined components: the people itself, its religious ideals, and the sancta or folkways in which those ideals are embodied and symbolized. This is Kaplan's version of the classic trinity of Jewish thought: God, Israel, and Torah. Kaplan insisted on both the continued necessity for all three of these elements in any viable approach to Jewish existence, and the need for each to be reinterpreted or reconstituted in light of the intellectual, social, and moral canons of modernity.

Kaplan vigorously rejected the charge of some of his critics that his naturalist Judaism was atheistic, or that it made of God a mere symbol. He insisted that God is indeed real, not, however, as a supernatural person or force, but rather as "that power in nature and in man which makes for man's this-worldly salvation."[21] Nevertheless, the focus of Kaplan's Judaism is on the Jewish people as the discoverer and bearer of the spiritual insights which make its way of life salvific for the Jew, however the concept of salvation may have changed from era to era. Kaplan believed that the group is the essential mediator of such salvation, that only in the context of group existence can individuals achieve the consciousness of their place in the organic processes of life which issues forth in responsible living. Hence, the keys to a meaningful Jewish existence in the modern era are the reconstitution of the Jewish people as an organic group and the revitalization of its spiritual teaching through the process of naturalist transvaluation of its traditional expressions. Virtually all of Kaplan's writings and his organizational activities were devoted to one or both of these ends.

In calling for the reconstitution of Jewry as a transnational people, Kaplan proposed an actual constitutional convention to formulate a new "covenant of peoplehood," a modern renewal of the covenant first entered into at Sinai, with a constitution setting out the structural framework and functional responsibilities of the people and its leaders. Such a *de jure* reconstitution was necessary, he believed, to overcome the impact of Emancipation and integration into Western civilization which had undermined the traditional bases of Jewish solidarity. It was also needed to express the formal commitment of the people to its spiritual heritage. Jewish peoplehood, Kaplan insisted, is a religious category, not merely a social or political one. Jews need the Jewish people for their spiritual and moral orientation in the secular world, to give their existence a purposive significance.

Within this context, Kaplan defined a critical role for what he called a "greater Zionism" as the primary instrument for achieving Jewish unity. The fulfillment of Zionism came not with the establishment of the State of Israel alone, but will only come when Jews in Eretz Yisrael and the Diaspora assume their organic relationship to one another as the hub and the spokes of a unified, yet diverse Jewish people. Kaplan's Zionism, like that of most American Jews, repudiates the so-called "negation of the Diaspora" of much classical Zionist thought. It envisions a "living, interactive and creative people" with Israel as a "spiritual catalyst" for a vibrant Jewry in the Diaspora as well.[22]

In order to achieve such a vital Jewish existence in America, both a restructuring and a reconceptualization of the character of American Jewish life are necessary. Kaplan called for American Jews to form "organic

Jewish communities," formal structures in which all Jews, regardless of ideology or economic standing, would be included. Kaplan saw potential strength in the diversity of ideological standpoints in American Jewish life, provided the various camps could learn to work as a fellowship beyond their divisions, accepting pluralism of belief, but acting in concert for the benefit of all Jews. In effect, Kaplan wished to make the "federation concept" the organizing principle for all of American Jewish life.

At the same time, Kaplan affirmed that American Jews could never live in an exclusively Jewish civilization. Rather, they must, he claimed, learn to live in two civilizations at once. Adjustment to America meant, for Kaplan, neither assimilation nor self-segregation, but social and economic integration combined with cultural differentiation—precisely the ideal which so many American Jews have persistently sought. He went even beyond this, however, in urging that American Jews seek as part of their integration into the American fabric a role in helping to lend religious weight and dignity to the American dream itself. Kaplan applied the technique of seeking a humanistic spiritual message in collective sancta such as holidays to both the Jewish and the American calendars. Just as the holy days of the Jewish year could be celebrated as symbolic crystallizations of the meaning of God in Jewish religion (as the Power making for righteousness, freedom, justice, etc.), so too the sacred days of the American calendrical cycle—New Year's, Washington's Birthday, Memorial Day, Independence Day, Labor Day, Thanksgiving—should each take on an explicit spiritual significance for the American people. Jews, Kaplan believed, could willingly promote and celebrate the holidays of this American religion without in the least abandoning their own unique heritage.

Preserving and renewing that heriatge was in Kaplan's view important not only for the Jew, who could only find spiritual fulfillment through identification with the Jewish people's civilization, but for the world as well. Kaplan rejected the concept of Jewish "chosenness" as another relic of an outmoded supernaturalistic worldview. But he strongly embraced the notion of a Jewish vocation and destiny. In his final book in particular, the mission of Jews as an exemplary people, embodying and expressing the ideals and practices of ethical nationhood, moves to the center of Kaplan's vision. In a time of crisis and threatened mass annihilation, all religion must strive to lead mankind to the wisdom of international concord. But the Jewish people, both because of their transnational character and because of the biblical heritage in which the ideal of nations living as ethically responsible entities is first adduced, has a special role to play in this educational mission. "In Torah," Kaplan wrote, "Jews have a potent instrument with which to humanize and civilize the human being."[23] In humanistic terms, devotion to Torah is devotion to a conception of human existence in which spiritual and moral values form the core of humanity's aspiration. Jews cannot be a "normal" people because they have a special world-historical vocation. They have (Kaplan quotes his pupil, Alan Miller) been "cast . . . into the role of being witnesses of the Divine."[24] There can be no Jewish renewal, Kaplan asserted, without the acceptance of this vocation, without the Jewish people "accepting ethical nationhood as its wisdom or religion."[25]

The congruences between Kaplan's philosophy of Judaism and the religious sensibility of civil Judaism are manifold. One wonders, therefore, why Kaplan's thought has not been more widely and explicitly embraced as a public theology for the Jewish polity. The answer may lie in the unremitting rationalism of Kaplan's schema. The very characteristics which make Kaplan's thought so suitable for highly secularized modern Jews, render it somewhat unsatisfying on the emotional level. Though many of the adherents of the civil religion endorse almost instinctively Kaplan's Copernican revolution which places the people, and not God, at the core of the Jewish religious experience, they are not necessarily comfortable with a philosophy which so thoroughly removes the elements of transcendence and mystery from that experience. Though Kaplan is the epitome of a "timely" thinker, vitally concerned with understanding Judaism as an historical phenomenon and with maintaining its relevance in the modern age, he is himself a creature of his own historical era and its now questionable assumptions. He recognizes the deep spiritual inadequacy of secular culture, but not the fact that his program of demythologizing is predicted on the absolute superiority of the same "scientific" worldview which has undermined all talk of spirituality. The open-endedness of civil Jewish rhetoric, its failure to establish the referents of its symbols in traditional transcendent terms, does not mean that the adherents of civil Judaism seek the explicitly naturalistic interpretations on which Kaplan insists. Indeed, in an important sense, Kaplan's naturalistic, functionalist, sociological approach to Judaism is *incongruent* with the existential root of their Jewish commitment. Their attachment to Judaism is far more visceral, far more rooted in a concrete response to specific historical events, than Kaplan's philosophy would suggest.

Kaplan's thought is, in the end, remarkably *un*historical in the existential sense, almost uninterested in the lived experience of the American Jew in an age of turmoil and uncertainty. It is didactic and exhortative, prescribing logical, but often wildly impractical, solutions in a tone of moral earnestness, but political and psychological unrealism. Though one cannot doubt Kaplan's genuine anguish in the face of a world of escalating violence—both general and directed specifically against the Jew—there is little sense of *angst*, of tension, of ambiguity within the framework of Kaplan's thought itself. Its passion is of the "high-minded" variety. If it is unfair to accuse Kaplan, as some critics have, of being insensitive to the reality of evil and of maintaining a progressivist optimism about the perfectability of human nature and society in the face of overwhelming evidence to the contrary, it is nevertheless true that his thought lacks almost entirely a "tragic" dimension. Thus, for all its acuity in elaborating and synthesizing some of the most fundamental propositions of the civil Jewish faith, Kaplan's thought is, by itself, an inadequate theological transposition of a religious sensibility more complex and tumultuous than its simple and unreflective rhetoric might lead us to suppose.

This critique of Mordecai Kaplan's philosophy of Judaism as a sufficient basis for constructing a public theology for contemporary civil Judaism should not obscure its substantial contribution to such a venture. In its emphasis on the primacy of the experience of Jewish peoplehood and the necessity of appropriating that peoplehood in religious terms, Kaplan's thought goes right to the heart of the neo-Sadducean religious posture. Kaplan's focus on the human role in the spiritual process, his insistence on the importance of community, his ethical activism, his post-Halakhic pluralism, all resonate powerfully with the civil Jewish worldview and ethos. These themes must be central to any civil Jewish theology, but they need not be linked only to Kaplan's naturalistic Judaism.

## Martin Buber: Hebrew Humanism

To demonstrate the potential for theological elaboration of the civil Jewish sensibility in very different directions, we can cite the work of a Jewish thinker, Martin Buber, who at first glance bears almost no intellectual resemblance to Kaplan. Buber is perhaps the most misunderstood Jewish philosopher of the modern era. Because of his attempts to transmit what he believed to be the spirit of Hasidism (the popular Jewish mystical movement which began in Eastern Europe in the eighteenth century) to the modern Jew, and because of his espousal of the I-Thou relationship as the core of the true religious life, Buber has often been taken to be a mystic. Nothing could be further from the truth. Buber was a religious humanist, and the animating force behind his Jewish philosophy was the aspiration to see the Jewish people renew itself in history by accepting once again its theo-political mission as a nation.

The scope of Buber's intellectual product during the course of his lifetime was enormous, impossible even to summarize in a few pages.[26] But its unifying thread may be found in Buber's insistence that the meaning of human existence is to be found in the encounter between the individual and what he meets in the world. "All real living," he wrote in the classic *I and Thou*, "is meeting."[27] Buber's religious philosophy is a philosophy of relationship, not to some deity beyond time and space, but to the beings of the world, and, through the fullness of our presence in the concrete situated reality, to the Eternal You who addresses us. Buber's language is often difficult and obscure, but the direction in which he points leads to what Donald Moore has termed a "religious secularism,"[28] an unremitting focus on the human social-historical arena as the place of our redemption precisely through our attentiveness to the demand it places on us and the potential for relationship contained within it. The primary aspiration of all history, Buber wrote, is community.[29] The overcoming of the distance between man and man and that between man and God are inseparable movements. Religious life is not a sanctuary from reality, but the hallowing of day to day existence.

Buber's philsophy of Judaism brings this general teaching into the specific realm of modern Jewish life.[30] The Jewish people, he believed, could renew itself in the modern world only by embracing and proclaiming its ancient teaching: that men are charged to perfect their portion of the universe, and that Israel is to show the way in the fulfillment of this task by building a community of justice and peace. The conviction informed Buber's Zionism over a period of more than six decades. It formed the core of his message of courage and hope to the Jews of Germany in the 1930s who found both their physical and their spiritual dignity under assault from Nazism.

For Buber, the essential message of Judaism is that there can be no separation of the life of the spirit from the real world. The spirit is nothing other than man's totality made conscious, and that spirit must act through the elemental realities of life—all of man's urges and capacities —in order to shape and transform life. But this task is not one for the individual; it is the task for humans as social beings, since the consummation of human existence is the fulfillment of our relationships in true community. Israel, uniquely in the ancient world, heard this charge and accepted it as a nation. Only as a nation—not as a "spiritualized" bearer of a universal message—can it continue to pursue this charge: "For only an entire nation, which comprehends peoples of all kinds, can demonstrate a life of unity and peace, of rightousness and justice to the human race, as a sort of example and beginning."[31] This vocation defines the role of the Jewish people and the necessity for its survival and renewal.

Buber was aware of the powerful modern pull of "normalization," of seeking to find a category—"nation" or "creed"—which would permit Jews to find security in the modern world. He insisted, however, that security for the Jewish people could only be found in the pursuit of its convenantal vocation. For this, a real, rounded community life was necessary—a life with autonomy and a land (hence Buber's firm Zionism)— but as the basis and the medium, not the consummation, of the pursuit of redemption.

Is this, though, a vocation which makes sense—or can be made convincing—to the modern Jew, particularly the modern Jew whose faith is at best uncertain and who cannot accept a traditional understanding of revelation and Torah? Buber knew that for many, if not most, modern

Jews a traditionalist faith was impossible. But he also recognized that no rationalist schema could provide the impetus for such a Jew—or for the Jewish people—to accept this vocation and this destiny. Buber urged, therefore, that Jews give up the quest for a secure knowledge of what Jewishness demands and listen once again to the voice which emerges from the lived moment, a voice in which, he was sure, they would hear the command of the hour. Buber wished to rehabilitate revelation and transcendence for the modern Jew by restoring their historical character. "Historic destiny is the secret correlation inhering in the current moment. . . . We are carried along by a meaning we could never think up for ourselves, a meaning we are to live—not to formulate."[32]

Buber struggled to preserve the reality of religious experience as dialogical encounter from slipping, on the one hand, toward a fundamentalist affirmation of revelation as the giving of propositional knowledge and legal prescriptions, or, on the other, toward a secularist assertion of an exclusively human origin for all meaning. His stance has brought him sharp criticism from traditional Jews and from philosophers who find his concept of revelation vague and intellectually insubstantial. Yet Buber may have captured quite incisively the experience of exactly those modern Jews who cannot indentify the source of their deep commitment to Jewish survival, who cannot define precisely the task they are prepared to embrace, but who affirm, with Buber, that it can be "sensed, pointed out, and presented."[33]

In making room for the mystery of faith, in asserting that a meaning which cannot be rationally formulated or evaluated can nevertheless make a claim upon us which we are prepared to acknowledge, Buber's thought removes from civil Judaism a potentially crushing intellectual burden. That which cannot be explicated, can still be appropriated. Buber did not demand an "orderly" world for the world to be meaningful. Far more than Kaplan's, his thought makes room for the contradictions of reality, for evil, even—in the face of the Holocaust—for what Buber called the "eclipse of God."[34] Buber's was not an "easy faith." In the twentieth century God's light was indeed nearly impossible to behold through the swollen mass of human creations. And after Auschwitz, Buber acknowledged in anguish, one could perhaps "believe" in God, but speaking to and hearing God was virtually inconceivable. Yet, Buber insisted, even the contradictions of the world can be experienced as a theophany, a demand that this world—with its evil—be grappled with and redeemed. And, though he denigrated those who in the face of the eclipse of God could say only "See there, it grows lighter," he found "a revelation through the hiding of the face" which gave hope that the voice of God, coming in a form unlike any before, might yet again be heard and recognized.[35]

Buber sought both to liberate Jewish religiosity from the shackles of conventional religious forms and thought, and to bring it directly and insistently into the arena of daily life. He did not want Jewish spiritual life to become a "superstructure, a non-obligatory transfiguration, an object of pride which imposes no duties."[36] He wanted the power of the Jewish spirit to impose itself on the "secular" world and to assault its pretensions at self-sufficiency. In the merging of the spiritual and the physical, in their operating together, he saw the only possibility for the survival of the Jewish people and the fulfillment of its destiny.

Buber's thought provides a vocabulary for understanding the Jewish experience in the modern world which is rooted in the tradition, yet addressed to Jews for whom that tradition is not immediately accessible. Like Kaplan's thought, Buber's philosophy places at its core the Jewish return into history in the modern world. It attempts to define the conditions for making that return a spur to a collective and individual renewal, a Jewish revival which can carry forward Judaism's ancient religious vocation into a modern world which has shattered the Pharisaic-rabbinic civilization which for so long kept the awareness of that vocation alive. It proclaims that Jewish survival indeed matters, that the unique destiny of this people awaits its fulfillment in a restored nation and a revitalized teaching. Buber attempted to provide the language in which that teaching could be communicated to the modern Jew who still feels its power, but who does not know how to draw the threads of his or her experience together into a unified religious stance. He espoused less Jewish "religion" than Jewish "living," defined not in terms of a set of unalterable prescriptions, but as ever-renewed attentiveness to what this time and this place demands of the Jew and the Jewish people.

For civil Judaism seeking theological articulation, Buber's thought is an important resource. It can serve as a link to the sources of Judaism and to one of the powerful religious options of our time: religious existentialism. Buber's thought can mediate civil Judaism's encounter with such concepts as "revelation" and "spirit," concepts it must deal with if its professions of faith in a Jewish destiny are not to be purely rhetorical or metaphorical. Buber's religious philosophy helps open a pathway to the transcendent for those who find traditional formulations impossible to appropriate. It takes many of the themes of the civil religion and integrates them with a compelling vision of purposeful Jewish existence, and inserts that vision, in turn, into a philosophy of human life which encompasses virtually every dimension of human concern and experience.

Yet, the breadth and scope of Buber's vision may be too bold for civil Judaism. Though Buber sought to anchor his thought firmly in the concrete reality of daily life, his poetic sensibility and intellectual reach move it into areas of philosophical and religious exposition where many will not and cannot follow. This is the dilemma of any theological elaboration of folk or civil religion. In saying enough to render the rhetoric and symbols of such religion intellectually significant, one may say too much for the adherents of the faith. Whether the language of I and Thou can ever become a language of Jewish public theology is uncertain. In most of his Judaic writing, Buber himself did not seek to use that vocabulary. Yet it is the critical bridge in his thought between the language of the Bible and a contemporary humanistic philosophical anthropology. Buber did not need to demythologize as Kaplan did, because he had an alternative spiritual vocabulary which did not demand rationalist reduction. But that vocabulary is itself problematic and elusive, and thus for many contemporary Jews Buber's thought remains inaccessible.

Perhaps more important, Buber, like Kaplan, is a creature of his time and place. Though he lived most of his life in the Disapora (and visited America), Buber's Jewish philosophy addresses only tangentially the specific situation of the contemporary American Jew. He was far from insensitive to the problematics of Diaspora Jewish life and the profound impact of the encounter of Judaism and Jews with modern Western civilization. His primary response was, however, his Zionism. Though he did much to urge German Jews to recover their integrity as Jews through spiritual renewal at the personal and communal level, and though he wrote with admiration of Hasidism's efforts to establish a model community within the Diaspora context, he viewed the latter venture as a inevitable failure and the former as secondary to the Jewish revival centered in Eretz Yisrael.

Much that Buber said can be brought to bear directly on the situation of the American Jew, but unlike Kaplan, the American Jew was not a focus of his concern. For civil Judaism, rooted as deeply as it is in the particular experience of the American Jew (including experiences which have come only after Buber's death), his "Hebrew humanism" lacks the immediate resonances with American Jewish life which would be needed to make it fully persuasive as a theological framework.

## Emil Fackenheim: The Commanding Voice of Auschwitz

The existential situation of the contemporary American Jew has been informed by four major factors: (1) the entrance of Jews into the mainstream of American life; (2) the impact of the Holocaust and the State of Israel on American Jewish self-understanding and commitment; (3) the persistent struggle of American Jews to maintain a religious identity in the face of their overwhelming embrace of secular culture; and (4) the central role of the Jewish polity in defining and implementing the agenda of Jewish group life in America.

Neither Kaplan nor Buber was really in a position to address this situation in its full particularity. There are, however, other thinkers who, during the past two decades, have sought to do precisely that: to comprehend in their writings the situation of the contemporary American Jew and to expose its religious significance and message. Their work, perhaps even more than Kaplan's and Buber's, is rooted in the religious sensibility, in the convictions and contradictions, with which civil Judaism is infused. Singly and collectively, their thought provides the clearest image of what Jewish public theology can offer in a contemporary dialogue of Judaisms.

Certainly the most classically philosophical voice among these contemporary public theologians is that of Emil Fackenheim. In works like *Encounters of Judaism and Modern Philosophy*[37] and *To Mend the World: Foundations of Future Jewish Thought* [38] he has undertaken dense and intellectually challenging examinations of the theological message of Judaism and its capacity to withstand the assaults of modern thought and modern history. These are important works, especially (for our purposes) the latter, which constitutes Fackenheim's most systematic effort to date to explicate his own theological stance. Yet Fackenheim's most critical contribution to Jewish public theology (as he himself acknowledged) came in a single, apparently simple, insight: that the Jewish response to the Holocaust has constituted the most important and telling religious and theological event of the contemporary era.

Judaism, Fackenheim asserts, is a religion which hinges on the experience of God's presence in history. The formative elements of the Jewish religious consciousness are what Fackenheim calls "root experiences" —events which are perceived and reappropriated by Jews throughout the generations as manifestations of the divine presence. The Exodus from Egypt and the Sinai covenant constitute the preeminent "root experiences" of Judaism. In them God was manifest as both a saving and a commanding presence, and only to the extent that the Jew can truly feel that presence can these events of the past legislate to the present and the future.[39]

The very notion (not to mention the experience) of the divine presence in history is wrought with paradox and contradiction. How can one reconcile divine transcendence and divine involvement in the world, divine power and human freedom? The answer, Fackenheim claims, is to be found in "midrashic thinking," a mode of reflection on root experiences and their contradictions which refuses to destroy these in the name of intellectual comprehension, but rather expresses the contradictions openly and consciously. Through midrashic thinking God's presence in history has been preserved despite its "irrationality" and through the vicissitudes of historical fate which the Jewish people has faced.[40]

Much of Fackenheim's theological work has been devoted to demonstrating how Jewish faith can withstand the challenges posed by secularist philosophical and subjectivist reductionist attempts to eliminate God's presence from history. Ultimately, he concludes, the stances of secularism and of faith are "mutually irrefutable."[41] The real challenge to Jewish faith and midrashic thinking in the contemporary world comes, however, not from intellectual critics, but from history itself: from the unimaginable, unprecedented horror of Auschwitz and the

Holocaust. In attempting to come to grips with the Holocaust in its singularity all forms of midrashic response of the past break down. Neither *midrashim* of divine powerlessness, nor of the redeeming power of martyrdom, nor of punishment, nor escape to otherworldiness can suffice to preserve God's presence in history when the history is that of Auschwitz.[42]

The path back from the abyss which the Holocaust represents, claims Fackenheim, lies in careful attention to how Jews have actually responded to that event. The Holocaust constituted a decisive repudiation of the quest for "normalcy" which has preoccupied Jews since the Emancipation. The attraction of secularism for the modern Jew has resided largely in its promise of normalizing the Jewish condition. But in the Holocaust Jews as Jews, whether secular or religious, nationalist or assimilationist, were singled out for a unique fate: total annihilation. The Jews who remained alive after the death camps might have taken the events as a signal to redouble their efforts to escape that singularity, if not for themselves, then for their grandchildren. But they did not. Even secular Jews, Fackenheim asserts, have not fled from their Jewishness, and affirming Jewishness on any level, "is to accept his singled-out condition; it is to oppose the demons of Auschwitz."[43]

This radical oppositon, this commitment to Jewish survival, even by the secular Jew, is a form of witness, if not directly for God, then against the devil. It is an opposition, Fackenheim suggests, which "cannot be grasped in terms of humanly created ideals but only as an *imposed commandment.*"[44] From Auschwitz there issues forth a commanding voice imposing that 614th commandment which the adherents of the civil religion hear so clearly: Thou shalt not grant Hitler a posthumous victory. As Fackenheim defines it, the 614th commandment has four elements: (1) Jews must survive as Jews; (2) Jews must remember the victims; (3) Jews must not despair of man and the world (lest the forces of Auschwitz triumph for lack of opposition); and (4) Jews must not despair of God (lest Judaism perish).[45] The latter two of these demands are, Fackenheim recognizes, especially difficult to sustain. But here contemporary Jews must adopt their own "mad" midrashic stance: the contradictions must be faced and endured. A "mad" midrashic stance is initially one of protest against the anti-world of Auschwitz and its God, but it leads to a determination to restore the world through action, through a political praxis. The word of midrashic madness which emanates "in the anti-world which ought not to be but is . . . points to acts to restore a world which ought to be but is not, committed to the faith that what ought to be must and will be."[46] That this faith is not pure absurdity was confirmed for many Jews in the moment of truth which came as they experienced the clash between Auschwitz and what occurred in Jerusalem in 1967: a moment of "wonder at a singled out, millennial existence which, after Auschwitz, is still possible and actual."[47]

In his identification of the 614th commandment and the "mad" commitment of the Jew to restore (or as he puts it in his most recent book, to mend) the world (both phrases translate the traditional Jewish concept of *tikkun olam*), Fackenheim draws from the living response of the Jewish people to the events of the recent past a bold theological message: that the boundaries between the secular and the religious have been redefined, and both have been overcome by the reality of Jewish faithful action today. The reassertion of Jewishness which began in North America in the late 1960s "cuts across traditional barriers such as old and young, Orthodox, Conservative, and Reform, and even religious and secularist. It reveals, as it were, a secular holiness which has crept by stealth, as will the Messiah, into our midst."[48] This renewed Jewish assertiveness, the commitment to affirm both Jewishness and life itself in the face of their negators, is the religious response of this era.

For Fackenheim, the way forward for the modern Jew lies in recognizing that the very terms of Jewish existence in the world have changed and that with that change, old boundaries are increasingly irrelevant. Fackenheim wishes to make sure, however, that the full religious import of the new situation is understood by the Jews who are living in it. Jews are responding to a new historical reality: "For the first time almost since biblical times, [the] duality [of a spiritual *Heilsegeschichte* and the flesh and blood history of a people] is once again a collective experience —by the same, still existing people."[49] The intertwining of the "religious" and the "secular" must be sustained, and can be sustained only by finding the points where the two have come together in reality in our time. Here again, the Holocaust is decisive for Fackenheim, not merely because it constitutes the rupture in the fabric of relationship between God, man, and the world which must be overcome, but because in the resistance of the Jewish victims, both spiritual and physical, an act of *tik kun*, of restoration, has already been made actual. Their *tikkun* is the ultimate ground of our own, he states, just as the death of the innocent millions makes the rupture forever unmendable.[50]

It is as a people committed to the tenuous and tension-ridden quest for *tikkun*, for mending the world, that the Jewish people must define its role in contemporary history. Fackenheim indentifies three elements to the *tikkun*: (1) a recovery of Jewish tradition; (2) recovery as a recuperation from an illness; and (3) a fragmentariness which renders both recoveries at risk and forever incomplete. The three together define a new Jewish condition which is epitomized in the State of Israel, the one indispensable *tikkun* today. The Jewish *tikkun* takes place in history, but witnesses to eternity. It is carried out largely in the secular domain, but it testifies to transcendence. In this fashion, Jewish existence again takes on world-historical significance, particularly in an age when all human forces face a failure of nerve, a loss of confidence in the future.[51]

For American Jews, participation in this work demands a confrontation with their own ambivalence. The bridging of the gap between the sacred and the secular means that the post-Emanicpation effort to normalize Jewry as either a faith community or an ethnic collectivity must fail. Emancipation must be emancipation of Jews as a people. The Holocaust makes such full emancipation a moral necessity; Israel makes it a spiritual and political possibility. For the American Jew, the "ambivalence" which seeks both full integration of Jews into American society as individuals and collective survival as an identifiable group must be recognized as a reflection of the *world's* ambiguous response to the Jewish struggle for complete emancipation. It is, in a sense, an appropriate response for a people not yet fully liberated. The ambivalence of the American Jew will, therefore, be overcome not when either aspiration is repudiated, but when he or she seeks and achieves integration precisely as an "American Jew," with the Jewish element of that compound secure.[52]

For civil Judaism, Fackenheim's philosophy of Judaism is (or should be) both compelling and challenging. Fackenheim asks contemporary Jews to understand their position in the modern world in light of Jewry's historic self-definition as witness to God's presence in history. Fackenheim acknowledges the radical character of the assault which modernity has mounted—intellectually, sociologically, historically— on that role. He concedes that no simple reappropriation of the religious sensibility of the past, complex and sophisticated as it was, is possible or appropriate. But he demands that contemporary Jews—and certainly the adherents of civil Judaism—reflect on their own instincts and behavior, and contends that they will find there the kernal of a new religious stance which opens a path to a renewed encounter with the old. Fackenheim does not advocate a return to the past; it is impossible. Jews and Judaism have turned a new page in their history by creating a Jewish state, but the new page enables a rereading of other pages as well. Joseph Mengele, when he carried out his selections on Yom Kippur, boasted that he had assumed God's place as judge over life and death. The State of Israel makes it possible for the Jew who prays on Yom Kippur after Auschwitz to restore the throne of judgment to God. The secular achievement thus makes possible the affirmation of transcendence. But Israel in turn would not exist without the inspiration its builders—including the secularists among them—drew from the Book, the biblical text. Thus, the legacy of faith makes possible the historical achievement.[53]

Fackenheim's philosophy requires that civil Judaism rethink its origins and its implications. He would ask it to deepen itself as a Judaic meaning system neither by simply becoming more "traditional" nor by seeking to redefine the traditional religious vocabulary to enable it to fit a modern worldview. Rather, like Buber, Fackenheim challenges contemporary Jews to struggle to understand how they participate in the same religious experience to which the tradition points.

Even more than Buber, Fackenheim recognizes the difficulty of making this connection. History itself has placed a seemingly impenetrable barrier between the modern Jew and the fundamental religious stance of Jewish tradition. Yet that same history, he argues, also shows us how to begin to break through that barrier. Understood aright, the assertiveness of the post-Holocaust Jew witnesses not to God's final demise, but to the abiding reality of his commanding, and perhaps even saving presence.

Civil Judaism, with its absolute commitment to Jewish survival and its plea for Jews to seize control of their own destiny, is a testimony of faith. But, Fackenheim warns, Jewish faith in the contemporary era cannot and should not be an easy one. The implication of Fackenheim's theology is, therefore, that the adherents of civil Judaism must face the full import of their commitment to faith: They must grapple with the demons of the modern world; they must consider carefully the nature and quality of their testimony—to whom and what does it witness?; they must learn the "mad midrash" which can sustain faith and prevent it from deteriorating into merely another form of secular hubris.

Kaplan, Buber, and Fackenheim share a common teaching: The ostensibly secular experience of the Jewish people in the modern era is not really secular at all. If a civil Jewish theology is to be grounded in the Jewish return to history and polity, this message is the absolutely necessary first principle of such theology. It is a message which the adherents of civil Judaism appear increasingly ready to hear and to absorb. But it is also one which must be made to speak to the whole experience of the contemporary American Jew.

Fackenheim's theology goes farther than either Kaplan's or Buber's in responding to this challenge. In articulating the 614th commandment, he has captured the essence of the determination to survive which dominates the civil Jewish faith. In identifying the work of *tikkun* as the Jewish witness and mission in the contemporary world, he has provided a master image from out of the Judaic tradition for pulling together the several elements of the civil Jewish ethos.

Yet, some of its very strengths also render Fackenheim's thought somewhat problematic as public theology. Fackenheim's vision is dominated on the one hand by the Holocaust and state of Israel, and on the other by a sense of radical challenge emanating from the secularist philosophies of the modern era. It is not clear, however, whether these are in fact the starting points from which all American Jews today (and certainly all civil Jews) approach the task of defining the nature of their Jewish commitment. Insightful as it is, Fackenheim's thought is not really aimed at those Jews who live in a more prosaic world than he describes, who begin not from anguish and questioning, but from relative contentment. This does not mean that Fackenheim errs in putting forward his vision of the critical choices which the contemporary Jew must face. It means only that a civil Jewish theology must seek additional ways to focus and to elaborate the religious implications of civil Jewish faith.

### Eugene Borowitz: The Existential Jew

This challenge has been taken up by another contemporary North American theologian, Eugene Borowitz, especially in his book analyzing American Jewry's self-understanding, *The Mask Jews Wear*.[54] For Borowitz, the key to building a more theologically articulate faith on the foundation of the sensibility manifest in civil Judaism is to strip away American Jewry's self-deceptions, its "modern Marronohood," and to reveal the profound commitment to Jewish belief and behavior which lies beneath. The outcome of this process of self-revelation is a renewed understanding of the power of Judaism to shape a personal and communal lifestyle which is at once secularized in content and religious in substance.

Borowitz finds a correlation between the willingness of Jews to look at a "new mix of American and Jewish ways of life" beginning in the late 1960s and the discovery during that period that America itself was a more imperfect society than many Jews had believed and hoped. For American Jews, the core of their Jewishness had long been ethical commitment. The Jew felt "commanded," even if the source of that commandment was the "moral law" rather than Jewish law. But the same ethical concern which helped Jews feel comfortable in America caused a sense of discomfort as America's ethical failings became manifest. And so a search began: a search to find a community with which to share moral values that no longer seemed so evidently grounded simply in American secular culture, values which appeared, in fact, to be in danger of being lost in American society.[55]

For some of these Jews, the Jewish community provided an answer to that search. What group, after all, has a better record of devotion to ethical excellence, of moral persistence than the Jews? Attachment to the Jewish community and to Judaism offers, Borowitz suggests, a model of "responsible alienation." Being a Jew means standing apart in some measure from every social system. The Jew stands separate "to be reminded of the values of his people, to be renewed in Judaism's high sense of what a human being ought to be."[56] The observance of Jewish ritual, e.g., the Sabbath, and the study of Jewish texts *lishma* (for their own sake) both express and maintain that separateness from the social mores of a thoroughly pragmatic and hedonistic society. Borowitz thus appeals to both the ethical sensitivity of American Jews and their persistent sense of being at least in some measure "strangers" in their land to suggest that these characteristics are precisely what links them to the faith of their ancestors.

The positive corollary of the sense of "responsible alienation" is the commitment to build communities which are models of "social righteousness." Jewish ethical values have always received their validation by being tested in the social arena. When they enjoyed relative autonomy, Jews sought to create just communities through the medium of Jewish law. Today, continued Jewish devotion to social activism serves, for Borowitz, as another clue that even the "non-religious" Jew has not really strayed far from the fundamental ethos of the faith.[57]

What Borowitz describes in this attempt to establish the essential Jewishness of the contemporary American Jew clearly reaches its quintessence in the civil Jewish sensibility. Civil Judaism, as we have noted, claims precisely this lineage for its sense of Jewish exceptionalism and its devotion to social justice. Borowitz suggests as well that the ethnic consciousness of civil Judaism is also a fitting manifestation of its comprehension of what being a Jew today must entail. Borowitz argues that the ethnic elements of Jewishness is indeed central, and intrinsically linked to the ethical dimension of Judaism. Jews have remained an ethnos throughout their history because that is the form best suited to insuring their "faithful survival" as bearers of Judaism's moral dream.[58] The bond of ethnic ties is reinforced by the power of a shared cultural legacy, a legacy which constitutes a teaching. Together, peoplehood and culture "give the individual Jew moral stamina, and messianic assurance. They summon us to continue the task our forbears began, and they teach us how not to despair in the face of frustration or failure."[59] The existence of the Jewish people, its survival, is a guarantee that the Jewish moral vision will be accomplished.

Like Fackenheim, Borowitz views the Jew who reasserts his or her ethnic bonds as one who by that very act witnesses for hope and stands against the negatives of existence. For many Jews, he acknowledges, a Jewishness of association, of good deeds and high culture, represents the summit of their self-conscious commitment. The critical question, however, is whether a purely secular Jewishness can provide the sense of the elemental worthwhileness of Jewish living which is necessary to sustain even this commitment. In insisting that the answer to this question is "no," Borowitz aims to push the American Jews whom he describes— among whom are no small number of civil Jews—to consider the deeper religious significance of their ethical concern and ethnic attachment.[60]

American Jews, as we have noted and Borowitz affirms, do not like to talk about God. Their discomfort with theology and with the religious institutions which speak a theological language does not, however, mean that they are without faith. For Borowitz, the characteristic passions of American Jews—their "uncommon interest . . . in high humanistic achievement," their "devotion to the notion that Jews ought to exemplify high moral values," their pride in the State of Israel because it has not been a nation like all the nations—are not merely the historic residue of Jewish tradition, but "signals of transcendence."[61]

Like Fackenheim, Borowitz sees in the Jewish response to the Holocaust perhaps the clearest indication of the true character of its faith. Jews did not become atheists; they sloughed off suggestions of the "death of God." Indeed, their refusal to accept the death of moral value which would necessarily accompany God's demise led back to a religious consciousness—the consciousness that these values emanated from a commanding source which Fackenheim has focused upon. Jewish survival after Auschwitz is a form of religious witness, an insistence that the message of redemption be kept alive. As long as Jews are in history and refuse to abandon God, then men cannot ignore him.[62]

In 1967, Borowitz claims, the message of redemption took on positive meaning. Jews felt even more powerfully the presence of God again. They recognized a "transcendent reality operating in history that they had almost come to believe could no longer make itself felt there."[63] To be sure, the moment passed and may even have been repressed, but in that moment Jews could again feel the fragments come together, could sense the meaning in life and the need to struggle for it, could recognize their unity and what God requires of the Jewish people.

Borowitz urges that American Jews not preoccupy themselves with the false problem of seeking to "understand" God in rationalistic terms. The Jewish understanding of God is anchored in the reality of relationship: in the Covenant. The concept of Covenant is the centerpiece of Borowitz's philosophy of Judaism. "The individual Jew and his sense of value, the Jewish people and its ethos, all come together in the Jew's relationship with God."[64] Through the Covenant the Jew receives both values and a social anchor in the Jewish people. The Covenant is the basis of Jewish integrity.

In the contemporary era the affirmation of the covenantal relationship will necessarily reflect the expansion of human autonomy which characterizes modernity. Jews will be more active participants in the covenantal partnership. But the claiming of this right is not atheism. The assumption of greater human responsibility does not end the relationship; it is in fact central to the Covenant.[65]

Borowitz calls on the ostensibly secular or religiously uncertain American Jew to recognize that

> establishing our Jewish integrity . . . will come when we make the Covenant the basis of our existence, when we link our lives with our people, joining in its historic pact with God. This commitment focuses Jewishness in an act of self—not in ideas, or practice, or birth alone; but all of these will now take their significance from an utterly fundamental relationship of self with God and people.[66]

This is not a plea for a return to traditionalism, but for an endeavor to move Jewish faith from the margins to the center of the individual's being. What would result from this existential commitment to the Covenant within the framework of modernity, Borowitz is unprepared to predict. It surely would not solve all of life's problems, but it would give the Jew, he claims, an invaluable personal resource in facing them. It would enable Jews to achieve, in setting the parameters for their lives, "a new sense of commandment, personally imposed but transcendentally grounded."[67]

In Borowitz's Jewish philosophy we find, then, a bold attempt to synthesize self, folk, and faith. Borowitz speaks to Jews who have not yet discovered the hidden roots and path to fulfillment of their own commitments and aspirations. He proposes that both the roots and the path may be found in the fundamental Judaic vision of divine-human partnership through the Covenant with Israel. By choosing to reaffirm their participation in that ancient drama, contemporary Jews can tie together the fragments of their existence, can affirm both selfhood and peoplehood, both autonomy and the tradition.

This is a philosophy which offers much to civil Jews. It enables them to see their own commitments as the core of a dynamically growing Judaism which propels them at once back to a stronger relationship with the sources of their faith, and forward to a fuller realization of its implications for their lives. It asks such Jews not for a "leap of faith" but a confrontation with what they already believe and do. Out of this, Borowitz contends, will come a recognition that there has always been more there than perhaps met the eye. The civil Jewish commitment to ethnos and ethos can be the platform for a recovery of a thoroughly modern yet traditional religious sensibility, integrated by the master integrating symbol of the Judaic tradition itself: the Covenant.

Borowitz speaks, like Kaplan, quite specifically to the American Jew, and offers a model of Jewish living which validates distinctiveness without abandoning participation. He goes beyond Kaplan, however, in his grasp of the complex dimensions of the contemporary American Jewish situation and the often conflicting impulses of the American Jew. Borowitz affirms that the primary "signals of transcendence" for the Jew today—and the tests of whatever faith the Jew espouses—are likely to emanate from the domain of collective history, from the Holocaust, the rebirth of Israel, and the participation of American Jews in the American social drama. The Jewish return into history has been decisive for shaping the meaning of Jewishness in our time, Borowitz agrees. Nothing else could be expected from a covenantal faith in which the destiny of the individual Jew is inexorably linked to that of Jews everywhere, and especially in Israel, in practical, concrete, political terms. "The destiny of the Household of Israel is a theopolitical matter now as it was in Biblical times."[68]

Borowitz is, nevertheless, sensitive to the fact that faith is ultimately an existential, not merely a sociological issue. Though anchored in what we have called a "neo-Sadducean" sensibility, Borowitz's philosophy, like Martin Buber's, provides a bridge toward a more "neo-Pharisaic" consciousness and concern as well. What is ultimately required for Jewish integrity in our day is commitment to the covenantal partnership on a personal as well as communal level. Borowitz speaks not only to the collectivity, but to the individual. The path he prescribes is one which is directed toward both the pursuit of the Jewish people's historic destiny and the fulfillment of the Jewish individual's quest for personal wholeness. Within the framework of a modern, secularly-infused, pluralistic approach to Jewish faith, Borowitz's philosophy offers civil Judaism a route toward theological self-consciousness which would make not only possible, but nearly mandatory, its participation in a contemporary dialogue of Judaisms. The critical question thus becomes whether it is possible for the adherents of the civil Jewish faith to move toward the whole-hearted acceptance of the covenantal commitment and consciousness which Borowitz urges upon them.

## Irving Greenberg: The Voluntary Covenant

This question—how the contemporary Jew can reaffirm the traditional Jewish covenantal relationship with God in a secular, post-Holocaust era—is the central concern in the writings of the last figure we wish to examine as a contributor to Jewish public theology: Irving (Yitz) Greenberg. More than any other contemporary theologian, Greenberg has directed his work explicitly toward the Jewish polity and its leadership. He has not yet produced a systematic statement of his ideas. The essays he has written, however, go further than any other body of theological writing in placing the polity and the civil Jewish faith at the core of the Jewish experience of our time, and in seeking to build on that faith a full-scale Jewish theological response to the contemporary situation.[69]

The primary teaching of Judaism, Greenberg asserts, is redemption, the vision of "a world in which every human being is in the image of God, i.e., of infinite value, equal and unique." Since such a vision cannot be realized at once, since evil exists and can only be redeemed step by step, Judaism has adopted a way as well as a goal: the way is the Covenant, the commitment of God and the Jewish people to work together until redemption is achieved.[70] The Jewish role in the process of redemption is thus central: Jews testify, model a way, and teach the world the goal of final perfection.[71]

The Covenant concept is not a static one in Jewish history. It is transformed as it unfolds under conditions of crisis. We live, says Greenberg, at such a moment of transformation, and this fact must inform our religious consciousness in a radical fashion.[72] The central problem for any contemporary covenantal theology is to spell out the nature of the claim which the Covenant can still make on the modern Jew. In practical terms, the challenge is one of specifying what the Covenant demands behaviorally of the individual Jew and the Jewish people today.

The thrust of Greenberg's answer to this question is very much in keeping with those suggested by Kaplan, Buber, Fackenheim, and Boro-witz: namely, that Jews must continue to witness to the validity of moral values in an amoral world and to the hope that those values will one day be affirmed and realized by all. This is an answer congruent with the es-sential ethos of the civil religion, one which defines the Jewish role in terms of the kind of social activism and ethical commitment with which the polity is eminently comfortable.

It is in theological terms that Greenberg seeks to go beyond Boro-witz's call for reaffirmation of the Covenant. The question which Green-berg, and perhaps Fackenheim, would insist must be raised is whether, after Auschwitz, one can speak of a Covenant between God and Israel in any meaningful sense at all.[73] This is a question which Borowitz ad-dresses only tangentially. For Greenberg, however, it is on this question and the answer to it that an understanding of the religious situation of the contemporary Jew must be founded. The Covenant must indeed be reaffirmed if Judaism is to endure. But how, he asks, can it be in such a God-bereft era?

Greenberg asks this question because he takes history with the utmost seriousness. Traditional rabbinic Judaism affirms that nothing decisive can happen in history between the revelation at Sinai and the messianic redemption. The return of the Jewish people into history challenges that affirmation; for Greenberg, as for Fackenheim, Auschwitz shatters it. Greenberg asserts even more boldly than Fackenheim that contem-porary, post-Holocaust Jews live in a different era from that in which traditional Judaism took shape, different even from that of the "modern" Jew whose historical and spiritual agenda was shaped by Emancipation and the quest for normalization. For Greenberg, the Holocaust is a de-cisive turning point in Jewish history, one which ushers in a new era which calls for an altogether different understanding of the nature of the Covenant and of its claims on the Jew.[74]

In his writings, Greenberg has spoken of our time as a "third era in Jewish history," following the biblical and rabbinic epochs which pre-ceded it. He attempts to justify this dramatic claim by noting that each era is characterized by a specific confluence of the factors that define the Jewish condition: the political situation of the Jews, their theological self-understanding, the type of leadership which is authoritative, and the institutions which embody the values and serve the needs of the Jewish community.[75] Each era is inaugurated by an epoch-shaping event: for the biblical era, the Exodus from Egypt, for the rabbinic era, the destruction of the Temple and defeat of Jewish messianic hopes. The transition from the biblical to the rabbinic eras was marked by a radical transformation in the total Jewish condition: From a situation of nation-hood and political (semi-) autonomy, Jewry passed into one of power-lessness. From a theological perspective which emphasized the manifestation of divinity in the Temple and relationship with God through the cult, Jews (or at least those who did not abandon Judaism altogether) moved to one which emphasized God's accessibility through prayer, study, and good deeds. From leadership by kings, priests, and occasional prophets, the community turned to leadership by scholars: the rabbis. From a people united institutionally by a sanctuary and the institutions of state, the Jews became a people of the synagogue and the schoolhouse.[76]

Jews today, Greenberg contends, are living in a third such era, one ushered in by both an event of destruction, the Holocaust, and one of redemption, the establishment of the State of Israel. The religious meaning of this third era can be recognized both in these events, and in an understanding of how the terms of the divine-human relationship have changed from era to era. In the biblical age, God was manifest, the clearly dominant partner in the covenantal relationship with Israel. The challenge implicit in the destruction of the second Temple in 70 c.e. was directed against both the manifest deity and the Covenant which bound him to Israel. The rabbinic response was theologically brilliant: they sacrificed the manifest deity, the God of public miracles and of prophecy, in order to salvage the Covenant. Holiness, previously concentrated in God and the Temple, was diffused into the domains of day-to-day living, and the Jewish people emerged as a full Covenant partner with a new measure of responsibility—through the *halakhah*—for its fulfillment in the world.[77]

This rabbinic reformulation of the Covenant relationship sustained the Jewish people through centuries of political powerlessness. Emancipation challenged it, but did not replace it, because it left the fundamental condition of Jewish powerlessness unaltered. The events of the twentieth century, however, have, according to Greenberg, destroyed the rabbinic synthesis and along with it even the rabbinic understanding of the covenantal relationship. The rabbis responded to the awesome tragedy of destruction and exile by proclaiming that God had gone into exile, as it were, with his people. But in the Holocaust even that theological metaphor could not withstand God's absolute absence. In its wake, one could only judge that God, not the Jewish people, had abandoned the Covenant. Hence, its obligations imposed on the Jew were suspended; no authority could claim the right to enforce them.[78]

The lesson of the Holocaust is that if holiness is to be found anywhere in the world it will be in the "secular" domain, where humans enjoy full responsibility. The rabbinic diffusion of the sacred into the profane world is, in the third era, taken a step farther. This must become, Greenberg contends, an era of "holy secularity"—an era in which religious commitment and faith are manifested through secular acts:

> Every act of social justice, every humane or productive factory, every
> sport contest in community centers, every act of human socializing and

dignity will become a secularized halacha as Jewish religious insight deepens and the sacred dimensions of the profane are uncovered.[79]

Like Fackenheim and Borowitz, Greenberg sees in the Jewish decision after the Holocaust to create and defend the state of Israel a sign of its determination to wrest life and meaning from out of the ashes. Israel is in this sense a reaffirmation of faith, but faith as a call to holy secularity, to testing the capacity of Jews to serve as the dominant figures in a renewed covenantal relationship. The Covenant of the third era must be and has become a "voluntary Covenant." Without coercion or obligation, Jews have reassumed the task of being a covenantal people; they have decided to take upon themselves the challenge of determining whether the values and ideals of the tradition can be sustained in the modern world.[80]

> The ability of Jews to reconcile realities and Covenantal ideals; the ability to generate the human, moral, and religious resources to carry on the struggle; and the ability to set about perfecting the world, however modestly, will be the test of Judaism in the third era.[81]

In order to undertake this task Jews must have power. The Holocaust demonstrated that the era of Jewish powerlessness must end; Israel has meant that it was ended. Now Israel represents the great test of whether classic Jewish ideals and models can in fact shape society in the modern world. For this reason, and for its existential meaning as the Jewish people's fundamental act of life and creation after Auschwitz, Israel is the central Jewish reality of the third era.[82] But even in the Diaspora, Jews can, in exercising power, psychologically pass beyond exilic Judaism. In America, the Jewish polity has committed itself to this goal: making sure that Jews have sufficient power to insure both their survival and the chance to play their covenantal role.[83] Greenberg warns that the ground rules of "morality" which apply to the powerless cannot be applied in the same way to those who exercise power. Moral purity is impossible, but moral responsibility in the exercise of power is a valid and vital goal.[84]

In calling this the era of the "voluntary Covenant," Greenberg clearly means to emphasize both its distinctiveness in Jewish history and its connectedness to the Jewish past. "Holy secularity" implies that the sacred, the divine presence, remains real, even though it is more broadly spread and more deeply embedded in the world than ever before. The observances and teachings of the biblical and rabbinic eras must continue to be examined for their capacity to shape values and inform lives with dignity and joy, and to cultivate a sensitivity to the sacred in its hidden dimensions.[85]

Nevertheless, Greenberg insists, the terms of Jewish existence in the contemporary era have changed decisively. A new synthesis of political condition, theological self-understanding, leadership, and institutional life is in the process of being effected. Greenberg lists several implications of the voluntary Covenant for Jewish belief and behavior today:

1. The survival of Jews regardless of their self-definition is in its own right testimony to the existence of the hidden God.
2. The voluntary Covenant is the theological base for a genuine Jewish pluralism and a genuine Jewish unity. Since no one can authoritatively define which self-assumed obligations will in fact lead toward the realization of the values implicit in the Covenant, all forms of commitment must be respected as covenantal experiments. The post-Emancipation lines which have divided Jews are, while not totally meaningless, largely irrelevant to the tasks of the third era.
3. As a corollary of human co-creativity in the Covenant, Jews have a responsibility to correct models or behavior patterns in the tradition (e.g., discrimination against women) which demean the image of God.
4. Jews must take up the challenge of achieving "messianic breakthroughs." Such breakthroughs will necessarily be partial, flawed, hidden, and must be sought while avoiding excessive utopianism and anti-nomianism. But the achievement of justice, peace, and human dignity demands a sense of messianic urgency.
5. New events, new observances, new *mitzvot*—more naturalistic, flawed, and secular—must be incorporated within the Covenantal framework as part of the work (and risk) of "secular sanctification."[86]

This program is one, Greenberg suggests, in which all of the institutions of Jewry must be involved, but his primary goal is the sensitization of that institutional network which we have called the Jewish polity to its central role in its achievement. In the synthesis of the third era, the polity and its leadership constitute the focal point for Jewish power and for the activities which manifest "holy secularity."[87] It is, therefore, vital that contemporary Jews, and espcially the leaders of the polity, recognize the religious dimensions of their commitment and their mission. By understanding and accepting the role they have assumed as participants in the new voluntary Covenant, Jews today can serve as continuators of the covenantal tradition as it moves toward its final redemptive goal.[88]

There is little that is entirely original in the details of Greenberg's Jewish philosophy. It echoes many of the themes we have already seen in the work of Fackenheim and Borowitz. In its present schematic form it lacks the profound philosophical underpinnings of Buber or Fackenheim, or the detailed social analysis of Kaplan or Borowitz. What makes it unique and significant is its straightforward assertion that Jews live today in a new era in Jewish history. This claim gives Greenberg's call for the reassumption of covenantal responsibilities a weight and an urgency which might otherwise be obscured in debate over what such a reassumption entails. Greenberg's historiosophy is problematic; it is a bold man who will assume the risk of characterizing the meaning and significance of his own historical time in the global terms which Greenberg employs. Yet, whether Jews today truly live in a third era of Jewish history or not, they have assumed a new political stance, they have created new institutions, they have generated new leadership, and they have developed a synthesis of worldly activism and religious passion which has reshaped the modern Jewish scene.

Greenberg does not endorse civil Judaism as an adequate religious expression of the voluntary Covenant. But he recognizes in it and in those who are its adherents the generative force for the more Judaically informed, religiously self-conscious "holy secularity" he seeks to inspire. In this respect, he is perhaps the first true public theologian of the contemporary American Jewish civil religion. Other individuals too, men like Daniel Elazar, Leonard Fein, and David Hartman, have begun to fill this role. Each brings somewhat different nuances and sensibilities to his teaching, but they, together with all of the figures whose thought we have cited, appear to share a common message: The essential meaning of Jewishness today lies in a reaffirmation of the Jewish people's historic mission to be a "kingdom of priests and a holy nation," to effect *tikkun olam*, the mending of the world.

The fulfillment of that mission demands that the secularity of the modern world be embraced and transfigured. The Jewish people's return to history and to power over its own destiny makes possible the reassumption of its historic vocation, and makes necessary that vocation's translation into new forms of action and commitment. In the renewal of Jewish responsibility in and for the world, the boundary between the religious and the secular, a boundary imposed by history on a resistant covenantal faith, can now be breached once again. In the breaching of that boundary, the fullness of Judaism as a messianic, theo-political endeavor can be restored.

### From Survival to Covenant

Our brief examination of the work of these five modern Jewish thinkers demonstrates that the "neo-Sadducean" sensibility can indeed serve as the kernal of a self-conscious and articulate contemporary religious posture. For the Jewish polity and for the adherents of civil Judaism this is an important and a challenging conclusion. It implies that those who embrace the tenets of the civil Jewish faith, who are moved by its myths and rituals, must view their commitment with a new religious seriousness. What they espouse is indeed no mere institutional ideology, nor simply a rhetoric of mobilization, but the schematic core of a Jewish meaning system which deals with the most serious issues of Jewish life in the contemporary world.

Civil Judaism has not yet achieved this level of self-consciousness. Indeed, as a civil religion it is almost surely incapable of achieving the depth of vision, memory, commitment, and reflection which would be required for it to stand as a significant philosophy of Jewish existence in its own right. This is why the Jewish polity needs to expose itself to public theology and to religious thinkers who will push its activists and citizens to explore the underpinnings and implications of their commitment. The relationship between civil religion and public theology is an ongoing and reciprocal one. Civil religious faith requires a public theological enterprise to constrain its tendencies to degenerate into formulaic rhetoric and celebratory ritual. Public theology needs the civil religious faith and the polity which carries it in order to fulfill its aspiration to impact upon the self-consciousness and behavior of a living community.

In the case of the relationship between contemporary American civil Judaism and the endeavors in Jewish theology examined above, this reciprocity is clear. Both civil Judaism and the religious approaches we have cited are "post-denominational." They are anchored in and addressed to a Jewry whose structural center lies in the public realm: in the state of Israel, in the institutions of the American Jewish polity. The theologies of Kaplan, Buber, Fackenheim, Borowitz, Greenberg, and the others who might be coupled with them make no sense without the institutional revolution which has brought the Jewish polity (in its largest sense) again to the forefront of Jewish life. That revolution in turn must, if it is to achieve its own aims of insuring a meaningful Jewish existence in the modern world, achieve an explicitly religious self-understanding.

The emergence of Jewish civil religions in Israel and in North America is no accident. Civil Judaism and its Israeli counterpart grow out of the rediscovered polity,[89] and the need to validate the Jewish return to history and power. The deepening of those civil religions through exposure to an enterprise of public theology constitutes the logical (but not thereby inevitable) next stage in their evolution. Certainly, it is the necessary prelude to their participation in a full-scale dialogue of Jewish meaning systems in the modern world.

This is a process which has already begun, though only in nascent form. For American civil Judaism, the continuation of that process demands a more intense confrontation with both the secular world in which it is active and the religious tradition from which it emerges. This is the clear message of the theological essays we have explored. The religious significance of civil Judaism lies precisely in its capacity to mediate the historical encounter of Judaism and the modern secular world in a new way. The civil religion represents, we have suggested, an effort to hold in balance the fundamental tensions of that encounter: tensions between Jewish particularism and universalism, between tradition and autonomy, between messianic expectation and human initiative, between perceiving "signals of transcendence" and facing the "eclipse of God."

Civil Judaism cannot avoid being afflicted at its core by these tensions; it cannot become an "easy faith" without undermining its own raison d'être.

Civil Judaism is, thus, a faith for the "ambivalent American Jew" in an even more profound way than we suggested in chapter 3. It is a religious posture and an activist program which faces a series of ongoing challenges: teaching Jews how to live in two civilizations; penetrating the structures of national and organizational life with the power of Jewish values; insuring that the Jewish people endures for its work of *tikkun olam* in a world which assaults both the people and its faith; reaffirming the Covenant in a time when it is difficult even to speak of God, much less to effect a divine-human partnership. The elements of problematic and risk inherent in the civil Jewish commitment—and especially in a deepening of that commitment—cannot, however, be avoided. They are what accords civil Judaism its religious integrity as a bridge between the sacred and the profane.

But is the path toward a more serious religiosity one which the adherents of civil Judaism are likely to wish to take? We believe that many will, if only because the visceral impact of their present commitment demands that they question themselves more seriously about the roots of their concern. Civil Judaism's theological aspirations are muted, largely as a self-protective mechanism, but the myths which it has adopted can only be sustained over time as part of a transcendental consciousness. Because of the fact that the civil religion simultaneously affirms a secular consciousness as well, these myths—of destruction and rebirth, of American Jewish exceptionalism, of Jewish election—will always be "broken myths."[90] Civil Jewish faith may never be comfortable intellectually with the affirmation of transcendence, but emotionally, its commitment has already been made and is manifest in the lives and actions of many of its adherents.

American civil Judaism is part of contemporary Jewry's reentry into the realm of theo-political history, the realm in which Judaism originally took shape three millennia ago. No orientation to human existence carries with it greater power to inspire devotion and sacrifice, or greater risk, than one which sees redemption at stake in every human action, every historical event. Yet this conviction—that what Jews do matters ultimately—may be the only answer which can sustain a Jewish commitment to endure as Jews in the modern world. Only by viewing themselves as the people of the Covenant, as the effectors of *tikkun olam*, can contemporary Jews make sense of their determination to survive. Civil Judaism has reflected and helped to shape American Jewry's passage from a community of adjustment to a community of survival. It is now poised to mold and to mirror an even more portentous transition: from being a community of survival to a truly covenantal community once again.

American Jewish civil religion represents neither the sole legitimate religious option available to the contemporary American Jew, nor the only valid interpretation of the meaning and message of the Judaic tradition for our time. It has, however, surely redeemed the "neo-Saducean" —or perhaps better, "neo-biblical"—religious sensibility as a vital component of the Judaic affirmation in the modern world. If it is not yet eager to enter into a contemporary dialogue of Judaisms, it may be because its faith stance and the institutional expression of that faith in the work of the Jewish polity seem so "unreligious" in terms of what Jews have been accustomed to think of as religious belief and practice. We have sought to dispell that illusion. Civil Judaism is not a completed faith and may never be one. But linked to a theologial consciousness which can ground its tenets in a hard-won reaffirmation of Jewish destiny and faith, civil Judaism can, perhaps must, be a central part of the two-centuries-old endeavor to regather the fragments of Jewish existence which have been torn asunder in the modern era. It is unlikely that the founders of the American Jewish polity and the first articulators of its values believed they were doing more than trying to forge a measure of communal unity amidst the chaos of their day. What they have made possible, however, is something far grander: a contemporary dialogue of Judaisms in which, perhaps, the wholeness of Jewish life itself can be restored and the Jewish journey toward redemption propelled yet another step forward.

# APPENDIX:
## DOCUMENTS USED IN CONTENT ANALYSIS

*Note:* The listing gives the author (individual or organization), title, publishing organization or organizational affiliation of the author, and date of publication or delivery.

1. Mort Mandel, "Entering the Eighties," Council of Jewish Federations, 1979.
2. Palm Beach County Board of Rabbis, "Let It Be Known," 1982.
3. American Jewish Joint Distribution Committee, "The American Jewish Joint Distribution Committee - 1979," 1980.
4. Jerold Hoffberger, "Retrospect and Prospect," Council of Jewish Federations, 1978.
5. Frank Lautenberg, "We Are One," United Jewish Appeal, 1974.
6. Mort Mandel, "CJF and Federations: New Goals for a New Decade," Council of Jewish Federations, 1980.
7. Mort Mandel, "The Future of Federations," Council of Jewish Federations, 1981.
8. Jerold Hoffberger, "The State of Our Federations," Council of Jewish Federations, 1976.
9. Phil Bernstein, "Federations: What They Are and Are Not," Council of Jewish Federations, 1976.
10. Phil Bernstein, "The Principles of Jewish Federations," Council of Jewish Federations, 1976.
11. Martin Citrin, "Where Do We Go From Here," Council of Jewish Federations, 1979.
12. Sidney Vincent, "Paradox and Promise," Council of Jewish Federations, 1977.
13. Sanford Solender, "Themes From the Assembly," Council of Jewish Federations, 1979.
14. Edward Robin, "Why We Are Here," United Jewish Appeal Young Leadership Cabinet, 1982.
15. Council of Jewish Federations, "CJF/50," 1981.
16. Bert Gold, "Pressures Facing the American Jewish Community," Brandeis University, 1977.
17. Phil Bernstein, "Agenda for American Jews," Brandeis University, 1978.
18. Ralph Goldman, "Leadership for an Ever-Changing World," Brandeis University, 1979.
19. Irving Bernstein, "The Future of Jewish Philanthropy," Brandeis University, 1980.
20. Mrs. Laurence Tisch, "The Jewish Community in the 1980s," Brandeis University, 1981.
21. United Jewish Appeal, "This Year in Jerusalem," 1976.
22. Anti-Defamation League of B'nai B'rith, "Purpose and Program," 1976.
23. National Jewish Community Relations Advisory Council, "The NJCRAC: What It Is, How It Works," 1974.

24. American Jewish Joint Distribution Committee, "1981 Annual Report," 1981.

25. Sidney Vincent, "The Jewish Federation: Reflections on an American Institution," Brandeis University, 1976.

26. American Jewish Committee, "The American Jewish Committee: Seventy Years," 1976.

27. Jewish Welfare Board, "JWB - Involved With the Quality of Jewish Family Life Worldwide," 1979.

28. Jewish Welfare Board, "JWB - Serving the Jewish Community," 1979.

29. Jerold Hoffberger, "Major Challenges Ahead," Council of Jewish Federations, 1977.

30. United Jewish Appeal, "Year of Jewish Renewal," 1978.

31. Charles Zibbell, "Tzedakah and the Jewish Community," Jewish Federation of New Orleans, 1974.

32. Anti-Defamation League of B'nai B'rith, "ADL: Purpose and Program," 1981.

33. American Jewish Joint Distribution Committee, "1980 Annual Report," 1980.

34. Michael Adler, "Caucus Introduction," United Jewish Appeal Young Leadership Cabinet, 1982.

35. David Greene, "Welcome to YLC Members," United Jewish Appeal Young Leadership Cabinet, 1982.

36. Jewish Welfare Board, "Priorities, Budget, Services 1980," 1980.

37. Council of Jewish Federations, "Resolutions of the 49th General Assembly," 1980.

38. Council of Jewish Federations, "Resolutions of the 50th General Assembly," 1981.

39. Organization for Rehabilitation Through Training, "ORT Yearbook, 1981," 1981.

40. Rabbi Robert Kahn, "Beyond Rachmanut . . . Beyond Tzedakah," United Jewish Appeal, 1981.

41. Hebrew Immigrant Aid Society, "Centennial Year HIAS Annual Report," 1980.

42. Jewish Federation of St. Louis, "Jewish St. Louis: A Guide," 1975.

43. United Jewish Appeal, "Proclaim Liberty," 1976.

44. United Jewish Appeal, "United Jewish Appeal - 1977," 1976.

45. United Jewish Appeal, "1980 Campaign Background," 1979.

46. Irving Bernstein, "UJA National Conference Address," United Jewish Appeal, 1982.

47. United Jewish Appeal, "Now. More Than Ever. We Are One." 1979.

48. United Jewish Appeal, "We Are One," 1980.

49. American Jewish Congress, "Keep The Faith," 1970.

50. American Jewish Committee, "The American Jewish Committee: Here and Now," 1970.

51. Jewish Labor Committee, "The Jewish Labor Committee Story," 1970.

52. Council of Jewish Federations, "Highlights—CJF Board and Committee Meetings," 1982.

53. American Jewish Congress, "Not Charity But Justice," 1968.

54. Charles Miller, "An Introduction to the Jewish Federation," Council of Jewish Federations, 1976.

55. Martin Citrin, "Community and Campaign," Council of Jewish Federations, 1982.

56. Anti-Defamation League of B'nai B'rith, "ADL Working For You," 1982.

57. Organization for Rehabilitation Through Training, "ORT Yearbook 1982," 1982.

58. David Greene, "Dear Chevre," United Jewish Appeal Young Leadership Cabinet, 1982.

59. Irving Bernstein, "UJA Young Leadership Conference Speech," United Jewish Appeal, 1982.

60. Robert Loup, "Dear Friend and Colleague," United Jewish Appeal, 1982.

61. Charles Zibbell, "New Directions in Federation Planning for Jewish Education," Council of Jewish Federations, 1969.

62. Mort Mandel, "Forging a Sturdy Chain," Council of Jewish Federations, 1979.

63. Phil Bernstein, "Federations in the Next Decade," Council of Jewish Federations, 1976.

64. Bernard Olshansky, "The Role of Jewish Community and Leadership in Assuring Jewish Continuity," Council of Jewish Federations, 1976.

65. David Zeff, "The Planning Process," Council of Jewish Federations, 1962.

66. United Jewish Appeal, "UJA Israel Independence Day Haggadah," 1978.

67. Irving Bernstein, "Young Leadership Cabinet Retreat Speech," United Jewish Appeal, 1979.

68. Irving Bernstein, "Highlights of Recent News and Events," United Jewish Appeal, 1979.

69. Neil Cooper, "Speech to UJA New Gifts Institute," United Jewish Appeal, 1982.

70. Council of Jewish Federations, "Summary Session—47th General Assembly," 1978.

71. Council of Jewish Federations, "Semi-Centennial Minutes," 1982.

72. Martin Citrin, "A Blow Against Terrorism," Council of Jewish Federations, 1982.

73. Council of Jewish Federations, "What's New in Federations," 1982.

74. Combined Jewish Philanthropies of Greater Boston, "CJP Means Caring," 1982.

75. Sidney Vincent, "Shaping a More Creative and Responsive Community: The Role of Leadership," Council of Jewish Federations, 1975.

76. Frank Lautenberg, "O Jerusalem, We Shall Never Be Still," United Jewish Appeal, 1976.

77. Council of Jewish Federations, "Resolutions of the 45th General Assembly," 1976.

78. Jerold Hoffberger, "Justice For All," Council of Jewish Federations, 1976.

79. Irwin Field, "The Spirit of Denver," United Jewish Appeal, 1979.

80. Council of Jewish Federations, "Resolutions of the 51st General Assembly," 1982.

81. Council of Jewish Federations, "Summary Session—46th General Assembly," 1977.

82. Max Fisher, Robert Russell, Jerome Cardin, "Project Renewal," Council of Jewish Federations, 1978.

83. Sidney Vincent, "Jewish Culture in North America: Actual and Potential," Council of Jewish Federations, 1978.

84. Council of Jewish Federations, "Resolutions of the 47th General Assembly," 1978.

85. Sidney Vincent, "Planning for Small Cities—New Directions for the 80s," Council of Jewish Federations, 1978.

86. Earl Raab, Al Chernin, Sanford Solender, "Domestic Social Problems," Council of Jewish Federations, 1978.

87. Irwin Field, "Jewish Renewal At Home and Abraod," United Jewish Appeal, 1978.

88. Albert Ratner, "The Jewish Response: A Personal Review," Council of Jewish Federations, 1979.

89. Irwin Field, "1980—The Keystone Campaign of a Decade," United Jewish Appeal, 1979.

90. United Israel Appeal, "The Triumph of a Dream," 1979.

91. United Jewish Appeal, "UJA Annual Report—1981," 1981.

92. United Jewish Appeal, "UJA Annual Report—1980," 1980.

93. Council of Jewish Federations, "Resolutions of the 46th General Assembly," 1977.

94. Council of Jewish Federations, "Resolutions of the 48th General Assembly," 1979.

95. Stuart Handmaker, "A Personal View of the Role of the President," Council of Jewish Federations, 1979.

96. United Jewish Appeal Young Leadership Cabinet, "Young Leadership Cabinet Communique," 1980.

97. United Jewish Appeal, "UJA Annual Report—1979," 1979.

98. United Jewish Appeal, "The Critical Difference," 1978.

99. United Jewish Appeal, "If You Think All Our Problems Are Solved," 1977.

100. Federation of Jewish Agencies of Greater Philadelphia, "75 Years of Continuity and Change: Our Philadelphia Jewish Community in Perspective," 1976.

101. Council of Jewish Federations, "Report on the Review of the Purpose, Function, Program and Organization of the Council of Jewish Federations," 1979.

102. Council of Jewish Federations, "General Assembly Digests," 1982.

103. Council of Jewish Federations, "Highlights—CJF Board and Committee Meetings," 1982.

104. Morris Zeldich, "What Makes a Jewish Community," Council of Jewish Federations, 1958.

105. Arthur Rotman, "Forging Links: The Jewish Community Center Builds Jewish Community," Jewish Welfare Board, 1982.

106. United Jewish Appeal, "Record—Quarterly of the UJA Women's Division," 1979.

107. United Jewish Appeal Young Leadership Cabinet, "Facts About the Cabinet," 1979.

108. Council of Jewish Federations, "A Look at the CJF," 1980.

109. United Jewish Appeal, "Covenant for Continuity," 1980.

110. United Jewish Appeal, "1983 Campaign Theme," 1982.

111. United Jewish Appeal, "UJA Campaign Guide For Students," 1979.

112. Arthur Katzenberg, "Urgent Information Re Israel Crisis," Combined Jewish Philanthropies of Greater Boston, 1982.

113. Stanley Horowitz, "Insuring Jewish Commitment: The Federation Role," Council of Jewish Federations, 1982.

114. Jewish Agency for Israel, "Report on the Pincus and Joint Education Funds," 1981.

115. Martin Citrin, "Visions of the Future," Council of Jewish Federations, 1982.

116. Monty Hall, "Handle With Care," Jewish Federation Council of Los Angeles, 1982.

117. Federation of Jewish Philanthropies of New York, "1981–82 Annual Report," 1982.

118. Bert Gold, "New Realities in American Jewish Life," American Jewish Committee, 1980.

119. American Jewish Committee, "The American Jewish Committee: An Inside Look," 1981.

120. American Jewish Committee, "Decades of Decision: A Brief History of the American Jewish Committee," 1982.

121. American Jewish Committee, "The American Jewish Committee 1906–1981," 1981.

122. Council of Jewish Federations, "Summary Session—45th General Assembly," 1976.

123. Allied Jewish Community Services of Montreal, "Toward a New Consensus," 1982.

124. Howard Squadron, "Farewell Address as President of the Conference of Presidents," 1982.

125. Edgar Bronfman, "Address to the South African National Jewish Congress," World Jewish Congress, 1983.

126. Federation of Jewish Philanthropies of New York, "1982–83 Annual Report," 1983.

127. Council of Jewish Federations, *Birkat Hamazon* (Grace After Meals)," 1983.

128. Alan Ades, "United Jewish Appeal Northeast Regional Conference Address," United Jewish Appeal, 1983.

129. Darrell Friedman, "Coping With Change," Council of Jewish Federations, 1983.

130. Myron Brodie, "Federations Confront the Challenge of Change," Council of Jewish Federations, 1983.

131. Leon Dulzin, "The Jewish Agency for Israel," Jewish Agency for Israel, 1983.

132. Martin Citrin, "A Year of Challenges," Council of Jewish Federations, 1983.

# NOTES

## 1. Civil Religion and the Modern Jewish Challenge

1. See, among others: Jacob Katz, *Tradition and Crisis: Jewish Society at the End of the Middle Ages* (New York: Free Press of Glencoe, 1961) and *Out of the Ghetto: The Social Background of Jewish Emancipation* (Cambridge: Harvard University Press, 1973); Michael Meyer, *The Origins of the Modern Jew: Jewish Identity and European Culture in Germany, 1749–1824* (Detroit: Wayne State University Press, 1979); Joseph L. Blau, *Modern Varieties of Judaism* (New York: Columbia University Press, 1964); Steven M. Cohen, *American Modernity and Jewish Identity* (New York: Tavistock Publications, 1983); Calvin Goldscheider and Alan S. Zuckerman, *The Transformation of the Jews* (Chicago: The University of Chicago Press, 1984).

2. Cf. Jacob Neusner, *Between Time and Eternity: The Essentials of Judaism* (Encino, California: Dickenson Publishing Company, 1975), p. 116.

3. For a detailed account of the modernization process and its effects on Jewish demography, ideologies, economic, and political life, see Goldscheider and Zuckerman, pp. 29–153.

4. Meyer, p. 8.

5. Paul R. Mendes-Flohr and Jehuda Reinharz, eds., *The Jew in the Modern World: A Documentary History* (New York and Oxford: Oxford University Press, 1980), p. 241.

6. Mendes-Flohr and Reinharz, pp. 114, 118.

7. Cf. Arnold M. Eisen, *The Chosen People in America: A Study in Jewish Religious Ideology* (Bloomington: Indiana University Press, 1983), chap. 1.

8. Blau, p. 25.

9. Eliezer L. Ehrmann, ed., *Readings in Modern Jewish History: From the American Revolution to the Present* (New York: Ktav Publishing House, 1977), p. 33.

10. Cf. Blau, p. 98.

11. Mendes-Flohr and Reinharz, p. 300ff.

12. Cf. the discussion on this question in Arthur Hertzberg's Introduction to his anthology *The Zionist Idea: A Historical Analysis and Reader* (New York: Atheneum, 1971), pp. 15–100.

13. Blau, p. 128.

14. Neusner, pp. 129–30.

15. Mendes-Flohr and Reinharz, p. 388.

16. Ibid.

17. Blau, p. 97.

18. Ibid. p. 98.

19. See the discussion in the next section for a more detailed consideration of the process through which civil religion may emerge in situations of religious pluralism. For a full discussion see Phillip E. Hammond, "The Rudimentary Forms of Civil Religion," and "Pluralism and Law in the Formation of American Civil Religion," in Robert N. Bellah and Phillip E. Hammond, *Varieties of Civil Religion* (San Francisco: Harper & Row, 1980), pp. 121–37, 138–63.

20. The literature on civil religion, and especially American civil religion is voluminous, and often contentious. The analysis which follows largely adopts the definitional and empirical approach of Bellah, Hammond, and others who regard civil religion as an important and enduring religious phenomenon. Critiques of Bellah's work have generally been of two types: (1) Normative critics have questioned Bellah's characterization and positive appraisal of the theological content and functional role of American civil religion. This has been especially characteristic of some denominational religious leaders who do not accept Bellah's claim that the civil religion represents a viable transcendent faith. (2) Sociological critics, most notably Richard Fenn, have argued that Bellah's picture of a unifying American faith, while possibly valid at one point in the nation's history, is no longer supportable. These critics fail to find any overarching moral order or transcendent meaning system uniting all of modern, secularized society, and hence regard civil religion as at best a phase in the long-term process of social differentiation and secularization. We will not attempt in this work to enter into these debates in any depth, since they focus largely on the specific phenomenon of American civil religion—if it is and what it is. For statements and analyses of the various positions, see the following: Robert N. Bellah, "Civil Religion in America," *Daedalus* (Winter 1967): 1–21; the reprint of this essay with comments by D. W. Brogan, Leo Pfeffer, John R. Whitney, Phillip E. Hammond, and a reply by Bellah in *The Religious Situation: 1968*, ed. Donald R. Cutler (Boston: Beacon Press, 1968), pp. 331–93; John Coleman, "Civil Religion," *Sociological Analysis* (Summer 1970): 67–77; Robert N. Bellah, *The Broken Covenant: American Civil Religion in Time of Trial* (New York: Seabury, 1975); Russell B. Richey and Donald G. Jones, eds., *American Civil Religion* (New York: Harper & Row, 1974); Richard K. Fenn, *Toward a Theory of Secularization* (Storrs, Conn.: Society for the Scientific Study of Religion, 1978); Bellah and Hammond, *Varieties of Civil Religion*; Gail Gehrig, *American Civil Religion: An Assessment* (Storrs, Conn.: Society for the Scientific Study of Religion, 1979); Michael W. Hughey, *Civil Religion and Moral Order: Theoretical and Historical Dimensions* (Westport, Conn.: Greenwood Press, 1983); as well as symposia in *Sociological Analysis* (Summer 1976): 111–82; *Religious Education* (September-October 1975) and (May-June 1976).

21. Hammond, "Pluralism and Law," p. 139.

22. Cf. Charles S. Liebman and Eliezer Don-Yehiya, *Civil Religion in Israel: Traditional Judaism and Political Culture in the Jewish State* (Berkeley: University of California Press, 1983), p. 214.

23. Hammond, "The Rudimentary Forms," pp. 121–37; "Pluralism and Law," pp. 141–44. Hammond suggests that religious sentiments are likely to be attached to precisely those institutions which are most effective in resolving social conflicts, i.e., which provide concrete foci of unity in the society. The legal system, he argues, often plays this role within American society and hence is a prime locus of American civil religion. A similar role, we contend, has been played by philanthropy in American Jewish life. Thus, as we will describe in detail in the next chapter, its emergence as the institutional and ideological core of American Jewish civil religion is in line with Hammond's argument.

24. The first use of the term "civil religion" is usually credited to the French political philosopher Jean-Jacques Rousseau, who included a chapter "Of Civil Religion" in *The Social Contract*. Rousseau viewed the existence of a set of universally affirmed, though theologically minimalist, dogmas of faith as a requisite for sustaining the cohesion of the social order and for inculcating citizens with appropriate civic virtues. He urged political leaders to promulgate such a faith. This notion of civil religion as a deliberately engineered political faith differs somewhat from the Durkheimean approach which focuses on the natural emer-

gence of religion as the symbolic expression of social unity. Both approaches are relevant to the depiction of civil religion's place in contemporary society, and, as we shall see, among American Jewry. In our understanding, a healthy, functioning civil religion can be neither simply an expression of popular sentiment nor an artificially contrived ideology imposed for the purpose of maintaining social cohesion. While rooted in a sense of unity which must be to some degree natural and organic, a civil religion represents as well a conscious program for sustaining and directing that solidarity toward socially worthy ends. The tension implicit in the alternative perspectives of Durkheim and Rousseau is, nevertheless, worth keeping in mind. In various times and places, civil religion may hew more toward one or another of the two models, and should the gap between popular self-understanding and political program grow too great, civil religion itself may be impossible to sustain. On this point, see N. J. Demerath III and Rhys H. Williams, "Civil Religion in an Uncivil Society," *The Annals of the American Academy of Political and Social Science*, vol. 480, Religion in America Today, ed. Wade Clark Roof (Beverly Hills: Sage Publications, July 1985), pp. 154–66.

25. Michael Novak, *Choosing Our King: Powerful Symbols in Presidential Politics* (New York: Macmillan Publishing Company, 1974), p. 127. Gail Gehrig, basing her definition on that of John Coleman, defines American civil religion as "the religious symbol system which relates the citizen's role and American society's place in space, time, and history to the conditions of ultimate existence and meaning" (p. 18). Bellah defines civil religion in general as "that religious dimension . . . through which [a people] interprets its historical experience in the light of transcendent reality" *(The Broken Covenant, p. 3). All of these definitions treat civil religion as a transcendent faith with universal dimensions. This is not, however, the only sense in which the term has been used. In the introduction to their collection of readings on American civil religion, Richey and Jones cite five different meanings given to the concept: (1) civil religion as "folk religion," (2) civil religion as religious nationalism, (3) civil religion as the democratic faith, (4) civil religion as Protestant civic piety, and (5) civil religion as the transcendent universal religion of the nation (pp. 14–18). We agree with Gehrig and others that the last of these is the most encompassing and conceptually significant of the understandings of civil religion. The others may be regarded as variants which can indeed be attested in the American historical experience, but which fall short of the full meaning of the concept. (Cf. Gehrig, pp. 2–4, 17–19.)

26. Liebman and Don Yehiya, p. 5.

27. Ibid. Gehrig too lists integration and legitimation as central functions of civil religion (indeed, of any religion). In keeping with her definition of civil religion in transcendent, universal terms, she posits a third function which she labels the "prophetic" role of religion (judging and criticizing a society which strays too far from the professed values of its religious faith). Whether American civil religion in fact performs a prophetic function is a major source of debate among various scholars (pp. 37–40). We address the question of civil religion's potential prophetic role in a somewhat different context below.

28. This formulation is based on the definition of religion given by the anthropologist Clifford Geertz. See "Religion as a Cultural System," in *The Interpretation of Cultures* (New York: Basic Books, 1973), pp. 87–125.

29. This assertion is, as we noted above, the basis for a major critique of Bellah's work. Is America still a society which is integrated by a shared moral order? If not, the critics contend, then the civil religion of which Bellah writes is an historical anachronism or an elite ideology, not a functioning meaning system for the nation as a whole. Two issues embedded within the debate between Bellah and his critics have relevance to our consideration of Jewish civil religion. The

first is the question of whether a civil religion must be recognized and affirmed as such by a broad segment of the populace in order actually to function as integrator and legitimator of the polity. There is disagreement, but not a great deal of empirical evidence, as to whether Americans at large do in fact endorse the tenets of the belief system which Bellah identifies as America's historic civil religion. We will raise this question concerning the American Jewish civil religion in chapter 4. The second issue focuses on the question of whether civil religion should be defined in functional or substantive tgerms. If one defines civil religion in terms of its presumed functions (i.e., as a meaning system which integrates and legitimates the social order), then the empirical judgment that no such integrating moral order can be found in contemporary society indeed defines civil religion out of existence. Bellah, on the other hand, defines civil religion in substantive terms, as a particular set of beliefs about the nation and its relationship to transcendent reality. Therefore, he regards the capacity of the civil religion to serve as a unifying force in American society as historically contingent. At times, especially times of crisis, Americans may indeed rally around the beliefs of the civil religion. But at other times, the prophetic message of the civil religion may fail to win uniform assent, even be divisive. The tenets of the civil religion are likely to be interpreted in different ways by different subgroups (denominational, ethnic, and class) in American society. (Indeed, as Demerath and Williams suggest, the symbols and rhetoric of the civil religion, like those of any religion, are available for mobilization as weapons in social and political conflict.) Thus, rather than always unifying society, civil religion may at times be crippled and ineffectual. (Bellah views the present as one such period in American life and speaks of the civil religion as a "broken covenant." See *The Broken Covenant* and "Response to the Panel on Civil Religion," *Sociological Analysis* [Summer 1976]: 153–59.) We would agree that the extent to which any civil religious system actually fulfills an integrative (or legitimating, or mobilizing) function is historically variable. That it is not or is only partially successful in performing these functions at any given moment does not, however, imply that the civil religion no longer exists as an identifiable meaning and symbol system, nor that it will never again emerge as a powerful social force.

30. Cf. Bellah, "Religion and the Legitimation of the American Republic," *Varieties of Civil Religion*, pp. 3–23; and Liebman and Don Yehiya, p. 215.

31. Thus, one can speak of a civil religious meaning system in the same way one speaks of "Judaism" or "Christianity" (as in "Judaism teaches . . . "). There is, to be sure, a measure of reification in such usage which does violence to the fact that all expressions of religious belief ultimately constitute particular, situated statements. There is in reality no such thing as "the American Jewish civil religion," just as there is no such thing as "Judaism." Yet, there is enough validity in the construct to justify our adopting the language convention of treating "the civil religion" as an entity with a life of its own.

32. Martin Marty, "Two Kinds of Two Kinds of Civil Religion," in *American Civil Religion*, ed. Richey and Jones, pp. 139–57.

33. This caution applies as well to the analysis of American Jewish civil religion which follows. The focus of that analysis will be on the civil religion as it has been embodied and interpreted primarily within the domain of Jewish Federations and the United Jewish Appeal. Although most other institutions and segments of the American Jewish community would, we believe, affirm the same fundamental tenets, they undoubtedly do so with some variation in emphasis and interpretation. Thus, we will be discussing one version of American Jewish civil religion, albeit the one which is the most widely articulated and influential today.

34. Cited in Bellah, "Religion and the Legitimation of the American Republic," p. 14.

35. See Liebman and Don Yehiya, especially pp. 123–61.

36. The description and analysis of the American Jewish community as a voluntary polity has been pioneered by Daniel J. Elazar. See especially *Community and Polity: The Organizational Dynamics of American Jewry* (Philadelphia: The Jewish Publication Society of America, 1976). Elazar uses the term "polity" to designate the entire American Jewish institutional structure—including its explicitly religious institutions—in its political dimension. This is entirely appropriate, since the religious-congregational sphere does play a role in the political processes of the Jewish community, just as the churches do in American life as a whole. In the discussion which follows, however, our emphasis in using the term "polity" is on the network of Jewish organizations and agencies which are conventionally thought of as non-religious, especially the Jewish federations and the local and national institutions closely linked to them. It is these organizations which serve as the functional equivalent of a Jewish "state" in America, and which are generally recognized as standing somewhat apart from the Jewish "churches."

## 2. From Philanthropy to Polity, from Adjustment to Survival

1. Deborah Dash Moore, *B'nai B'rith and the Challenge of Ethnic Leadership* (Albany: State University of New York Press, 1981), p. 7.

2. Rabbi Liebman Adler, quoted in Louis Wirth, *The Ghetto* (Chicago: University of Chicago Press, 1928 [1956]), pp. 172–73.

3. Cited in Milton Goldin, *Why They Give: American Jews and Their Philanthropies* (New York: Macmillan, 1976), p. 52.

4. Alfred J. Kutzik, "The Social Basis of American Jewish Philanthropy," (Ph.D. diss., Brandeis University, 1968), pp. 607–08.

5. Cited in ibid., p. 331.

6. Ibid., p. 631.

7. Barbara Miller Solomon, *Pioneers in Service: The History of the Associted Jewish Philanthropies of Boston* (Boston: Associated Jewish Philanthropies, 1956), p. 7.

8. Kutzik, p. 607.

9. Max Senior, quoted in Harry L. Lurie, *A Heritiage Affirmed: The Jewish Federation Movement in America* (Philadelphia: The Jewish Publication Society of America, 1961), p. 38.

10. A detailed recounting of the development and guiding principles of the federation movement may be found in Lurie and in Philip Bernstein, *To Dwell in Unity: The Jewish Federation Movement in America Since 1960* (Philadelphia: The Jewish Publication Society of America, 1983).

11. Solomon, p. 32.

12. Lurie, p. 409.

13. Charles S. Liebman, *The Ambivalent American Jew: Politics, Religion, and Family in American Jewish Life* (Philadelphia: The Jewish Publication Society of America, 1973), vii.

14. Kutzik, p. 373.

15. Robert Morris and Michael Freund, eds., *Trends and Issues in Jewish Social Welfare in the United States, 1899–1958* (Philadelphia: The Jewish Publication Society of America, 1966), p. 9.

16. A. H. Fromenson, "East Side Preventive Work," in Morris and Freund, p. 123.

17. Solomon, p. 88.

18. Morris and Freund, p. 9.

19. Jacob Billikopf, "Advanced Settlement Work," in Morris and Freund, pp. 124–29.

20. For an overview of some of the initial efforts at undertaking coordinated action in response to overseas crises, see Abraham Karp, *To Give Life: The UJA in the Shaping of the American Jewish Community* (New York: Schocken Books, 1981). The history of the American Jewish Committee is detailed in Naomi Cohen, *Not Free To Desist: The American Jewish Committee, 1906–1966* (Philadelphia: The Jewish Publication Society of America, 1972).

21. Cf. the citation from Brandeis's essay "The Jewish Problem and How To Solve It," in Paul R. Mendes-Flohr and Jehuda Reinharz, eds., *The Jew in the Modern World: A Documentary History* (New York and Oxford: Oxford University Press, 1980), pp. 393–94.

22. Cited in Goldin, p. 58.

23. Ibid., p. 132.

24. On the maneuverings to establish the first American Jewish Congress and its initial meeting, see Morris Frommer, "The American Jewish Congress: A History, 1914–1950" (Ph.D. diss., Ohio State University, 1978), pp. 51–112.

25. Deborah Dash Moore, *At Home in America: Second Generation New York Jews* (New York: Columbia University Press, 1981), p. 153.

26. Solomon, p. 96.

27. Lurie, pp. 83–84.

28. Goldin, p. 85.

29. Cited in Kutzik, pp. 609–10.

30. Oscar Handlin, "Changing Patterns in Group Life in America and their Implications for the American Jewish Community," *Journal of Jewish Communal Service* (Summer 1958): 348.

31. Morris and Freund, p. 207.

32. Morris Waldman, "New Issues in Federation," in Morris and Freund, pp. 172–76.

33. The academic debate is essentially over whether assimilation is a "straight-line" process which eventually must lead to the integrating group's loss of ethnic identity (or its reduction to a purely symbolic, residual level) or whether a meaningful ethnic identity can be retained even in the face of substantial social integration. The social theorists at the University of Chicago in the 1920s and 1930s, under the intellectual leadership of Robert Park, saw full assimilation as inevitable and in large measure desirable. Louis Wirth's *The Ghetto* reflects this perspective. In recent years, Herbert Gans, among others, has argued that American Jews (and members of other ethnic minorities) are in fact assimilating in a more or less "straight-line" fashion and that manifestations of so-called ethnic revival represent a largely residual "symbolic ethnicity." See Herbert J. Gans, "Symbolic Ethnicity: The Future of Ethnic Groups and Cultures in America," in *On the Making of Americans: Essays in Honor of David Ries -man,* ed. Herbert J. Gans, Nathan Glazer, Joseph R. Gusfield, and Christopher Jencks (Philadelphia: University of Philadelphia Press, 1979), pp.193–220. This view has been challenged by a number of other sociologists of American Jewry, including Cohen and Goldscheider and Zuckerman in the works cited above. Cf. also, Chaim Waxman, "The Fourth Generation Grows Up: The Contemporary American Jewish Community," *Annals of the American Academy of Political and Social Science* (March 1981): 84.

34. Harry L. Glucksman, "Tendencies in the Jewish Center Movement," in Morris and Freund, pp. 225–30.

35. Lurie, pp. 94–95.

36. Ibid., p. 96.

37. Cf. Maurice J. Karpf, *Jewish Community Organization in the United States: An Outline of Types of Organizations, Activities, and Problems* (New York: Bloch Publishing Company, 1938), pp. 109–14.

38. Lurie, pp. 97–98.

39. Karpf, p. 114.

40. Kutzik, pp. 610–11.

41. I.M. Rubinow, quoted in Graenum Berger, ed., *The Turbulent Decades: Jewish Communal Services in America, 1958–78* (New York: Conference of Jewish Communal Service, 1981), p. 517.

42. Hyman Kaplan, "Visible Effects of the Present Immigration Policy in the Work of Jewish Family Agencies," in Morris and Freund, p. 187.

43. Morris D. Waldman, discussion of "What Have Been the Effects in Jewish Social Agencies of Membership in Community Chests and Councils of Social Agencies," by Raymond Clapp, in Morris and Freund, pp. 252–54.

44. Karp, pp. 61–67; Marc Lee Raphael, *A History of the United Jewish Appeal, 1939–1982*, Brown Judaic Studies, 34 (Missoula, Mont.: Scholars Press, 1982), pp. 2–5.

45. Karp, p. 63.

46. Samuel Kohs, "Jewish Community Chests," in Morris and Freund, pp. 257–58.

47. Cf. Deborah Dash Moore's discussion of this period in the history of the New York Jewish community in *At Home in America*.

48. See, for example, Dorothy Kahn, "Our Contemporary Ancestors," in Morris and Freund, pp. 239–43; Kutzik, pp. 689, 718–19.

49. Lurie, p. 419.

50. John Slawson, "What Makes Jewish Social Work 'Jewish'? Communal Aspects," in Morris and Freund, pp. 214–18.

51. Cf. H.L. Lurie, Solomon Lowenstein, and Frances Taussig, "The Present Status of Jewish Social Work: The Need for Critical Examination. A Symposium," in Morris and Freund, pp. 307–09.

52. Ben Selekman, "The Federation in the Changing American Scene," *American Jewish Year Book*, vol. 36, 1934–35, ed. Harry Schneiderman (Philadelphia: The American Jewish Committee and the Jewish Publication Society of America, 1935), p. 65.

53. Harry Greenstein, *Proceedings of the Organizing Conference of the National Council of Jewish Federations and Welfare Funds* [=CJFWF], New York, 1932, p. 21. [Subsequent citations from the Proceedings or papers of the General Assemblies of the National Council of Jewish Federations and Welfare Funds (later the Council of Jewish Federations and Welfare Funds, and today the Council of Jewish Federations) will be noted by the title of the presentation (if any), year and page number.]

54. Samuel Goldsmith, ibid., p. 23.

55. Joseph Proskauer, *Proceedings of the National Conference on Jewish Welfare*, sponsored by the CJFWF, 1935, p. 13.

56. Judge Henry Fisher, *General Assembly Proceedings*, 1934, CJFWF, p. 12.

57. *General Assembly Proceedings*, 1933, CJFWF, p. 3.

58. Ibid., p. 7

59. Emanuel Gamoran, *General Assembly Proceedings*, 1934, CJFWF, p. 12.

60. Fisher, pp. 12–13.

61. Solomon Lowenstein, *Proceedings of the National Conference on Jewish Welfare*, 1935, CJFWF, p. 17.

62. Samuel Goldsmith, ibid., p. 21.

63. Sidney Hollander, "Reshaping Federation: The Changing Scene," *General Assembly Proceedings*, 1936, p. 13.

64. Harry Greenstein, *General Assembly Proceedings*, 1937, p. 17.

65. Morris Waldman, "Problems Facing the Jews Throughout the World and Their Implications for American Jewry," in Morris and Freund, p. 363.

66. Indeed, many federations cut their allocations for Jewish education as campaigns declined during the depression.

67. George Backer, *General Assembly Proceedings*, 1937, pp. 7–8. Even more extreme than Backer's view was one offered anonymously by a Jewish communal professional in the *Jewish Social Service Quarterly* in 1930. This author suggested that the "distinctiveness" of the Jewish way of life was solely the product of economic and social restrictions, and a vestige of the ghetto. Holding on to separateness and adhering to vague "traditions" was preventing Jewish social work from having its desired impact in furthering adjustment to modern American life. "Facing Reality," in Morris and Freund, pp. 218–19.

68. William Shroder, "The National Council Meets the Community," *General Assembly Proceedings*, 1936, CJFWF, p. 6.

69. Samuel Rosenman, *General Assembly Proceedings*, 1937, CJFWF, p. 9.

70. Ibid.

71. Ibid.

72. Waldman, "Problems Facing the Jews," p. 363.

73. I.M. Rubinow, *General Assembly Proceedings*, 1936, CJFWF, p. 23.

74. Joseph Willen, ibid., p. 21.

75. James Marshall, *General Assembly Proceedings*, 1938, CJFWF, p. 75.

76. Cited in Kutzik, pp. 945–46. American participation in World War II called forth no less bold a statement from Philip Bernstein, who was subsequently to become the professional head of CJFWF. The war, he stated, was being fought for the values underlying not only democracy and social work, but Judaism as well. "And as Jews we must bring to that task the leadership, the resources, the experience, and the great moral message which has been our heritage, and which the world needs now and will need more than ever in the days to come" ("The Impact of War Upon Jewish Social Service," in Morris and Freund, p. 462).

77. David Heyman, *General Assembly Proceedings*, 1934, pp. 14–15.

78. *General Assembly Proceedings*, 1936, p. 9.

79. Goldsmith, *Proceedings of the National Conference on Jewish Welfare*, 1935, CJFWF, p. 22.

80. Raphael, pp. 16–19.

81. Such efforts for a more comprehensive unity were pursued. Growing out of the shocked response of American Jewish leaders to news of the Nazi extermination program, an American Jewish Conference was convened in 1943 with over five hundred delegates representing nearly every element in the organized community in order to develop some coordinated response to the desperate plight of European Jewry. Henry Monsky, the professional head of B'nai B'rith and spearhead behind the effort, made a powerful plea for unity and praised the democratic character of the assembly. He argued that "our people's salvation depends upon a united front" and cited the "magnificent fortitude" with which "the Jews in the stricken lands [have] manifested once again the will of Israel to survive." He urged as well that divisions over ideology and the self-definition of the Jewish group be set aside. "We are an integral group, call it what you will— religious or national—it matters not, for we do have a common inheritance, a common history, a common religion, common traditions and a common cause, and we must strive for a common basis of action" *(The American Jewish Confer-*

*ence: Its Organization and Proceedings of the First Session*, ed. Alexander S. Kohanski [New York: American Jewish Conference, 1944], p. 70). The practical work of rescue might have provided such a basis. But the conference soon foundered when its pro-Zionist majority adopted positions unacceptable to the leaders of the American Jewish Committee, who withdrew from the conference shortly thereafter. Though the conference endured for a few years beyond the war, it rapidly became an inconsequential factor in American Jewish life.

82. *General Assembly Proceedings*, 1938, CJFWF, pp. 37ff.

83. Ibid., pp. 49–50.

84. Isaac Franck, "The Community Council Idea," in Morris and Freund, p. 426.

85. Ibid., p. 431.

86. Harry L. Lurie, "Developments in Jewish Community Organization," in Morris and Freund, pp. 415–25.

87. William Shroder, "The Communities Pass Their Test," *General Assembly News and Notes*, 1941, CJFWF, pp. 3–4.

88. Sidney Hollander, *General Assembly Papers*, 1944, CJFWF, p. 11.

89. Karp, p. 89.

90. Raphael, p. 39.

91. *General Assembly Resolutions*, 1949, CJFWF, p. 4.

92. Stanley Myers, "Agenda for American Jewry," *General Assembly Papers*, 1950a, CJFWF, pp. 2–5. [In 1950 CJFWF moved the date of its annual assembly from early Winter to November. Hence there were two General Assemblies designated as the 1950 assembly. They are referred to in the notes as 1950a and 1950b.]

93. Isadore Sobeloff, "The Changing Jewish Community: An Appraisal," *Journal of Jewish Communal Service* (Fall 1956): 11ff.

94. *Federation of Jewish Agencies of Greater Philadelphia Annual Report*, 1965, cited in Kutzik, pp. 895–96.

95. "A Rationale for the Jewish Family Agency," CJFWF, 1953, cited in Kutzik, pp. 925–26.

96. Stanley Myers, *General Assembly Papers*, 1950b, CJFWF, p. 8.

97. Ibid., pp. 4–5.

98. Philip Bernstein, "Current and Prospective Trends in Jewish Communal Service," in Berger, pp. 464, 468.

99. Irving Kane, "In Quest of Purpose," *General Assembly Papers*, 1960, CJFWF, pp. 1–13.

100. Ibid., p. 2.

101. Louis Stern, "Major Issues Facing the Organized Jewish Communities," *General Assembly Papers*, 1963, CJFWF, p. 15.

102. Hyman Safran, "Updating Federations: How Relevant to Changing Issues and Communities," *General Assembly Papers*, 1964, CJFWF, pp. 11–12.

103. David Zeff and Irving Greenberg, "The Jewish Casework Agency: Problems and Prospects in a Time of Paradox," in Berger, pp. 619–23.

104. Julian Freeman, "Report to the General Assembly," *General Assembly Papers*, 1950b, CJFWF, p. 16.

105. Jerome Curtis, *General Assembly Papers*, 1950b, CJFWF, p. 17.

106. Joseph Schwartz, *General Assembly Papers*, 1950b, CJFWF, pp. 1–2.

107. Herbert Friedman, *General Assembly Papers*, 1960, CJFWF, p. B–7.

108. Many leaders shared Isadore Sobeloff's assessment that "Israel and its developing society may furnish us with an enriching factor, but its influence for us may not be dominant" ("Jewish Community Organization—Its Past, Current Trends, Directions," *General Assembly Papers*, 1954, CJFWF, p. 11).

109. *General Assembly Resolutions*, 1957, CJFWF.

110. Kane, p. 7.

111. Sidney Z. Vincent, *Personal and Professional: Memoirs of a Life in Community Service* (Cleveland: The Jewish Community Federation of Cleveland, 1982), pp. 127–28. The phrase "mir zeinen doh!" is a refrain in the Yiddish "Song of the Partisans," sung by the Jewish resistance during World War II. It has become a testament of faith in Jewish survival in the wake of the Holocaust.

112. Max Fisher, "Our Overseas Responsibilities in a Time of Change and Challenge," *General Assembly Papers*, 1965, CJFWF, pp. 8, 15, 19.

113. See the discussion of the myths of the American Jewish civil religion in chapter 5.

114. Kane, p. 9.

115. Edwin Wolf, *General Assembly Papers*, 1962, CJFWF, p. 7.

116. William Goldfarb, "Jewish Education and a Changing Society," *General Assembly Papers*, 1964, CJFWF, pp. 1–14.

117. Donald Hurwitz, "Jewish Community Organizations—Their Relevance to Key Issues," Document prepared for the General Assembly, 1964, CJFWF, IV–4.

118. The CJFWF established the National Foundation for Jewish Culture in 1959 as part of the effort to stimulate cultural activities. For most of its existence, however, the foundation has not received the funding from local federations which proponenets of Jewish culture deem necessary for significant achievements. The national agencies charged with planning for Jewish education have complained perennially as well of inadequate financial support. A similar situation existed in many local communities, where despite some increases in funding for educational institutions, few dramatic changes in allocation priorities took place.

119. In a sense, the dire predictions and calls for increased support for Jewish education and culture frequently heard at General Assemblies and other forums represent a classic type of prophetic civil religious rhetoric, measuring the performance of the polity against its stated aspirations.

120. Julian Freeman, "Twenty Years of Cooperation: A Restatement of Basic Principles," *General Assembly Papers*, 1951, CJFWF, p. 7.

121. Milton Weil, "The Glamor and Drama of Home Services," *General Assembly Papers*, 1952, CJFWF, p. 5.

122. Saul Cherniak, "The Role of the Synagogue in the Jewish Community," *General Assembly Papers*, 1954, CJFWF, pp. 11, 19.

123. Irving Kane, "Domestic Issues in America Today," *General Assembly Papers*, 1957, CJFWF, p. 3, 5.

124. *General Assembly Papers*, 1963, p. 5.

125. Philip Bernstein, *General Assembly Papers*, 1965, CJFWF, p. 3.

126. Louis Stern, "The Changing Jewish Community and the Contribution of Federations," *General Assembly Papers*, 1965, CJFWF, p. 8.

127. Louis Stern, "The Federation Commitment in our Changing World," *General Assembly Papers*, 1962, CJFWF, pp. 3–4.

128. Irving Blum, "Federation Support—Reality and Responsibility," *General Assembly Papers*, 1966, CJFWF, pp. 4, 10.

### 3. The Civil Jewish Faith

1. The Young Leadership Cabinets are comprised of several hundred men and women between the ages of twenty-five and forty, who have demonstrated a strong commitment to the UJA and their local Jewish communities. The members of the cabinets are expected to make significant contributions to the feder-

ation/UJA campaign, to work for the campaign and Jewish institutions both nationally and locally, to educate themselves as Jews and community leaders, and to work with other young people in their communities. In 1978, the cabinets initiated the idea of a bi-annual conference in Washington, D.C. for their members and other young polity activists which would focus on political issues of Jewish concern. On the cabinets, their members, and activities, see, Gary Rosenblatt, "The Youngers of Zion: UJA's Young Leadership Cabinet and How It Got That Way," *Moment* (June 1977): 37–40, 66–70; Jonathan Woocher, "The 1980 United Jewish Appeal Young Leadership Cabinet: A Profile," *Forum* (1981): 57–67.

2. Edward Robin, "Why We Are Here" (Speech delivered at the 1982 UJA Young Leadership Washington Conference, Typescript).

3. The speech, given by Hillel Levine, then a graduate student and now a professor of Jewish Studies, was entitled "To Share a Vision," and is printed in *Jewish Radicalism: A Selected Anthology*, ed. Jack Nusan Porter and Peter Dreier (New York: Grove Press, 1973), pp. 183–94.

4. Sanford Solender, "Themes From the Assembly," *General Assembly Papers*, 1979, CJF, p. 4. [In 1977, the Council of Jewish Federations and Welfare Funds (CJFWF) changed its name officially to the Council of Jewish Federations (CJF).]

5. Mort Mandel, "Entering the Eighties," *General Assembly Papers*, 1979, CJF, p. 10.

6. Philip Bernstein, "Federations: What They Are and Are Not," CJFWF, 1976, p. 2.

7. Charles Zibbell, "Highlights of the Workshops and Forums," *General Assembly Papers*, 1974, CJFWF, p. 2.

8. Martin Citrin, "A Year of Challenges," *General Assembly Papers*, 1983, CJF, p. 8.

9. Sidney Vincent, "Shaping a More Creative and Responsive Community—The Role of Leadership," *General Assembly Papers*, 1975, CJFWF, p. 2.

10. Martin Citrin, "Where Do We Go From Here," CJF, 1979, p. 4.

11. Ibid.

12. Martin Citrin, "Community and Campaign," CJF, 1982, p. 4.

13. "Proclaim Liberty," United Jewish Appeal, 1976, p. 1.

14. Citrin, "Community and Campaign," pp. 4–5.

15. Irving Bernstein, *UJA National Conference Address*, United Jewish Appeal, 1982, p. 2.

16. Philip Bernstein, "The Principles of Jewish Federations," CJFWF, 1976, p. 2.

17. Frank Lautenberg, General Chairman's Message, in "United Jewish Appeal–1977," United Jewish Appeal, 1976, p. 3.

18. Frank Lautenberg, "Jewish Responsibility in 1976," *General Assembly Papers*, 1975, CJFWF, pp. 1–2.

19. Albert Ratner, "The Jewish Response: A Personal Review," CJF, 1979, p. 5.

20. "The United Jewish Appeal–1977," p. 8.

21. Charles S. Liebman and Eliezer Don-Yehiya, *Civil Religion in Israel: Traditional Judaism and Political Culture in the Jewish State* (Berkeley: University of California Press, 1983), pp. 137–48.

22. Simon Rawidowicz, "Israel: The Ever-Dying People," *Studies in Jewish Thought* (Philadelphia: The Jewish Publication Society of America, 1974), pp. 210–14. On the American Jewish adoption of this syndrome, cf. Marshall Sklare, "American Jewry—The Ever Dying People," *Midstream* (June/July 1976):

17–27; Deborah Lipstadt, "American Jewry—From Ever Preyed Upon to Ever Dying People," in Jonathan Woocher, Deborah Lipstadt, and Deborah Dash Moore, eds., *Sacred People, Secular World: American Judaism in the Making* (Chappaqua, N.Y.: Rossel Books, forthcoming).

23. Max Fisher, "The Role of an American Jewish Leader in Today's World," *General Assembly Papers*, 1967, CJFWF, p. 2.

24. "If You Think All Our Problems Are Solved," United Jewish Appeal, 1977, p. 2.

25. Citrin, "A Year of Challenges," p. 8.

26. Charles Zibbell, "Strengthening Jewish Commitment," *Journal of Jewish Communal Service* (Spring 1973): 200.

27. Robert Rifkind, Statement at a meeting of the Jewish Communal Affairs Commission, American Jewish Committee, February 25, 1982.

28. "Proclaim Liberty," p. 3.

29. Mort Mandel, "CJF and Federations: New Goals," *General Assembly Papers*, 1980, CJF, p. 9.

30. Citrin, "A Year of Challenges," p. 8.

31. Gordon Zacks, "Young Leadership Looks at the Future of the Jewish Community," *General Assembly Papers*, 1969, CJFWF, pp. 6–7.

32. Cf., e.g., the statement by Irving Rabb, a prominent communal leader from Boston, at the 1974 General Assembly: The Jewish community, he argued, was groping toward "a new understanding of the Jewish mission in America and in the world." Increasingly, leaders are asking "is survival enough? why is it important that we survive?" The answer, Rabb proposed, lay in an understanding of Jewish history and values: "what we are, what we have contributed in the past, where we succeeded in making an impact on the upward mobility of humanity and where we failed" ("Enrichment and Training of Veteran Leadership for Jewish Decision-Making," *General Assembly Papers*, 1974, CJFWF, pp. 4–5).

33. Charles Zibbell, "The Crisis in Jewish Life—The Aftermath of the Yom Kippur War," *Journal of Jewish Communal Service* (Fall 1974): 24.

34. Ratner, pp. 2–3.

35. Citrin, "Community and Campaign," pp. 6–7.

36. Max Fisher, "The Triumph of a Dream," United Israel Appeal, 1979, p. 21.

37. Martin Citrin, "Visions of the Future," *General Assembly Papers*, 1982, CJF, p. 7.

38. Frank Lautenberg, "O Jerusalem, We Shall Never Be Still," United Jewish Appeal, 1976, p. 1.

39. Peter Berger, *A Rumor of Angels: Modern Society and the Rediscovery of the Supernatural* (Garden City, N.Y.: Doubleday and Company, 1969).

40. Frank Lautenberg, "We Are One," United Jewish Appeal, 1974, p. 3.

41. Ibid.

42. "Toward a Working Agenda: Report of the CJP Committee on Communal Objectives," Combined Jewish Philanthropies of Greater Boston, 1984, p. 17.

43. Mandel, "CJF and Federations," p. 6.

44. Citrin, "Visions of the Future," p. 10.

45. Citrin, "A Year of Challenges," p. 3.

46. Several of the essays of Ahad Ha'am, one of the most important Zionist thinkers of the late nineteenth and early twentieth centuries, are excerpted in Arthur Hertzberg, ed., *The Zionist Idea: A Historical Analysis and Reader* (New York: Atheneum, 1971), pp. 247–77.

47. Zibbell, "The Crisis in Jewish Life," p. 21.

48. Jerome Cardin, "Guidelines for 1979 Community Campaigns," *General Assembly Papers*, 1978, CJF, p. 9.

49. Lautenberg, General Chairman's Message, p. 3.

50. Alan Ades, Speech delivered at the UJA Northeast Leadership Conference, October 22, 1983, pp. 1–2.

51. Philip Bernstein, "Federation Agenda for the 1970s," *General Assembly Papers*, 1968, CJFWF, p. 6.

52. Raymond Epstein, "Major Issues Facing Federations and the Council," *General Assembly Papers*, 1974, CJFWF, p. 1.

53. Bernard Olshansky, "The Role of Jewish Community and Leadership in Assuring Jewish Continuity," *General Assembly Papers*, 1976, CJFWF, p. 8.

54. Herschel Blumberg, cited in a press release of the National Jewish Resource Center, New York, 1984, p. 2.

55. Citrin, "Visions of the Future," pp. 10–11.

56. Charles Zibbell, "Tzedakah and the Contemporary Jewish Community," Jewish Welfare Federation of New Orleans, July 1975, p. 1.

57. Philip Bernstein, "The Principles of Jewish Federations," p. 2.

58. Citrin, "Community and Campaign," p. 2.

59. "Toward a Working Agenda," p. 5.

60. Stanley Horowitz, "Insuring Jewish Commitment: The Federation Role," *General Assembly Papers*, 1982, CJF, p. 3.

61. Philip Bernstein, "The Principles of Jewish Federations," p. 6.

62. Louis Fox, "Issues Confronting Our Communities and the Assembly," *General Assembly Papers*, 1968, CJFWF, p. 6.

63. Jordan Band, "The Human Rights Revolution: Reassessing the Jewish Role," *General Assembly Papers*, 1967, CJFWF, p. 1.

64. Citrin, "A Year of Challenges," p. 7.

65. Jerold Hoffberger, "Justice For All," *General Assembly Papers*, 1976, CJFWF, p. 1.

66. Fisher, "The Role of an American Jewish Leader," p. 5.

67. Philip Bernstein, "Federation Agenda," p. 7.

68. Zacks, p. 8.

69. Sidney Vincent, "Planning for Small Cities—Directions for the '80's," *General Assembly Papers*, 1978, CJF, p. 3.

70. Cf. Jerold Hoffberger, "Retrospect and Prospect," *General Assembly Papers*, 1978, CJF, p. 8.

71. The full list of documents analyzed in this fashion may be found in the Appendix.

72. This question is obviously linked to the larger one of defining "religion" itself, about which there has been much inconclusive debate. Both substantive definitions (which generally invoke some notion of a transcendent reality) and functional approaches (which often allow for the absence of such a reality) can be defended conceptually and historically. Cf. Peter Berger, "Some Second Thoughts on Substantive versus Functional Definition of Religion," *Journal for the Scientific Study of Religion* (June 1974): 125–33.

73. Martin Marty, "Two Kinds of Two Kinds of Civil Religion," in *American Civil Religion*, ed. Russell B. Richey and Donald G. Jones (New York: Harper and Row, 1974), pp. 139–57.

74. Charles S. Liebman, "Reconstructionism in American Jewish Life," in *Aspects of the Religious Behaviour of American Jews* (New York: Ktav Publishing House, 1974), pp. 254, 276.

75. Charles S. Liebman, *The Ambivalent American Jew: Politics, Religion, and Family in American Jewish Life* (Philadelphia: The Jewish Publication Society of America, 1973).

76. Ellen Lasser LeVee, "Rationality: American Jewry's False Messiah," (typescript, 1985), chap. 4, pp. 12–16.

77. Liebman, *The Ambivalent American Jew*, pp. 23–27.

78. Cf., in addition to Richey and Jones, *American Civil Religion*, and many of Bellah's writings cited above, Conrad Cherry, ed., *God's New Israel: Religious Interpretations of American Destiny* (Englewood Cliffs, N.J.: Prentice-Hall, 1971).

79. David Altshuler, "Judaic America, American Judaism: Covenantal Siblings Confront Modernity," in Woocher, Lipstadt, and Moore.

80. Deborah Dash Moore, "American Jewish Civil Religion: An Ideology of Acculturation," in Woocher, Lipstadt, and Moore.

81. Ibid.

82. The importance of this congruence to American Jews in validating their Jewishness in American terms may help to explain the intense resistance which most American Jews have offered to any perceived attempts to "Christianize" American civil religion.

83. Peter L. Berger, *The Sacred Canopy: Elements of a Sociological Theory of Religion* (Garden City, N.Y.: Doubleday and Company, 1967), pp. 45–47.

## 4. The Civil Jewish Activist—a Portrait

1. Gail Gehrig, *American Civil Religion: An Assessment* (Storrs, Conn.: Society for the Scientific Study of Religion, 1979), pp. 16–17, 29–31, 40–43. Testing empirically the relationship of American civil religious beliefs to personal religious convictions has been made difficult by the lack of agreement as to what the characteristic beliefs of the civil religion are. Bellah has, e.g., been critical of the items used in some of the empirical studies cited by Gehrig. The difficulty is compounded by the fact that there are two types of beliefs which have been termed "civil religious." Bellah refers to these as "general civil religion" (belief in God or in a divine purpose in history, e.g.)—which provides a general moral basis for citizenship—and "special civil religion," in which religious symbols are attached specifically to the life of the nation or polity (e.g., America as the "new Israel") ("Response to the Panel on Civil Religion," pp. 155–56). Obviously, in the American context, the former is likely to be more widely attested than the latter. In the discussion which follows, we use the tenets outlined in chapter 3 as the basis for generating the items testing for civil Jewish belief. These contain both "general" and "special" dimensions in Bellah's terms. Belief in God, however, is treated as an extra-civil religious belief.

2. Peter L. Berger, *The Sacred Canopy: Elements of a Sociological Theory of Religion* (Garden City, N.Y.: Doubleday and Company, 1967), pp. 128–34; Richard Fenn, "Bellah and the New Orthodoxy," *Sociological Analysis* (Summer 1976): 160–66.

3. It might be objected that the focus on individuals already active (or indicating an interest in becoming active) in the Jewish polity introduces an element of circularity. That is, one could argue that these individuals become active *because* they accept the tenets of civil Judaism. Thus, demonstrating that they hold these beliefs is trivial, not to say tautological. While this objection may have some merit, it is by no means decisive. We would not deny that the population studied is among the most likely to manifest civil Jewish beliefs—*if those beliefs are in fact personally consequential.* It is the latter proposition which is at issue. Individuals become active in Jewish communal life for a wide variety of reasons, many of which have little or no connection at all with civil religious beliefs as such (e.g., social status, business connections, family tradition, opportunities to associate with peers, sense of civic responsibility). If we are able to show that a preponderance of those becoming active do in fact hold civil Jewish convictions,

this argues that such beliefs are not simply institutional rhetoric, but rather components of personally consequential meaning systems. That there are other Jews for whom the tenets of civil Judaism are less meaningful in terms of their personal world views and value commitments we would not doubt. Nevertheless, in the absence of more encompassing studies, it is still important, we would argue, to demonstrate that civil Judaism is personally, as well as institutionally, endorsed by at least some body of American Jews.

4. Additional details on the study itself and the methods of analysis employed may be found in Jonathan Woocher, "The 'Civil Judaism' of Communal Leaders," *The American Jewish Year Book, 1981,* ed. Milton Himmelfarb and David Singer (New York and Philadelphia: The American Jewish Committee and the Jewish Publication Society of America, 1981), pp. 149–69; Jonathan Woocher, "'Jewish Survivalism' as Communal Ideology: An Empirical Assessment," *Journal of Jewish Communal Service* (Summer 1981): 291–303; and Jonathan Woocher, "The 1980 UJA Young Leadership Cabinet: A Profile," *Forum* (1981) 57–67.

5. Not eating pork or shellfish, both prohibited by Jewish dietary laws (kashrut), may be regarded as reflecting a commitment to the maintenance of those laws to at least a minimal extent.

6. Fred Massarik, *Jewish Identity: Facts for Planning* (New York: Council of Jewish Federations and Welfare Funds, 1974), p. 10.

7. Marshall Sklare, *America's Jews* (New York: Random House, 1971), p. 114.

8. Cf. the observation of Daniel Elazar: "After three hundred years of secularization and assimilation there is strong evidence that a revived concern with Jewish tradition is leading to its restoration as a vital norm. While different groups will be entitled to define 'Jewish tradition' in various ways, identification with that tradition and acceptance of the responsibility for maintaining, fostering, and extending it seem to be reemerging as central norms in Jewish life, embraced by all Jewish organizations and enforced by them." Daniel J. Elazar, *Community and Polity: The Organizational Dynamics of American Jewry* (Philadelphia: The Jewish Publication Society of America, 1976), p. 335.

9. A standard five point Likert scale was used to measure strength of agreement or disagreement.

10. Empirical studies of American civil religion have found such a relationship between endorsement of its tenets and denominational religious commitment. Civil religious belief is apparently both genuinely *religious* (hence related to other religious convictions), yet sufficiently distinct from other dimensions of religiosity to be identifiable as a constellation of beliefs in its own right. Cf. Gehrig, pp. 30–31.

11. The Communities group was selected for this further analysis because of its larger size and the greater diversity of its responses on a number of the questions in the survey. It is difficult to conduct correlational analyses among various items if the scores of respondents on those items nearly all cluster around a single value. The several attitudinal indices referred to in the body of the text were created through factor analysis of the fifty items on the survey questionnaire. The behavioral indices discussed subsequently consist of the number of rituals observed by the respondent (from the list provided in the questionnaire) and a measure of communal involvement based on synagogue and other organizational activity, Jewish political activity, and total number of hours spent per week on Jewish affairs. Further details on the construction of all of the indices may be found in Woocher, "The 'Civil Judaism' of Communal Leaders," pp. 161–62.

12. See, e.g., Harold Himmelfarb, "Measuring Religious Involvement," *Social Forces* (June 1975): 606–18.

13. We do not wish to enter here into the debate over the extent to which attitudes *determine* behaviors and vice versa. Regardless of any causal relationships, we should expect some correspondence between these two components of identity if professions of faith are to be taken seriously as reflective of deeply-held convictions.

14. The matrix enables one to see the strength of relationship between the scores on each pair of indices. The higher the number, the stronger the relationship. The numbers presented are Pearson product-moment correlation coefficients (r).

15. In exploring these relationshps, we must be careful not to imply a direct causal pathway in either direction between strength of adherence to the tenets of the civil religion and intensity of Jewish identification along the several other dimensions we have noted. Correlations as such do not establish causation, and though we may speculate concerning the dynamics of Jewish commitment, we cannot demonstrate from statistical data of this type how various behavioral and attitudinal patterns influence one another. Thus, we cannot say whether those who adhere more strongly to civil Judaism are thereby inspired to greater degrees of Jewish activity and observance (or to accept Jewish tradition as normative or to deepen their affirmation of transcendent reality), or whether the lines of influence move in the opposite directions. Impressionistic evidence suggests that for many of the respondents the relationshps have been reciprocal; i.e., attitudes both modify and are modified by behavior, and changes in commitment do tend to embrace both personal and communal, civil Jewish and "extra-consensual" dimensions of Jewish self-expression.

16. One finding which appears anomalous is the relatively low ranking given the problem of "lack of unity among Jewish religious denominations," in light of the prominent civil Jewish concern with Jewish unity. This may reflect the fact that with respect to the concerns which dominate the civil religious ideology itself, the denominations are not perceived to be seriously disunified. The areas where the denominations are clearly at odds with one another, i.e., theology and the authority of the Jewish legal tradition, are, as we have seen, areas of lesser importance for civil Judaism and arenas wherein a plurality of views is regarded as legitimate. Unity at the denominational level is, thus, not what civil Jewish adherents tend to have in mind when they espouse Jewish unity. Since the survey was conducted, denominational unity has perhaps become a somewhat more salient issue because of its connection with attempts to amend Israel's Law of Return and other concerns affecting the integrity of the Jewish people as such. It would, therefore, be interesting to see whether its relative ranking would be higher today than in the period when the survey was undertaken. A similar analysis may be relevant when examining the comparably low ranking accorded "promoting unity among American Jews" among the list of proposed communal goals. In part, the ranking may reflect a perception that American Jews are substantially united on the issues which matter, and hence this need not be emphasized as a goal. Further, as much as the respondents feel a powerful sense of Jewish unity, they may be somewhat reluctant to tread on the freedom of conscience and pluralism in Jewish life which they also value by pushing for unity as a programmatic goal.

17. The full results of this section of the survey are reported in Woocher, "'Jewish Survivalism' as Communal Ideology," p. 299.

## 5. "Choose Life"

1. Mircea Eliade, *The Sacred and the Profane: The Nature of Religion* (New York: Harcourt, Brace & World, 1959).

2. The best example of this by far is the term "the Holocaust," which, as we shall see below, encapsulates a wealth of meanings linked to the death of European Jews at the hands of the Nazis.

3. Jacob Neusner, *Stranger at Home: "The Holocaust," Zionism, and American Judaism* (Chicago: The University of Chicago Press, 1981), p. 1.

4. Ibid.

5. See Jonathan Woocher, "'In Every Generation': The Seder as a Ritual of Anti-Structure," *Journal of the American Academy of Religion (Supplement)* (December 1977): 1263–92.

6. Jacqueline Levine, "Building Commitment—Women's Special Role," *General Assembly Papers*, 1970, CJFWF, p. 2.

7. Irving Bernstein, "UJA National Conference Address," p. 10.

8. "Proclaim Liberty," United Jewish Appeal, 1976, p. 1.

9. Max Fisher, "A *New* Program for Immigrant Absorption," *General Assembly Papers*, 1966, CJFWF, p. 15.

10. Gordon Zacks, "Young Leadership Looks at the Future of the Jewish Community," *General Assembly Papers*, 1969, CJFWF, p. 6.

11. Irving Bernstein, "UJA National Conference Address," p. 10.

12. Max Fisher, "The Decade Ahead: A Formidable Agenda," *General Assembly Papers*, 1971, CJFWF, p. 12.

13. Sidney Vincent, "The Agenda of Jewish Federations in War and Peace," *General Assembly Papers*, 1973, CJFWF, p. 2.

14. Stuart Handmaker, "A Personal View of the Role of the President," *General Assembly Papers*, 1982, CJF, p. 14.

15. Frank Lautenberg, General Chairman's Message, in "United Jewish Appeal—1977," United Jewish Appeal, 1976, p. 3.

16. Ibid.

17. Frank Lautenberg, "Jewish Responsibility in 1976," *General Assembly Papers*, 1975, CJFWF, p. 7.

18. Max Fisher, "We Have Chosen," *General Assembly Papers*, 1969, CJFWF, p. 7.

19. "Now. More Than Ever. We Are One." United Jewish Appeal, 1979, p. 7.

20. Lautenberg, "Jewish Responsibility in 1976," p. 1.

21. Bert Gold, Speech delivered at Brandeis University, July 18, 1985.

22. In saying this, we do not wish to dismiss the negative side of the American Jewish image of American society or the historical realities which underlie it. Particularly in the pre-World War II period (some might say prior to the 1960s), many Jews put very severe limits on their expectations of opportunity, and were justified in doing so. Only in the past few decades have Jews found that their horizons in America are indeed virtually unlimited, though even this has not erased the suspicion that such may not always be the case. Nevertheless, the central strand in the story American Jewry tells itself about itself and about America today is a decidedly positive one. Cf. Charles Silberman, *A Certain People: American Jews and Their Lives Today* (New York: Summit Books, 1985), pp. 28–156.

23. Martin Citrin, "Visions of the Future," *General Assembly Papers*, 1982, CJF, p. 3.

24. Edward Robin, "Why We Are Here," (Speech delivered at the 1982 UJA Young Leadership Washington Conference, Typescript), pp. 3–4.

25. Citrin, "Visions of the Future," p. 3.

26. Jerold Hoffberger, "Major Challenges Ahead," *General Assembly Papers*, 1979, CJF, pp. 9–10.

27. Hoffberger, "The State of Our Federations," *General Assembly Papers*, 1976, CJFWF, p. 3.

28. Howard Squadron, "Between Power and Influence: The American Jewish Community," *Congress Monthly* (January 1983): 10.

29. Stanley Frankel, "The Challenge of Young Leadership," Young Leadership Cabinet Communique, United Jewish Appeal (Spring 1980): 3.

30. Hoffberger, "The State of Our Federations," pp. 3, 8.

31. Ibid., p. 3.

32. Arthur Hertzberg, *Being Jewish in America: The Modern Experience* (New York: Schocken Books, 1979), pp. 12–27.

33. Arnold Eisen, *The Chosen People in America: A Study in Jewish Religious Ideology* (Bloomington: Indiana University Press, 1983).

34. That the myth has remained a powerful one, even among highly secularized American Jews, is nearly incontestable. Cf. Silberman, pp. 73–81. We should recall as well that 63% of the respondents to the Young Leadership surveys stated explicit agreement with the proposition that "the Jewish people is the chosen people."

35. Ibid., p. 181.

36. Arthur Hertzberg, "Jewish Identification After the Six-Day War," *Jewish Social Studies* (1969): 271.

37. Eugene Borowitz, "The Chosen People Concept As It Affects Life in the Diaspora," *Journal of Ecumenical Studies* (1975): 553–68.

38. Eisen, pp. 68–69.

39. Albert Chernin, "Jewish Community Relations—Boundaries and Priorities," in Berger, p. 608.

40. Albert Ratner, "The Jewish Response: A Personal Review," CJF, 1979, p. 1.

41. Hoffberger, "The State of Our Federations," pp. 2–3.

42. Cf. Philip Bernstein, "Federations: What They Are and Are Not," CJFWF, 1976, p. 8.

43. Isaac Franck, "The Challenge to Jewish Purposes of Communal Agencies in the Light of Evolving Public Policies and Trends," in Berger, pp. 575–76.

44. Sidney Vincent, "The Emerging Agenda for Jewish Communal Life—The Role of Jewish Communal Service," in Berger, p. 919. The motif of Jewish suffering as an expression of its chosenness, central in Deutero-Isaiah and interwoven thereafter with other motifs in the classical tradition's utilization of the concept, is occasionally (as here) a feature of the civil Jewish appropriation of the myth as well. More usually, however, the emphasis in civil Judaism is on the uniquenes of Jewish history as a whole, and there is almost no effort to accord suffering a positive value in its own right. Sacrifice, on the other hand, is often put forward as a moral value, especially for the privileged Jews of America.

45. Irving Blum, "Community Prospects: Paradox and Challenge," *General Assembly Papers*, 1972, CJFWF, pp. 14–15.

46. Charles Zibbell, "The Crisis in Jewish Life—The Aftermath of the Yom Kippur War," *Journal of Jewish Communal Service* (Fall 1974): 24.

47. Sidney Vincent, *General Assembly Papers*, 1972, CJFWF, pp. 11, 16.

48. Stanley Horowitz, "Insuring Jewish Commitment: The Federation Role," *General Assembly Papers*, 1982, CJF, p. 2.

49. Raymond Epstein, "Major Issues Facing Federations and the Council," *General Assembly Papers*, 1974, CJFWF, p. 4.

50. Sidney Vincent, "The Jewish Federation: Reflections on an American Institution," (The Milender Seminar in Jewish Communal Leadership Address, Brandeis University, 1976), p. 14.

51. Mary Douglas, *Natural Symbols: Explorations in Cosmology* (New York: Random House, 1973), pp. 19–58.

52. Victor Turner, *The Ritual Process: Structure and Anti-Structure* (Chicago: Aldine Publishing Company, 1969), pp. 125–29, 166–203.

53. Ibid., pp. 126–33.

54. Ibid., p. 128.

55. Vincent, "The Emerging Agenda," p. 921.

56. The "mission" has in fact proved so successful that both the name and the basic design have been appropriated for other federation sponsored journeys to less exotic sites. The "Washington mission" has become increasingly popular in recent years (especially as federation leadership have come to see political action as an important complement to fundraising and communal activity in pursuing the Jewish communal agenda). In the "Washington mission" a group of community leaders travels to the nation's capital for a day (or two) of briefings by government officials, Jewish communal professionals who are engaged in lobbying and government relations, staff of the Israeli embassy, and meetings with their congressional representatives. Some federations also sponsor "local missions," which generally consist of visits to community agencies to see first-hand the services being provided to Jews and to receive briefings on current issues. All of these "missions" employ the same psycho-social dynamic embodied in many ritual performances to enhance motivations among participants: separation from daily routine, a crowded schedule, group togetherness, creation of a sense of "specialness" and urgency.

57. See, e.g., Wallace Markfield's satire of a typical fundraising event honoring a community "leader," reprinted in Raphael, pp. 48–61.

58. Eugene Borowitz, Louis A. Pincus Memorial Lecture, quoted in "Campaign Newsbrief," United Jewish Appeal, May 1984, p. 2.

59. Irving Bernstein, "Highlights of Recent News and Events," United Jewish Appeal, 1979, p. 4.

60. Cf. Silberman, p. 210.

61. It should be noted that this sense is generally most profound among those attending their first General Assembly. As with many public religious rituals, repetition sometimes mitigates the awe-inspiring qualities initially experienced. The tendency for the impact of the General Assembly to diminish for those who have attended many may also reveal some of the problematic characteristics of civil religious as opposed to traditional religious ritual. Lacking an explicitly transcendental frame of reference, the former can too easily become a play. GA veterans can sometimes be heard critiquing assemblies in just these terms: "lacked a good opening," "dull and routine." Nevertheless, even the most jaded attendees are not immune to the excitement which, often unexpectedly, can grip the assembled participants and lift them out of the mundane into what can only be called a transcendent solidarity and purposiveness.

62. Charles Zibbell, "Summary of Workshops on Insuring Jewish Commitment," *General Assembly Papers*, 1982, CJF, p. 1.

63. Sandford Solender, "Themes From the Assembly," *General Assembly Papers*, 1979, CJF, p. 6.

64. Charles Zibbell, "Highlights of the Workshops," *General Assembly Papers*, 1973, CJFWF, p. 2.

65. Sidney Vincent, "Paradox and Promise," *General Assembly Papers*, 1977, CJFWF, pp. 7–8.

66. On the development of Holocaust Memorial Day observances, see Mervin Verbit, "Shaping a New Religious Ritual: *Yom Hashoah* in American Jewish Practice," in Woocher, Lipstadt, and Moore.

67. The United Jewish Appeal commissioned and published an Israel Independence Day Haggadah in 1978, for use in family, congregational, or commu-

nal settings. The text was prepared by Rabbi Shlomo Goren (Ashkenazi Chief Rabbi of Israel at the time) and the UJA's Rabbinic Cabinet. Despite this formidable sponsorship, the Haggadah has not been widely adopted as a standardized ritual text for Israel Independence Day. This is again indicative of the barriers which come into play when polity institutions seek to move explicitly into the role of generators of religious ritual, especially for the "private" domain. It also reveals how difficult it is in general to "create" new rituals, even by adopting existing forms. Thus, it is understandable that most civil Jewish ritual (like its mythology) is implicitly rather than explicitly "religious."

68. Cf. Clifford Geertz, *Islam Observed* (New Haven: Yale University Press, 1968), pp. 97–98.

## 6. Toward a Dialogue of Judaisms

1. Cf. Jacob Neusner, *From Politics to Piety: The Emergence of Pharisaic Judaism* (Englewood Cliffs, N.J.: Prentice-Hall, 1973).

2. Cf. Daniel J. Elazar, "The New Sadducees," *Midstream* (August/September 1978): 20–21.

3. Ibid, p. 22.

4. Ibid, p. 24.

5. Perhaps the best evidence of this assertion has been the success of semi-outsiders in pushing the central institutions of the Jewish polity to adopt a more activist posture with respect to a number of specific issues—e.g., the rescue of Soviet and Ethiopian Jews, and support of intensive Jewish education—than they were initially inclined to take. The successes were achieved largely by appealing to the polity's own professed value commitments, and the positions of the advocates of change were accepted as substantively valid for precisely this reason, even where the tactics and rhetoric of these groups were rejected as excessive.

6. Will Herberg, *Protestant-Catholic-Jew*, rev. ed. (Garden City, N.Y.: Doubleday and Company, 1960).

7. One example of how this has occurred in connection with the bar/bat mitzvah—American Jewry's quintessential rite of passage and longtime target of critics for its frequent lack of religious substance—is the recent introduction of the concept of "twinning." Each bar/bat mitzvah is "twinned" with a young Soviet Jew who is unable to celebrate his or her bar/bat mitzvah because of the oppression in the Soviet Union. The synagogue ceremony will take note of the twinning relationship in one or more ways, the bar/bat mitzvah may make a contribution to help Soviet Jews, and, in general, the "twinning" serves as a graphic symbol of the young man or woman's assumption of Jewish responsibility. There is, of course, nothing incompatible between this concept and the traditional meaning of the bar/bat mitzvah as the occasion of reaching religious maturity, symbolized by one's mastery of Torah and readiness to fulfill its obligations. Yet, the introduction of the contemporary political element as a means of adding religious seriousness to what today often threatens to be merely a giant party illustrates the power of civil Jewish values even within the synagogue environment.

8. This is one of the characteristics which distinguishes civil religion from what might be termed "political religion," which does seek to monopolize the religious loyalties of its adherents.

9. Harold Kushner, "The American Jewish Experience: A Conservative Perspective," *Judaism* (Summer 1982): 297–98.

10. Harold Schulweis, "The Challenge of the New Secular Religions," *Conservative Judaism* (Summer 1979): 3–15.

11. Charles Liebman, "American Jews and the 'Modern Mind,' " *Midstream* (April 1981): 8–12.

12. There is debate about how to define the concept of the *ba'al teshuva*. Some would apply the term only to those who have embraced Orthodox traditionalism, i.e., *halakhic* Judaism. Others use the term more broadly to include as well individuals who, while not necessarily embracing Orthodox life-styles, have significantly deepened their commitment to living "Jewishly." Some have suggested that the term be applied to anyone who is more Jewishly observant than his/her parents were during the period of his/her upbringing.

13. Cf. Jacob Neusner, *Fellowship in Judaism: The First Century and Today* (London: Valentine-Mitchell, 1963).

14. Liebman, "American Jews and the 'Modern Mind,' " p. 12.

15. One of the strongest in recent years may be found in Samuel Dresner, "Federation or Synagogue: Alternatives in the American Jewish Community," *Forum* (1977): 73–95.

16. In making this claim, we obviously reject the notion that secularization will inevitably sweep away all religious consciousness and language in modern society. Secularization has perhaps irreversibly changed the ways in which most contemporary American Jews confront the Judaic religious tradition. There is good evidence, however, that it has not—either for Jews or for Western culture in general—succeeded in displacing religious values and sensibilities altogether. If anything, secularism as an ideological force is on the defensive today. Cf. Andrew Greeley, *Unsecular Man: The Persistence of Religion* (New York: Schocken Books, 1972).

17. Mordecai M. Kaplan, *Judaism As a Civilization: Toward a Reconstruction of American Jewish Life* (New York: Schocken Books, 1967).

18. Mordecai M. Kaplan, *The Religion of Ethical Nationhood: Judaism's Contribution to World Peace* (New York: The Macmillan Company, 1970).

19. Charles Liebman, "Reconstructionism in American Jewish Life," in *Aspects of the Religious Behaviour of American Jews* (New York: Ktav Publishing House, 1974) p. 279.

20. Among the most notable in addition to those already mentioned are: *The Greater Judaism in the Making: A Study of the Modern Evolution of Judaism* (New York: Reconstructionist Press, 1960); and *The Meaning of God in Modern Jewish Religion* (New York: Reconstructionist Press, 1962). The discussion of Kaplan's thought here is based upon these works, especially his own recapitulation of its central themes in *The Religion of Ethical Nationhood*.

21. Kaplan, *The Religion of Ethical Nationhood*, p. 17.

22. Ibid., p. 132.

23. Ibid., p. 156.

24. Ibid., p. 114.

25. Ibid.

26. Still the best single volume introduction to Buber's thought is Maurice Friedman's *Martin Buber: The Life of Dialogue* (New York: Harper and Row, 1960). Among the most important of Buber's books for an understanding of his philosophy of Judaism are: *I and Thou*, trans. with an Introduction by Walter Kaufmann (New York: Charles Scribner's Sons, 1970); *On Judaism*, ed. Nahum N. Glatzer (New York: Schocken Books, 1972); *Israel and the World: Essays in a Time of Crisis* (New York: Schocken Books, 1963); *Pointing the Way*, ed. and trans. with an Introduction by Maurice Friedman (New York: Harper and Row, 1963); *At the Turning: Three Addresses on Judaism* (New York: Farrar, Straus & Young, 1952); and *A Believing Humanism: Gleanings*, trans. with an Introduction by Maurice Friedman (New York: Simon and Schuster, 1969).

27. *I and Thou*, p. 62. (We have changed Kaufmann's translation of the Ger-

man back to that of the original English version translated by Ronald Gregor Smith.)

28. Donald J. Moore, *Martin Buber: Prophet of Religious Secularism* (Philadelphia: The Jewish Publication Society of America, 1974).

29. Martin Buber, *Paths in Utopia*, trans. R.F.C. Hull, Introduction by Ephraim Fischoff (Boston: Beacon Press, 1958), p. 133.

30. One might, in fact, put this in exactly the opposite terms: Buber's general philosophy represents his attempt to enable humanity as a whole to appropriate the fundamental message of Judaism as embodied preeminently in the Hebrew Bible.

31. Martin Buber, *Israel and the World*, p. 186.

32. Ibid., p. 95.

33. Ibid., p. 255.

34. Martin Buber, *Eclipse of God: Studies in the Relation Between Religion and Philosophy*, trans. Maurice Friedman (New York: Harper and Row, 1957).

35. Martin Buber, "Replies to My Critics," trans. Maurice Friedman, in *The Philosophy of Martin Buber*, ed. Paul Schilpp and Maurice Friedman (LaSalle, Ill.: Open Court Press, 1967), p. 716.

36. Buber, *Israel and the World*, p. 138.

37. Emil Fackenheim, *Encounters Between Judaism and Modern Philosophy* (New York: Basic Books, 1973).

38. Emil Fackenheim, *To Mend the World: Foundations of Future Jewish Thought* (New York: Schocken Books, 1982).

39. Emil Fackenheim, *God's Presence in History: Jewish Affirmations and Philosophical Reflections* (New York: Harper and Row, 1970), pp. 3–16.

40. Ibid., pp. 16–34.

41. Ibid., p. 44.

42. Ibid., pp. 69–79.

43. Ibid., pp. 80–81.

44. Ibid., p. 83.

45. Ibid., p. 84.

46. Emil Fackenheim, *The Jewish Return Into History: Reflections in the Age of Auschwitz and a New Jerusalem* (New York: Schocken Books, 1978), pp. 265, 269.

47. Fackenheim, *God's Presence in History*, p. 96.

48. Fackenheim, *The Jewish Return*, p. 142.

49. Fackenheim, *To Mend the World*, p. 18.

50. Ibid., pp. 299–302.

51. Ibid., pp. 310–13.

52. Fackenheim, *The Jewish Return*, pp. 129–75.

53. Fackenheim, *To Mend the World*, pp. 323–31.

54. Eugene B. Borowitz, *The Mask Jews Wear: The Self-Deceptions of American Jewry* (New York: Simon and Schuster, 1973).

55. Ibid., pp. 51–88.

56. Ibid., p. 96.

57. Ibid., pp. 98–105.

58. Ibid., pp. 122–23.

59. Ibid., p. 131.

60. Ibid., pp. 135—43.

61. Borowitz, "The Chosen People Concept," pp. 564–65.

62. Eugene B. Borowitz, *How Can a Jew Speak of Faith Today?* (Philadelphia: The Westminster Press, 1969), pp. 33–34.

63. Ibid., p. 55.

64. Borowitz, *The Mask Jews Wear*, p. 189.

65. Ibid., pp. 189–94.
66. Ibid., pp. 207–08.
67. Ibid., p. 214.
68. Borowitz, *How Can a Jew Speak of Faith Today?*, p. 54.

69. The most important sources for Greenberg's current thinking are a series of papers he has published in the "Perspectives" series of the National Jewish Resource Center (recently renamed the Center for Learning and Leadership), an organization which he founded and continues to direct: *On the Third Era in Jewish History: Power and Politics* (New York: National Jewish Resource Center, 1980); *The Third Great Cycle in Jewish History* (New York: National Jewish Resource Center, 1981); and *Voluntary Covenant* (New York: National Jewish Resource Center, 1982). The discussion of Greenberg's thought here is based on these papers and on a recently circulated manuscript, "Judaism as a Covenant of Life: The Relationship of History and Values."

70. Greenberg, "Judaism As a Covenant of Life," p. 3.
71. Greenberg, *Voluntary Covenant*, pp. 2–3.
72. Ibid, p. 5.
73. Ibid, pp. 14–15.
74. Greenberg, *The Third Great Cycle*, pp. 12–15.
75. Greenberg, *On the Third Era*, p. 1.
76. Ibid, pp. 1–2; Greenberg, *The Third Great Cycle*, pp. 3–12.
77. Ibid, pp. 6–12; Greenberg, *The Voluntary Covenant*, pp. 7–13.
78. Ibid, pp. 14–16.
79. Greenberg, *The Third Great Cycle*, p. 16–20.
80. Ibid., p. 17; Greenberg, *The Voluntary Covenant*, pp. 16–18.
81. Greenberg, *The Third Great Cycle*, p. 26.
82. Greenberg, *On The Third Era*, pp. 3–4; Greenberg, *The Third Great Cycle*, pp. 21–26.

83. The organized involvement of American Jewish communal leaders in American political activity has grown dramatically in recent years. Political involvement has come to stand alongside philanthropic activity as a defining characteristic of the Jewish polity activist. As Greenberg asserts, politics is seen both as a vital means of defending collective Jewish interests (not only in support of Israel, but in preserving American society as one hospitable to Jews) and as a way of advancing Jewish social ideals.

84. Greenberg, *The Third Great Cycle*, pp. 24–26; Greenberg, *On the Third Era*, pp. 4–6.
85. Greenberg, *The Third Great Cycle*, pp. 37–38.
86. Greenberg, *The Voluntary Covenant*, pp. 21–27.
87. Greenberg, *The Third Great Cycle*, pp. 28–29.
88. Greenberg, *The Voluntary Covenant*, p. 37.

89. The phrase is Daniel Elazar's. He, more than any other single figure, has drawn the attention of contemporary Diaspora Jews to the significance of the resurgence of the public-political dimension of Jewish life which has taken place in recent decades. He has also begun the work of mining the Jewish political tradition for the insights and models which can help guide the contemporary Jewish polity in its quest for self-definition in traditional Jewish terms. Perhaps his most important work in this regard has been his demonstration of the centrality of the concept of Covenant not only for Jewish theology, but for its political theory as well. (See, e.g., "The Covenant as the Basis of the Jewish Political Tradition," in *Kinship and Consent: The Jewish Political Tradition and Its Contemporary Uses* [Philadelphia: Turtledove Publishing, 1981], pp. 21–56.) The study and elaboration of the Jewish political tradition—in reality a theopolitical tradition throughout—may serve as another bridge linking the contem-

porary Jewish polity to Judaic religious tradition. That both Jewish theologians and political theorists are today pointing to the Covenant as the fundamental defining category of Jewish existence in the world lends weight to the claim that civil Judaism can find its own theological language along this path.

90. The phrase is Paul Tillich's. See his *Dynamics of Faith* (New York: Harper and Row, 1957), pp. 48–54.

# BIBLIOGRAPHY OF SOURCES CITED

## Documents

Ades, Alan. Speech delivered at the UJA Northeast Leadership Conference, October 22, 1983.

Band, Jordan. "The Human Rights Revolution: Reassessing the Jewish Role." *General Assembly Papers.* New York: CJFWF, 1967.

Bernstein, Irving. "Highlights of Recent News and Events." New York: United Jewish Appeal, 1979.

_____. "UJA National Conference Address." New York: United Jewish Appeal, 1982.

Bernstein, Philip. "Federation Agenda for the 1970s." *General Assembly Papers.* New York: CJFWF, 1968.

_____. "Federations: What They Are and Are Not." New York: CJFWF, 1976.

_____. "The Principles of Jewish Federations." New York: CJFWF, 1976.

Blum, Irving. "Community Prospects: Paradox and Challenge." *General Assembly Papers.* New York: CJFWF, 1972.

_____. "Federation Support—Reality and Responsibility." *General Assembly Papers.* New York: CJFWF, 1966.

Blumberg, Herschel. Speech to the Board of the National Jewish Resource Center. Press Release. New York: National Jewish Resource Center, 1984.

Borowitz, Eugene. Louis A. Pincus Memorial Lecture. In "Campaign Newsbrief." New York: United Jewish Appeal, May 1984.

Cardin, Jerome. "Guidelines for 1979 Community Campaigns." *General Assembly Papers.* New York: CJF, 1978.

Cherniak, Saul. "The Role of the Synagogue in the Jewish Community." *General Assembly Papers.* New York: CJFWF, 1954.

Citrin, Martin. "Community and Campaign." New York: CJF, 1982.

_____. "Visions of the Future." *General Assembly Papers.* New York: CJF, 1982.

_____. "Where Do We Go From Here." New York: CJF, 1979.

_____. "A Year of Challenges." *General Assembly Papers.* New York: CJF, 1983.

Combined Jewish Philanthropies of Greater Boston. "Toward a Working Agenda: Report of the CJP Committee on Communal Objectives." Boston, 1984.

Council of Jewish Federations and Welfare Funds. "1933 General Assembly Proceedings." New York, 1933.

_____. "1934 General Assembly Proceedings." New York, 1934.

_____. "1936 General Assembly Proceedings." New York, 1936.

_____. "1937 General Assembly Proceedings." New York, 1937.

_____. "General Assembly Papers, 1944." New York, 1944.

_____. "General Assembly Resolutions, 1949." New York, 1949.

_____. "General Assembly Resolutions, 1957." New York, 1957.

————. "General Assembly Resolutions, 1963." New York, 1963.

————. *Major Issues Facing Jewish Communities: A Symposium.* New York, 1963.

————. "Proceedings of the National Conference on Jewish Welfare." New York, 1935.

————. "Proceedings of the Organizing Conference of the National Council of Jewish Federations and Welfare Funds." New York, 1931.

Epstein, Raymond. "Major Issues Facing Federations and the Council." *General Assembly Papers.* New York: CJFWF, 1974.

Fisher, Max. "The Decade Ahead: A Formidable Agenda." *General Assembly Papers.* New York: CJFWF, 1971.

————. "A *New* Program for Immigrant Absorption." *General Assembly Papers.* New York: CJFWF, 1966.

————. "Our Overseas Responsibilities in a Time of Change and Challenge." *General Assembly Papers.* New York: CJFWF, 1965.

————. "The Role of an American Jewish Leader in Today's World." *General Assembly Papers.* New York: CJFWF, 1967.

————. "We Have Chosen." *General Assembly Papers.* New York: CJFWF, 1969.

Fox, Louis. "Issues Confronting Our Communities and the Assembly." *General Assembly Papers.* New York: CJFWF, 1968.

Freeman, Julian. "Report to the General Assembly." *General Assembly Papers.* New York: CJFWF, 1950.

————. "Twenty Years of Cooperation: A Restatement of Basic Principles." *General Assembly Papers.* New York: CJFWF, 1951.

Gold, Bert. Speech delivered at Brandeis University, July 18, 1985.

Goldfarb, William. "Jewish Education and a Changing Society." *General Assembly Papers.* New York: CJFWF, 1964.

Handmaker, Stuart. "A Personal View of the Role of the President." *General Assembly Papers.* New York: CJF, 1982.

Hoffberger, Jerold. "Justice For All." *General Assembly Papers.* New York: CJFWF, 1976.

————. "Major Challenges Ahead." *General Assembly Papers.* New York: CJF, 1979.

————. "Retrospect and Prospect." *General Assembly Papers.* New York: CJF, 1978.

Horowitz, Stanley. "Insuring Jewish Commitment: The Federation Role." *General Assembly Papers.* New York: CJF, 1982.

————. "Entering the Eighties." *General Assembly Papers.* New York: CJF, 1979.

Hurwitz, Donald. "Jewish Community Organizations—Their Relevance to Key Issues." In *Jewish Community Organizations: How Relevant to Major Issues?* New York: CJFWF, 1964.

Kane, Irving. "Domestic Issues in America Today." *General Assembly Papers.* New York: CJFWF, 1957.

————. "In Quest of Purpose." *General Assembly Papers.* New York: CJFWF, 1960.

Lautenberg, Frank. "General Chairman's Message." In "United Jewish Appeal–1977." New York: United Jewish Appeal, 1976.

————. "Jewish Responsibility in 1976." *General Assembly Papers.* New York: CJFWF, 1975.

————. "O Jerusalem, We Shall Never Be Still." New York: United Jewish Appeal, 1976.

————. "We Are One." New York: United Jewish Appeal, 1974.

Levine, Jacqueline. "Building Commitment—Women's Special Role." *General Assembly Papers.* New York: CJFWF, 1970.

Mandel, Mort. "CJF and Federations: New Goals." *General Assembly Papers.* New York: CJF, 1980.

Myers, Stanley. "Agenda for American Jewry." *General Assembly Papers.* New York: CJFWF, 1950.

Olshansky, Bernard. "The Role of Jewish Community and Leadership in Assuring Jewish Continuity." *General Assembly Papers.* New York: CJFWF, 1976.

Rabb, Irving. "Enrichment and Training of Veteran Leadership for Jewish Decison-Making." *General Assembly Papers.* New York: CJFWF, 1974.

Ratner, Albert. "The Jewish Response: A Personal Review." New York: CJF, 1979.

Rifkind, Robert. Statement at a meeting of the Jewish Communal Affairs Commission, American Jewish Committee, February 25, 1982.

Robin, Edward. "Why We Are Here." Speech delivered at the 1982 UJA Young Leadership Washington Conference. Unpublished manuscript, March 1982.

Safran, Hyman. "Updating Federations: How Relevant to Changing Issues and Communities." *General Assembly Papers.* New York: CJFWF, 1964.

Shroder, William. "The Communities Pass Their Test." In "General Assembly News and Notes." New York: CJFWF, 1941.

Sobeloff, Isadore. "Jewish Community Organization—Its Past, Current Trends, Directions." *General Assembly Papers.* New York: CJFWF, 1954.

Solender, Sanford. "Themes From the Assembly." *General Assembly Papers.* New York: CJF, 1979.

Stern, Louis. "The Federation Commitment in our Changing World." *General Assembly Papers.* New York: CJFWF, 1962.

_____. "Major Issues Facing the Organized Jewish Communities." *General Assembly Papers.* New York: CJFWF, 1963.

United Israel Appeal. *The Triumph of a Dream.* New York, 1979.

United Jewish Appeal. "If You Think All Our Problems Are Solved." New York, 1977.

_____. "Now. More Than Ever. We Are One." New York, 1979.

_____. "Proclaim Liberty." New York, 1976.

Vincent, Sidney, "The Agenda of Jewish Federations in War and Peace." *General Assembly Papers.* New York: CJFWF, 1973.

_____. "The Impact of Contemporary Issues on Jewish Life: Response." *General Assembly Papers.* New York: CJFWF, 1972.

_____. "The Jewish Federation: Reflections on an American Institution." The Milender Seminar in Jewish Communal Leadership Address. Waltham, Massachusetts: Brandeis University, 1976.

_____. "Paradox and Promise." *General Assembly Papers.* New York: CJFWF, 1977.

_____. "Planning for Small Cities—Directions for the '80's." *General Assembly Papers.* New York: CJF, 1978.

_____. "Shaping a More Creative and Responsive Community—The Role of Leadership." *General Assembly Papers.* New York: CJFWF, 1975.

Weil, Milton. "The Glamor and Drama of Home Services." *General Assembly Papers.* New York: CJFWF, 1952.

Wolf, Edwin. "Jewish Culture in America—Status and Outlook." *General Assembly Papers.* New York: CJFWF, 1962.

Zacks, Gordon. "Young Leadership Looks at the Future of the Jewish Community." *General Assembly Papers.* New York: CJFWF, 1969.

Zibbell, Charles. "Highlights of the Workshops." *General Assembly Papers.* New York: CJFWF, 1973.

_____. "Highlights of the Workshops and Forums." *General Assembly Papers.* New York: CJFWF, 1974.

_____. "Summary of Workshops on Insuring Jewish Commitment." *General Assembly Papers.* New York: CJF, 1982.


## Books, Articles, and Other Published Materials

Bellah, Robert N. *The Broken Covenant: American Civil Religion in Time of Trial.* New York: Seabury, 1975.
Bellah, Robert N. "Civil Religion in America." *Daedalus* (Winter 1967): 1–21.
_____. "Civil Religion in America." With "Commentaries" by D. W. Brogan, Leo Pfeffer, John R. Whitney, Phillip E. Hammond, and "Response" by Robert N. Bellah. In *The Religious Situation: 1968,* edited by Donald R. Cutler, pp. 331–93. Boston: Beacon Press, 1968.
_____. "Response to the Panel on Civil Religion." *Sociological Analysis* (Summer 1976): 153–59.
Bellah, Robert N. and Phillip E. Hammond. *Varieties of Civil Religion.* San Francisco: Harper and Row, 1980.
Berger, Graenum, ed. *The Turbulent Decades: Jewish Communal Services in America, 1958–78.* New York: Conference of Jewish Communal Service, 1981.
Berger, Peter L. *A Rumor of Angels: Modern Society and the Rediscovery of the Supernatural.* Garden City, N.Y.: Doubleday and Company, 1969.
_____. *The Sacred Canopy: Elements of a Sociological Theory of Religion.* Garden City, N.Y.: Doubleday and Company, 1967.
_____. "Some Second Thoughts on Substantive versus Functional Definition of Religion." *Journal for the Scientific Study of Religion* (June 1974):125–33.
Bernstein, Philip. *To Dwell in Unity: The Jewish Federation Movement in America Since 1960.* Philadelphia: The Jewish Publication Society of America, 1983.
Blau, Joseph L. *Modern Varieties of Judaism.* New York: Columbia University Press, 1964.
Borowitz, Eugene B. "The Chosen People Concept As It Affects Life in the Diaspora." *Journal of Ecumenical Studies* (1975): 553–68.
_____. *How Can a Jew Speak of Faith Today?* Philadelphia: The Westminster Press, 1969.
_____. *The Mask Jews Wear: The Self-Deceptions of American Jewry.* New York: Simon and Schuster, 1973.
Buber, Martin. *At the Turning: Three Addresses on Judaism.* New York: Farrar, Straus and Young, 1952.
_____. *A Believing Humanism: Gleanings.* Translated with an Introduction by Maurice Friedman. New York: Simon and Schuster, 1969.
_____. *Eclipse of God: Studies in the Relation Between Religion and Philosophy.* Translated by Maurice Friedman. New York: Harper and Row, 1957.
_____. *I and Thou.* Translatd with an Introduction by Walter Kaufmann. New York: Charles Scribner's Sons, 1970.
_____. *Israel and the World: Essays in a Time of Crisis.* New York: Schocken Books, 1963.
_____. *On Judaism.* Edited by Nahum N. Glatzer. New York: Schocken Books, 1972.
_____. *Paths in Utopia.* Translated by R.F.C. Hull, Introduction by Ephraim Fischoff. Boston: Beacon Press, 1958.
_____. *Pointing the Way.* Edited and translated with an Introduction by

Maurice Friedman. New York: Harper and Row, 1963.

_____. "Replies to My Critics." Translated by Maurice Friedman. In *The Philosophy of Martin Buber*, edited by Paul Schilpp and Maurice Friedman. LaSalle, Ill.: Open Court Press, 1967.

Cherry, Conrad, ed. *God's New Israel: Religious Interpretations of American Destiny.* Englewood Cliffs, N.J.: Prentice-Hall, 1971.

Cohen, Naomi. *Not Free to Desist: The American Jewish Committee, 1906–1966.* Philadelphia: The Jewish Publication Society of America, 1972.

Cohen, Steven M. *American Modernity and Jewish Identity.* New York: Tavistock Publications, 1983.

Coleman, John. "Civil Religion." *Sociological Analysis* (Summer 1970): 67–77.

Demerath III, N.J. and Rhys H. Williams. "Civil Religion in an Uncivil Society." In *The Annals of the American Academy of Political and Social Science.* Vol. 480, *Religion in America Today.* Edited by Wade Clark Roof, pp. 154–66. Beverly Hills: Sage Publications, July 1985.

Douglas, Mary. *Natural Symbols: Explorations in Cosmology.* New York: Random House, 1973.

Dresner, Samuel. "Federation or Synagogue: Alternatives in the American Jewish Community." *Forum* (1977): 73–95.

Ehrmann, Eliezer L., ed. *Readings in Modern Jewish History: From the American Revolution to the Present.* New York: Ktav Publishing House, 1977.

Eisen, Arnold M. *The Chosen People in America: A Study in Jewish Religious Ideology.* Bloomington: Indiana University Press, 1983.

Elazar, Daniel J. *Community and Polity: The Organizational Dynamics of American Jewry.* Philadelphia: The Jewish Publication Society of America, 1976.

_____. "The Covenant as the Basis of the Jewish Political Tradition. " In *Kinship and Consent: The Jewish Political Tradition and Its Contemporary Uses,* edited by Daniel J. Elazar, pp. 21–56. Philadelphia: Turtledove Publishing, 1981.

_____. The New Sadducees." *Midstream* (August/September 1978): 20–25.

Eliade, Mircea. *The Sacred and the Profane: The Nature of Religion.* New York: Harcourt, Brace and World, 1959.

Fackenheim, Emil. *Encounters Between Judaism and Modern Philosophy.* New York: Basic Books, 1973.

_____. *God's Presence in History: Jewish Affirmations and Philosophical Reflections.* New York: Harper and Row, 1970.

_____. *The Jewish Return Into History: Reflections in the Age of Auschwitz and a New Jerusalem.* New York: Schocken Books, 1978.

_____. *To Mend the World: Foundations of Future Jewish Thought.* New York: Schocken Books, 1982.

Fenn, Richard K. "Bellah and the New Orthodoxy." *Sociological Analysis* (Summer 1976): 160–66.

_____. *Toward a Theory of Secularization.* Storrs, Conn.: Society for the Scientific Study of Religion, 1978.

Frankel, Stanley. "The Challenge of Young Leadership." *Young Leadership Cabinet Communique* (Spring 1980): 3.

Friedman, Maurice. *Martin Buber: The Life of Dialogue.* New York: Harper and Row, 1960.

Frommer, Morris. "The American Jewish Congress: A History 1914–1950." Ph.D. Diss., Ohio State University, 1978.

Gans, Herbert J. "Symbolic Ethnicity: The Future of Ethnic Groups and Cultures in America." In *On the Making of Americans: Essays in Honor of* wood Cliffs, N.J.: Prentice-Hall, 1973.

*David Riesman*, edited by Herbert J. Gans, Nathan Glazer, Joseph R. Gusfield, and Christopher Jencks, pp. 193–220. Philadelphia: University of Pennsylvania Press, 1979.

Geertz, Clifford. *The Interpretation of Cultures*. New York: Basic Books, 1973.

_____. *Islam Observed*. New Haven: Yale University Press, 1968.

Gehrig, Gail. *American Civil Religion: An Assessment*. Storrs, Conn.: Society for the Scientific Study of Religion, 1979.

Goldin, Milton. *Why They Give: American Jews and Their Philanthropies*. New York: Macmillan and Company, 1976.

Goldscheider, Calvin and Alan S. Zuckerman. *The Transformation of the Jews*. Chicago: The University of Chicago Press, 1984.

Greeley, Andrew. *Unsecular Man: The Persistence of Religion*. New York: Schocken Books, 1972.

Greenberg, Irving. "Judaism as a Covenant of Life: The Relationship of History and Values." New York: National Jewish Resource Center, 1985.

_____. *On the Third Era in Jewish History: Power and Politics*. New York: National Jewish Resource Center, 1980.

_____. *The Third Great Cycle in Jewish History*. New York: National Jewish Resource Center, 1981.

_____. *Voluntary Convenant*. New York: National Jewish Resource Center, 1982.

Handlin, Oscar. "Changing Patterns in Group Life in America and Their Implications for the American Jewish Community." *Journal of Jewish Communal Service* (Summer 1958): 348.

Hertzberg, Arthur. *Being Jewish in America: The Modern Experience*. New York: Schocken Books, 1979.

_____. "Jewish Identification After the Six-Day War." *Jewish Social Studies* (1969): 267–271.

_____. ed. *The Zionist Idea: A Historical Analysis and Reader*. New York: Atheneum, 1971.

Himmelfarb, Harold. "Measuring Religious Involvement." *Social Forces* (June 1975): 606–18.

Hughey, Michael W. *Civil Religion and Moral Order: Theoretical and Historical Dimensions*. Westport, Conn.: Greenwood Press, 1983.

Kaplan, Mordecai M. *The Greater Judaism in the Making: A Study of the Modern Evolution of Judaism*. New York: Reconstructionist Press, 1960.

_____. *Judaism As a Civilization: Toward a Reconstruction of American Jewish Life*. New York: Schocken Books, 1967.

_____. *The Meaning of God in Modern Jewish Religion*. New York: Reconstructionist Press, 1962.

_____. *The Religion of Ethical Nationhood: Judaism's Contribution to World Peace*. New York: The Macmillan Company, 1970.

Karp, Abraham J. *To Give Life: The UJA in the Shaping of the American Jewish Community*. New York: Schocken Books, 1981.

Karpf, Maurice J. *Jewish Community Organization in the United States: An Outline of Types of Organizations, Activities, and Problems*. New York: Bloch Publishing Company, 1938.

Katz, Jacob. *Out of the Ghetto: The Social Background of Jewish Emancipation*. Cambridge: Harvard University Press, 1973.

_____. *Tradition and Crisis: Jewish Society at the End of the Middle Ages*. New York: Free Press of Glencoe, 1961.

Kohanski, Alexander S., ed. *The American Jewish Conference: Its Organization and Proceedings of the First Session*. New York: American Jewish Conference, 1944.

Kushner, Harold. "The American Jewish Experience: A Conservative Perspective." *Judaism* (Summer 1982): 296–98.

Kutzik, Alfred J. "The Social Basis of American Jewish Philanthropy." Ph.D. Diss., Brandeis University, 1968.

LeVee, Ellen Lasser. "Rationality: American Jewry's False Messiah." Draft of Ph.D. Diss., University of California, 1985.

Levine, Hillel. "To Share a Vision." In *Jewish Radicalism: A Selected Anthology*, edited by Jack Nusan Porter and Peter Dreier, pp. 183–94. New York: Grove Press, 1973.

Liebman, Charles S. *The Ambivalent American Jew: Politics, Religion, and Family in American Jewish Life*. Philadelphia: The Jewish Publication Society of America, 1973.

_____. "American Jews and the 'Modern Mind.'" *Midstream* (April 1981): 8–12.

_____. *Aspects of the Religious Behaviour of America Jews*. New York: Ktav Publishing House, 1974.

Liebman, Charles S. and Eliezer Don-Yehiya. *Civil Religion in Israel: Traditional Judaism and Political Culture in the Jewish State*. Berkeley: University of California Press, 1983.

Lipstadt, Deborah. "American Jewry—From Ever Preyed Upon to Ever Dying People." In *Sacred People, Secular World: American Judaism in the Making*, edited by Jonathan Woocher, Deborah Lipstadt, and Deborah Dash Moore. Chappaqua, N.Y.: Rossel Books, forthcoming.

Lurie, Harry L. *A Heritage Affirmed: The Jewish Federation Movement in America*. Philadelphia: The Jewish Publication Society of America, 1961.

Marty, Martin. "Two Kinds of Two Kinds of Civil Religion, " In *American Civil Religion*, edited by Russell B. Richey and Donald G. Jones, pp. 139–57. New York: Harper and Row, 1974.

Massarik, Fred. *Jewish Identity: Facts for Planning*. New York: Council of Jewish Federations and Welfare Funds, 1974.

Mendes-Flohr, Paul R. and Jehuda Reinharz, eds. *The Jew in the Modern World: A Documentary History*. New York and Oxford: Oxford University Press, 1980.

Meyer, Michael. *The Origins of the Modern Jew: Jewish Identity and European Culture in Germany 1749–1824*. Detroit: Wayne State University Press, 1979.

Moore, Deborah Dash. "American Jewish Civil Religion: An Ideology of Acculturation." In *Sacred People, Secular World: American Judaism in the Making*, edited by Jonathan Woocher, Deborah Lipstadt, and Deborah Dash Moore. Chappaqua, N.Y.: Rossel Books, forthcoming.

_____. *At Home in America: Second Generation New York Jews*. New York: Columbia University Press, 1981.

_____. *B'nai B'rith and the Challenge of Ethnic Leadership*. Albany: State University of New York Press, 1981.

Moore, Donald J. *Martin Buber: Prophet of Religious Secularism*. Philadelphia: The Jewish Publication Society of America, 1974.

Morris, Robert and Michael Freund, eds. *Trends and Issues in Jewish Social Welfare in the United States, 1899–1958*. Philadelphia: The Jewish Publication Society of America, 1966.

Neusner, Jacob. *Between Time and Eternity: The Essentials of Judaism*. Encino, Calif.: Dickenson Publishing Company, 1975.

_____. *Fellowship in Judaism: The First Century and Today*. London: Valentine-Mitchell, 1963.

_____. *From Politics to Piety: The Emergence of Pharisaic Judaism*. Engle-

_____. *Stranger at Home: "The Holocaust," Zionism, and American Judaism.* Chicago: The University of Chicago Press, 1981.

Novak, Michael. *Choosing Our King: Powerful Symbols in Presidential Politics.* New York: Macmillan Publishing Company, 1974.

"Pre-Convention Symposium: Civil Religion and Education." *Religious Education* (September-October 1975): 467–518.

Raphael, Marc Lee. *A History of the United Jewish Appeal, 1939–1982.* Brown Judaic Studies, 34. Missoula, Mont.: Scholars Press, 1982.

Rawidowicz, Simon. *Studies in Jewish Thought.* Philadelphia: The Jewish Publication Society of America, 1974.

*Religious Education,* Convention Issue on Civil Religion (May-June 1976).

Richey, Russell B. and Donald G. Jones, eds. *American Civil Religion.* New York: Harper and Row, 1974.

Rosenblatt, Gary. "The Youngers of Zion: UJA's Young Leadership Cabinet and How It Got That Way." *Moment* (June 1977): 37–40, 66–70.

Schulweis, Harold. "The Challenge of the New Secular Religions." *Conservative Judaism* (Summer 1979): 3–15.

Selekman, Ben. "The Federation in the Changing American Scene." In *The American Jewish Year Book,* Vol. 36, edited by Harry Schneiderman. Philadelphia: The American Jewish Committee and the Jewish Publication Society of America, 1935.

Silberman, Charles. *A Certain People: American Jews and Their Lives Today.* New York: Summit Books, 1985.

Sklare, Marshall. "American Jewry—The Ever Dying People." *Midstream* (June/July 1976): 17–27.

_____. *America's Jews.* New York: Random House, 1971.

Solomon, Barbara Miller. *Pioneers in Service: The History of the Associated Jewish Philanthropies of Boston.* Boston: Associated Jewish Philanthropies, 1956.

Squadron, Howard. "Between Power and Influence: The American Jewish Community." *Congress Monthly* (January 1983): 9–10.

"A Symposium on Civil Religion." *Sociological Analysis* (Summer 1976): 111–82.

Tillich, Paul. *Dynamics of Faith.* New York: Harper and Row, 1957.

Turner, Victor. *The Ritual Process: Structure and Anti-Structure.* Chicago: Aldine Publishing Company, 1969.

Vincent, Sidney Z. *Personal and Professional: Memoirs of a Life in Community Service.* Cleveland: The Jewish Community Federation of Cleveland, 1982.

Waxman, Chaim. "The Fourth Generation Grows Up: The Contemporary American Jewish Community." *The Annals of the American Academy of Political and Social Science* (March 1981): 70–84.

Wirth, Louis. *The Ghetto.* Chicago: University of Chicago Press, 1928 [1956].

Woocher, Jonathan. "The 'Civil Judaism' of Communal Leaders." In *The American Jewish Year Book,* Vol. 81, edited by Milton Himmelfarb and David Singer, pp. 149–69. New York and Philadelphia: The American Jewish Committee and the Jewish Publication Society of America, 1981.

_____. "'In Every Generation': The Seder as a Ritual of Anti-Structure." *Journal of the American Academy of Religion (Supplement)* (December 1977): 1263–92.

_____. "'Jewish Survivalism' as Communal Ideology: An Empirical Assessment." *Journal of Jewish Communal Service* (Summer 1981): 291–303.

_____. "The 1980 UJA Young Leadership Cabinet: A Profile." *Forum* (1981): 57–67.

Zibbell, Charles. "The Crisis in Jewish Life—The Aftermath of the Yom Kippur War." *Journal of Jewish Communal Service* (Fall 1974): 21–27.

————. "Stengthening Jewish Commitment." *Journal of Jewish Communal Service* (Spring 1973): 199–205.

————. *Tzedakah and the Contemporary Jewish Community.* New Orleans: Jewish Welfare Federation of New Orleans, 1975.

# INDEX

JONATHAN S. WOOCHER, is executive vice-president of the Jewish Education Service of North America. Formerly, associate professor of Jewish communal service at Brandeis University, he is the author of numerous articles on American Jewish communal religious life, and is co-editor of *Perspectives in Jewish Population Research.*